English Unlimited

B2 **Upper Intermediate**
Coursebook with e-Portfolio

Alex Tilbury & Leslie Anne Hendra with David Rea & Theresa Clementson
Course consultant: Adrian Doff

CAMBRIDGE
UNIVERSITY PRESS

Contents

Contents

How to use this coursebook

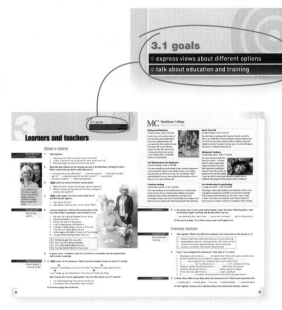

Every unit of this book is divided into sections, with clear, practical **goals** for learning.

The first four pages of the unit help you build your language skills and knowledge. These pages include speaking, listening, reading, writing, grammar, vocabulary and pronunciation activities. They are followed by a **Target activity** which will help you put together what you have learned.

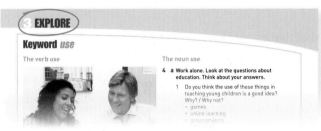

The **Explore** section of the unit begins with either a **Keyword** page, which looks at one or two of the most common and useful words in English or an **Across cultures** page, and then an **Explore speaking** or **Explore writing** page. The Explore section gives you extra language and skills work, all aiming to help you become a better and more culturally aware communicator in English.

The **Look again** section takes another look at the target language for the unit, helping you to review and extend your learning.
Sometimes you will also find this recycling symbol with the goals, to show when a particular goal is not new but is recycling language that you have met before.

The **e-Portfolio** DVD-ROM contains useful reference material for all the units, as well as self-assessment to help you test your own learning, and Wordcards to help you test your vocabulary learning.

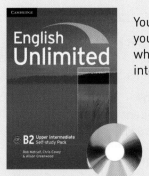

You can do more practice by yourself using the **Self-study Pack**, which includes a workbook and interactive DVD-ROM.

The DVD-ROM contains video and over 300 interactive activities.

1 Talented

1.1 goals
◉ talk about people's success
◉ discuss and evaluate ideas

Practice makes perfect?

READING

1 Talk in groups. Find out:

1 what each person in your group does.
2 how they spend their spare time.
3 some things they're good at.

2 Read the article on p7 about what makes people successful. Circle the correct options.

1 The best soccer players tend to be born at the beginning / end of the year.
2 Ericsson believes people become successful mainly through practice / natural talent.
3 The real reason people give up doing things is that they have no enthusiasm / talent for them.
4 Sports coaches prefer players born earlier in the year because they're more talented / mature.

3 Read again. Find out:

1 the three things that make up 'deliberate practice'.
2 what Ericsson's research suggests students should do, and why.
3 why January-born players are chosen for teams.
4 four ways in which the January-born players benefit from being chosen.

VOCABULARY

Routes to success

4 Match the verbs with the correct endings to make expressions from the article.

1	set	feedback	7	have	your interests
2	get	specific goals	8	follow	the will to succeed
3	concentrate on	results	9	receive	training
4	possess	talent	10	have	high self-esteem
5	put in	experience			
6	build up	a lot of practice			

Specific goals?

Set specific goals.

5 Test each other. Take turns to say the endings in 1–10 and remember the verbs.

SPEAKING

6 Talk together. Use expressions from 4 and your own ideas.

1 What does it take to do these things, in your opinion?
- play a sport to a high standard
- succeed in business
- speak a foreign language fluently
- be an excellent musician
- manage people effectively
- be a good teacher
2 Think of someone who is very successful. How did they succeed?
3 In what ways have you been successful? How do you explain your success?

6

A Star Is Made

by Stephen J. Dubner and Steven D. Levitt

If you examined the birth certificates of every soccer player in a World Cup tournament, you would find an unusual tendency: elite soccer players are more likely to have been born earlier in the year than later. If you then examined the European national youth teams that supply many World Cup players, this tendency would be even more noticeable. In recent English teams, for instance, half the elite teenage soccer players were born in January, February or March. In Germany, fifty-two were born in the first three months, with just four players born in the last three. What might account for this?

Swedish-born Anders Ericsson, a psychology professor at Florida State University, is leader of a group of scholars trying to answer an important question: when someone is very good at something, what actually makes them good? Early experiments by Ericsson suggested that the best way to learn was a process known as 'deliberate practice'. This is more than simply repeating a task. Rather, it involves setting specific goals, getting immediate feedback and concentrating equally on technique and results.

Ericsson and his colleagues therefore began studying expert performers in a wide range of pursuits, from soccer and surgery to piano playing and software design. They've come to a rather startling conclusion: practice really does make perfect. What we call 'talent' is highly overrated, as expert performers are nearly always made, not born. The research also suggests that when it comes to choosing a life path, you should do what you love. People often give up trying to do things they don't like, telling themselves they simply don't possess the talent. But what they really lack is the will to succeed and to put in the deliberate practice that would make them better. Ericsson's conclusions, if accurate, suggest that students should follow their interests earlier in their schooling to build up experience and receive meaningful feedback.

The insights of the researchers can explain the riddle of why so many elite soccer players are born early in the year. Since youth sports are organised by age group, teams have a cut-off birth date. In the European youth soccer leagues, the cut-off date is December 31. So when a coach is assessing two players in the same age group, one born in January and the other in December, the player born in January is likely to be bigger, stronger, more mature. Guess who the coach will pick. He may be mistaking maturity for ability but once chosen, those January-born players are the ones who, year after year, receive the training, the deliberate practice, the feedback – and have the accompanying self-esteem – that will turn them into elite players.

I'm not really convinced

LISTENING

1 🔊 **1.1** Listen to Derek and Jennifer's conversation.

1 Which sport has Derek started playing recently? Does he enjoy it?
2 Who's read the article? Who hasn't?
3 Who seems to find the ideas in the article convincing? Who's not so sure?

2 a 🔊 **1.1** Listen again. What's Derek's attitude to these ideas from the article?

1 Practice is important if you want to be good at something.
2 'Deliberate' practice is the best way to learn.
3 People are good at things they enjoy because they get more practice.

b Compare your answers, then read the script on p141 to check.

VOCABULARY

Reacting to ideas

3 a Look at the sentences from the conversation. Which can you use when an idea is:

a probably true?   b probably not true?   c too simple?
d not interesting or original?   e not clear?

1 That's **not saying anything new**.
2 That's **not the whole picture**.
3 It **makes a lot of sense**.
4 I'm not really **convinced**.
5 I **don't get** the bit about 'deliberate' practice.

b Now match these sentences with a–e.

6 I don't find it very **persuasive**.
7 It seems quite **simplistic**.
8 It sounds **logical**.
9 It's a bit **obvious**.
10 The part about 'deliberate' practice is hard to follow.

4 What do *you* think about the ideas in the article?

SPEAKING

5 Look at the summaries from a science news website on p118. Talk together and compare your reactions.

I've always been good at ...

1.2 goals
- talk about things you're good at
- describe and evaluate skills

LISTENING

1 🔊 **1.2** Listen to Darya, Cian and Hyun-Ae talking about things they're good at.

1 Match each person to a picture A–C.
2 Does each person talk about their working life, their life outside work, or both?

2 🔊 **1.2** Listen again. Find out:

1 when Darya realised what she was good at.
2 how she uses her ability now.
3 who Cian has represented in competitions.
4 how long a race stage can last.
5 how Hyun-Ae's childhood influenced her.
6 what she's doing now.

3 Do you think anyone can learn to be good at these things? Talk together.

GRAMMAR

Present perfect simple and progressive

4 Read examples 1–5 from the recording. Match them with discriptions a–e.

1 I've always **been** good with numbers.
2 I've **done** a couple of degrees, in psychology and social work.
3 I've recently **passed** my final engineering exams.
4 I've **been sailing** pretty consistently since I was nine.
5 I've **been studying** in the evenings so I'm quite tired.

You can use the **present perfect simple**:
a to summarise experiences in a period up to now. ___
b to describe finished events with a result now. ___
c to describe **states** which started in the past and continue up to now. ___
Verbs that commonly describe **states** include *be, know, understand, love, hate,* etc. They are not usually used in progressive forms.

You can use the **present perfect progressive**:
d to describe longer or repeated activities – finished or not – with a result now. ___
e to describe **activities** which started in the past and are still happening now. ___

5 a Complete Esmeralda's profile using the present perfect simple or progressive.

Esmeralda Vallejo, artist

I ^{1}_____ always _____ (be) interested in painting but I ^{2}_____ only _____ (do) it seriously for about five years. During that time, I ^{3}_____ (complete) various courses in techniques and materials and I ^{4}_____ (win) a few prizes in regional competitions. I'm not rich – not at all! – but since last year I ^{5}_____ (advertise) my work on the Internet and I now sell enough of my work to make a living, so I ^{6}_____ (give up) my part-time office job and I ^{7}_____ (become) a full-time artist. I'm feeling really excited about my work at the moment as I ^{8}_____ (experiment) with some new ideas – though I think some of my regular clients might be a bit shocked at the results!

Grammar reference and practice, p131

b Think of something you're good at. Write a paragraph like this about it, using the present perfect simple and progressive.

SPEAKING

6 a In groups, talk about the things you're good at and what you've done.

b Get into new groups. Tell each other about the people in your first group.

Transferable skills

VOCABULARY
Skills

1 a Look at the expressions from the recording in the box. Which group 1–3 describes:

a people skills? b physical abilities? c mental skills?

> 1 be **physically fit**, be **strong**, have plenty of **endurance**
> 2 be **good with numbers**, be able to **think logically**, be **focused**
> 3 be a **good listener**, be an **effective communicator**, have **the ability to compromise**

b Now add three more expressions from the box to each of the groups, 1–3.

> be able to **delegate** have **good eyesight** have a **good sense of balance**
> be able to **manage groups** have a lot of **self-discipline** have **quick reflexes**
> have plenty of **imagination** be **sensitive to** people's feelings be **well organised**

> Well, Cian's physically fit ... And he must have a good sense of balance.

2 Talk together. Which skills do you think Darya, Cian and Hyun-Ae probably have?

PRONUNCIATION
Stress

3 a Look at the highlighted expressions in 1a and 1b. Which words do you think are stressed? Which are not stressed? Underline the stressed syllables.

be good with numbers

b 🎧 **1.3** Listen and look at the script on p141 to check.

c What kinds of words are usually:

1 stressed? *nouns, ...*
2 not stressed? *pronouns, ...*

SPEAKING

4 Read part of a website for job seekers. What are transferable skills? Does everyone have them?

---

www.jobsfoundbyus.com/skills

Findajob

Transferable skills for job seekers

These skills are vitally important for all job seekers, students and people considering a career change. But what exactly are transferable skills? Basically, they're skills that you have naturally or that you've acquired from any activity in your life – classes, parenting, projects, hobbies, sports, other jobs – which you can then take and put to use in a job you'd like to do. For example, a full-time parent who'd like to move into a junior management position might have a number of relevant transferable skills like being well organised, good at managing their time and able to multi-task.

---

5 a Work alone. What transferable skills do you have that would be relevant to these jobs?

- a high-rise window cleaner • a landscape gardener • the mayor of a small town
- a stock market trader • a tele-sales agent • a writer

Decide which job would be most suitable for you.

b In groups, explain your ideas from 5a. Who would be the best person for each job?

> I could be a high-rise window cleaner. I've always been quite sporty so I've got a good sense of balance.

> Really? I'd be terrified of falling ...

Give advice about an interest or occupation

1.3 goals

⊚ talk about people's success ♻
⊚ describe and evaluate skills ♻
⊚ give advice about an interest or occupation

TASK LISTENING

1 Read the information about VideoJug. Which of the four guides mentioned would you be most interested in? Have you ever used a website like this?

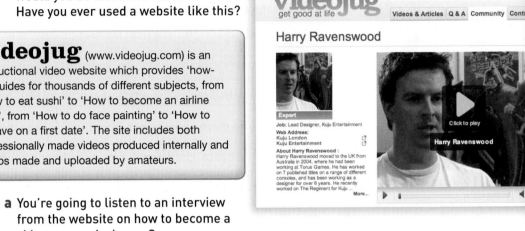

videojug (www.videojug.com) is an instructional video website which provides 'how-to' guides for thousands of different subjects, from 'How to eat sushi' to 'How to become an airline pilot', from 'How to do face painting' to 'How to behave on a first date'. The site includes both professionally made videos produced internally and videos made and uploaded by amateurs.

2 a You're going to listen to an interview from the website on how to become a video games designer. Can you guess the answers to these questions?

1 Does a game designer need qualifications?
2 How do I get my foot in the door at a games company?
3 Does a games designer need to know how to write computer code?
4 Does a games designer need to be a good artist?
5 I have an idea for a game. What should I do with it?

b ⚫ **1.4** Listen to check your ideas. Compare in groups, then listen again or read the script on pp141–2.

TASK VOCABULARY

Giving advice

3 Look at some of Harry's answers to the interview questions. Which questions in 2a is he answering?

1 *It helps to* be able to draw a little bit.
2 A broad qualification *can help you*.
3 If you can sketch even feebly, I think *it helps*.
4 A game designer *doesn't need* to know how to code, *but it helps*.
5 There are *a number of ways you can* get your foot in the door.
6 *A good way of* getting experience *is to* apply for work experience positions.
7 If you really want that game made, *try and* get a job in the industry ...
8 ... or hook up with a couple of mates and *see if you can* make it together.

4 Using the highlighted expressions in 3, choose one of your interests or your occupation and write four or five sentences giving advice about it.

TASK

5 a Imagine you're going to take part in an interview for VideoJug about the interest or occupation you chose in 4. Tell a partner what the topic is.

b Work alone. Make a list of questions to ask your partner about their chosen topic.

• Would you recommend ... as a career / a pastime?
• What advice would you give to someone who ...?
• Can anyone ...?
• How can you become a ...?

• How can you get into ...?
• Do you need a lot of ...?
• Is it ...?

c Exchange questions. Think about:

1 how to answer your partner's questions.
2 which language you can use from 3.

6 a Interview each other. Ask questions to find out more details.

b If possible, do your interviews again and make an audio or video recording. Listen to or watch the interviews as a class.

Keyword *think*

Meanings of *think*

1 a What do you think the people in these pictures are saying?

b Now find one sentence from A–D to go in each picture. Did you have similar ideas?

A
You **think** too much. Just choose one and let's go!
You're always **thinking about** your work. You need a holiday.

C
How did you **think of** the name for your company?
We really need to **think of** some ways to save money.

B
We're **thinking of** having a party on Friday. Are you free then?
My parents are **thinking about** buying a new car.

D
What do you **think about** jazz music? Do you like it?
So, what do you **think of** the octopus?

c Match each meaning of think with a pair of sentences A–D.

1   have an opinion or believe something
2   create an idea or a solution to a problem
3   consider doing something
4   use your mind to consider a topic

d Which meanings go with: a of? b about? c either of or about?

2 a Choose of or about. Sometimes both are possible.

1   What do you think of / about when you're doing exercise?
2   Have you ever thought of / about having your own website?
3   What do you think of / about your country's football team?
4   Can you think of / about three reasons why you started studying English?

Now write two or three more questions with think for the people in your class.

b Answer and discuss all your questions in groups.

Common expressions with *think*

3 a Look at the sentences together. Can you work out what the expressions mean?

1	I can't **think straight** if there's music on while I'm trying to work.	think + adverb
2	I find that **thinking aloud** helps me to solve problems.	
3	Where I live, people generally **think highly of** doctors ...	think + adverb + of/to/about
4	... but they **don't think much of** teachers.	
5	As I get older, I **think back to** my schooldays more and more.	
6	I know people who are always **thinking ahead to** their next holiday.	
7	If I won a lot of money, I'd **think twice about** telling my friends.	
8	I **thought long and hard about** what shoes to wear today.	
9	I really don't enjoy situations where I have to **think on my feet**.	think + prepositional phrase
10	The best school teachers encourage children to **think for themselves**.	

Check your ideas in a dictionary or ask your teacher.

b Test each other in pairs. Take turns to give definitions and say the expressions in 1–10.

It means think carefully, for a long time.

OK ... think long and hard?

4   Which sentences are true for you? Discuss 1–10 in groups.

1 If you were organising a party, what things would you need to think about?

a venue, food, ...

2 ● **1.5** Listen to Giulia and Brendan organising a party for their friend Indra.

1 What has Brendan already done or planned on his own?

2 What things do Giulia and Brendan plan together?

3 a Read the conversation in the opposite column. Which highlighted expressions 1–9 can you use:

1 to describe groups of things, after giving one or two examples?

2 in informal situations, when you can't remember or don't know:
   a the name of a person?
   b the name of a thing?

b Now add six more expressions to the groups in 3a.

> and all that   and whatnot   what's-her-name
> and stuff   thingummy   and so forth

4 Choose expressions from 3a and 3b to complete the conversation. There's more than one possible answer.

BRENDAN	Can you bring your CDs by ¹_____? The Brazilian guitarist?
GIULIA	Jobim? Sure. And I'll bring some salsa and meringue ²_____.
BRENDAN	Oh, and Stella's bringing some Indian pop – Bollywood music ³_____.
GIULIA	Perfect. Now what about games and activities ⁴_____?
BRENDAN	I think we're too old for games!
GIULIA	But what about a one-minute speech contest? On various topics.
BRENDAN	Could be fun. We'd need a ⁵_____ – erm, a video camera.
GIULIA	No, we can use our mobiles. OK, now what about drinks ⁶_____?

5 a In groups, choose one of these events to plan for, or think of your own event.

• a weekend hiking trip in the mountains
• a summer picnic near a lake
• a child's birthday party

b Talk together and make a list of things you'll need or want for your event, for example:

food and drink   equipment   office supplies
decorations   clothing   transport   entertainment

Use expressions from 3a and 3b.

6 Tell the other groups what you've planned.

Goals

⊚ use vague expressions to describe categories of things
⊚ use vague expressions when you can't remember a word

GIULIA	So, how much have you managed to do, Brendan?
BRENDAN	Well, I've sent the invitations.
GIULIA	Great.
BRENDAN	And the meal's all planned – the starters, meat dishes, vegetarian dishes ¹and so on.
GIULIA	By vegetarian dishes, do you mean salads ²and things?
BRENDAN	Yeah, salads of course, but also vegetarian soup, pasta, curry ³et cetera. I want a good variety.
GIULIA	Sounds perfect. And have you had a chance to think about decorations?
BRENDAN	No, I haven't got that far yet.
GIULIA	Right. Well, I think we should have balloons ⁴and that kind of thing. Oh, and flowers. Indra loves flowers.
BRENDAN	OK, and how about a ⁵thingy for her to wear? Like, erm, a badge that says 'Top of the class' or 'Best student', you know?
GIULIA	Maybe, but I can't see her wearing a badge. She's quite modest. I think we should stick with balloons ⁶and what have you.
BRENDAN	Hmm ... well, what about a Mexican ⁷whatsit? You know, erm, you hang it from the ceiling and hit it and out come sweets, toys ⁸and all sorts of things.
GIULIA	Oh, you mean a piñata. Yeah, that would be fun. You'd need a car to get it home, though. They're pretty big.
BRENDAN	No problem. I can ask ⁹what's-his-name ... er, Kerry's cousin. He's got a car and doesn't live too far from here.

> First, we need to decide on clothes, footwear et cetera.

> Yes, and we'd better take a whatsit, you know, to tell us which direction we're going in.

Review

VOCABULARY Skills

1 a Which expressions go with **be**? Which go with **have**? Make two lists.

> good with numbers   physically fit
> plenty of endurance   a lot of self-discipline
> a good listener   the ability to compromise

b Add more expressions to each list. Think about physical, mental and people skills. Then look back at p9 to check your ideas.

c Think of five people who you believe are really skilful at particular things on your lists. They can be well-known people or people you know personally.

my sister – really good listener

d Tell each other about the people you chose. Ask questions to find out more about them.

GRAMMAR Present perfect simple and progressive

2 a Read the paragraph and choose the correct options.

> I have a friend, Remi, who has been playing the guitar since he was ten. He ¹has released / has been releasing several CDs and he ²has organised / has been organising a number of festivals devoted to different kinds of guitar music. He ³has always had / has always been having a lot of talent and self-discipline, but in the last few years in particular I think he ⁴has become / has been becoming a really great guitarist. The last time I saw him was about three months ago because he ⁵has worked / has been working on a new CD. I can't wait to hear it.

b Think of someone you know about who's very talented. Write a short paragraph about:

- what the person has experienced and achieved
- how they've got to their present position
- what they've been working on recently.

Use the present perfect simple and progressive.

c Read each other's paragraphs. Ask questions to find out more.

Extension

SPELLING AND SOUNDS /dʒ/

3 a Complete the spelling of these words with: **j g dg**. Then check in a dictionary.

__ail	mana__er	in__ure
__ym	__igsaw	__ournal
bu__et	sub__ect	lo__ically

b Find words in 3a to match these spelling patterns for the beginning and middle of words.

1. You usually write **j** before *a*, *o* and *u*.
2. You usually write **g** before *e*, *i* and *y*.
3. In some words, you write **j** before *e* and *i*.
4. You write **dg** in the middle of some words.

c ● 1.6 Spellcheck. Listen and write twelve words. Then check your spelling on p142.

NOTICE *good at*, *good with*

4 a Look at the two patterns with **good** from script 1.2 on p141.

DARYA   I've always been good with numbers.

HYUN-AE   I'm good at helping people get on with each other.

Which pattern do you use before:

1. an activity or subject?
2. a group of things or people?

b Which of these expressions go after **good at**? Which go after **good with**? Make two lists.

> children   computers   cooking   my hands
> explaining things   maths   money   music
> people   sports   words   writing

c Talk to different people in your class. Find at least one person who's good at or good with each of the things in 4b.

Self-assessment

Can you do these things in English? ⊙Circle⊙ a number on each line. 1 = I can't do this, 5 = I can do this well.

⊙ talk about people's success	1	2	3	4	5
⊙ discuss and evaluate ideas	1	2	3	4	5
⊙ talk about things you're good at	1	2	3	4	5
⊙ describe and evaluate skills	1	2	3	4	5
⊙ give advice about an interest or occupation	1	2	3	4	5
⊙ use vague expressions to describe categories of things	1	2	3	4	5
⊙ use vague expressions when you can't remember a word	1	2	3	4	5

- For Wordcards, reference and saving your work → e-Portfolio
- For more practice → Self-study Pack, Unit 1

2.1 goals
⊚ describe events in detail
⊚ deal with misunderstandings
⊚ describe experiences of things going wrong

2 Misunderstandings

Not my day

LISTENING

1 What seems to be the problem in each picture? What might the people be saying or thinking?

2 🔊 **1.7** Listen to Rainer's two conversations, first with his colleague Pauline, then with his wife Liana.

1 What's the problem in each conversation?
2 What's the solution?
3 Who are the people in the pictures?

3 🔊 **1.7** Listen again. Are these statements true or false?

1 Chris's text message to Pauline was badly written.
2 In the office where Rainer works, most people have now got the flu.
3 Pauline will be able to go to her other appointments after the Layton meeting.
4 Rainer's mother phoned to say thank you for her present.
5 Liana chose the wrong thing in the catalogue.
6 They can't return the present because Rainer bought it for a special price.

4 If you were Rainer, what would you say to Chris? If you were Rainer's mother, would you keep the tree?

VOCABULARY

Dealing with misunderstandings

5 Complete the sentences from the conversations with the words on the right.

Explaining
1 I _____ you'd cancelled that meeting.   told
2 Chris _____ me he'd cancelled all meetings because of the flu.   said
3 You _____ you'd ordered that plant we talked about.   thought
4 I think he _____ all *his* meetings.   explains
5 That's _____ what he said. He said *all* meetings.   meant
6 I see. Well, that _____ it.   not
Solving
7 What _____ I call for a taxi? I can be there in twenty minutes.   logical
8 The _____ thing is to return the tree to the garden centre.   if
9 The other _____ is to take it to your office.   option

PRONUNCIATION

Contrastive stress

6 a 🔊 **1.8** You can stress a word strongly when you want to contrast it with something else. Listen.

PAULINE   Chris told me he'd cancelled all meetings.
RAINER   I think he meant all his meetings.
PAULINE   But that's not what he said. He said all meetings.

14

b Decide which two contrasting words would have strong stress.

1 It isn't your fault. It's Chris's fault.
2 The problem is, it isn't a plant. It's a tree.
3 It wasn't the normal price. It was a special price.

c 🔊 **1.9** Listen to check. Practise saying the sentences.

SPEAKING

7 a Work in pairs.

Student A – read your situations on p119.
Student B – read your situations on p120.

Think about which expressions from 5 you can use in each situation.

b Imagine you are in each situation and talk to each other.

I was sure I'd ...

GRAMMAR
Past simple and past perfect simple

1 Look at these examples. In each sentence, which verb form describes the earlier action or event?

> 1 I **assumed** it **had spread** through your whole office.
> 2 After Chris **had texted** me, I **made** other appointments for today.
> 3 She **said** she'**d received** it.
> 4 I **was sure** I'**d circled** the plant in the garden centre catalogue.
> 5 By the time I **got** to the office, the catalogue **had disappeared**.
> 6 I **knew** something **had gone** wrong but I couldn't imagine what.
>
> The past perfect is often used after past simple verbs describing speech and thoughts: *said told thought was sure assumed knew noticed realised ...*

2 a Read Carl's story about a disastrous journey. Choose the best options.

"My worst ever journey – though it was kind of funny, too – happened in India a few years ago. I wanted to get a train from Delhi to a town called Dehra Dun near the Himalayas. But half an hour before my train was due to leave, I ¹realised / had realised I ²came / had come to the wrong station. I ³was / had been sure my friend ⁴told / had told me to go to the station in New Delhi but in fact my train went from the Old Delhi station. I jumped in a taxi but when I ⁵got / had got to Old Delhi, my train ⁶already left / had already left.

So I bought a new ticket, waited a few hours and got on the next train. Everything was fine until I ⁷noticed / had noticed one of my bags ⁸disappeared / had disappeared. I ⁹remembered / 'd remembered that a strange man ¹⁰walked / had walked through the carriage some time before, so maybe he ¹¹took / 'd taken it. Unfortunately, there was an old camera in it with some pictures that I ¹²took / 'd taken of my grandmother just before she died, and also a hat some close friends ¹³gave / had given me. The other passengers were very kind and tried to help, but it was too late.

Later, we stopped at a little station in the countryside. Suddenly, a wave of water ¹⁴came / had come through the open window and soaked me to the skin! I ¹⁵forgot / 'd forgotten it was the Hindu festival of Holi, when people throw paints and water at each other. It's all meant to be fun, of course, but by that time I ¹⁶lost / 'd lost my sense of humour!"

Grammar reference and practice, p132

b 🔊 **1.10** Listen to check.

SPEAKING

3 a Think about an incident from your life when things went wrong, involving for example:

- a misunderstanding
- wrong information
- a lost or stolen item
- something you forgot to do or say
- a small accident
- transport problems

Plan the language you'll need to describe the incident.

b In pairs, describe your incidents. Ask questions to find out more.

4 Get into new pairs and describe your incidents again. Include the extra details that your first partner asked about.

Sen no Rikyū

morning glory flowers

Sen no Rikyū, tea master (1522–1591)

Toyotomi Hideyoshi, warlord (1536–1598)

LISTENING

1 a Look at the pictures. While taking her friend Jessica around a museum in Japan, Shiori tells her an old story about Rikyū, Hideyoshi, and Rikyū's flowers. Can you guess which of the two men:

1   asks for something?
2   reluctantly agrees to do something?
3   does something surprising?

4   gets angry?
5   learns something?

b ⏺ **1.11** Listen to the story. Did you guess correctly?

2 a Put the events of the story in order 1–8. Hideyoshi:

a   ___ arrived at the garden the next day.
b   ___ asked Rikyū to hold a tea ceremony.
c   ___ felt shocked and angry.
d   ___ noticed the flowers in the garden.
e   ___ saw a single flower in a vase.
f   ___ saw the flowers had been cut down.
g   ___ was riding past Rikyū's house.
h   ___ went into the tea house.

b ⏺ **1.11** Listen again to check.

3 a What do you think the meaning of the story could be? Talk together.

b ⏺ **1.12** Listen to Shiori's interpretation. What do you think of it?

VOCABULARY

Adverbs for describing actions

4 Match the adverbs in 1–5 with their opposites in the box.

1   He would **carefully** choose tea bowls and pots and so on.
2   **Suddenly**, he noticed that Rikyū's garden was full of these fantastic flowers.
3   He asked Rikyū to hold a tea ceremony, and Rikyū agreed **reluctantly**.
4   Rikyū had **deliberately** cut down all the flowers!
5   Rikyū was just sitting there **calmly**, waiting to make tea for him.

accidentally   furiously   carelessly   enthusiastically   gradually

5 You can put this kind of adverb in positions a–c. Find examples in the sentences in 4.

a   before the main verb which it describes
b   at the end of a clause
c   at the start of a clause, to give it special emphasis

SPEAKING

6 a Work in two groups, A and B.

As – imagine you're Sen no Rikyū.
Bs – imagine you're Toyotomi Hideyoshi.

Practise telling the story from your point of view. Include some of the adverbs from 4.

One day, I was out riding my horse when I saw …

b Get into A/B pairs and listen to each other's versions of the story.

Significant stories

GRAMMAR

Past progressive
and past perfect
progressive

1 **Look at the sentences in the box. Which verb form can you use to describe:**

a an activity in progress at a point in the past?

NOW

b a period of activity before a point in the past?

NOW

> **Past progressive**
> Hideyoshi **was riding** past Rikyū's house when he noticed the garden was full of flowers.
> When Hideyoshi got inside the teahouse, Rikyū **was sitting** there calmly.
>
> **Past perfect progressive**
> Hideyoshi was a rich, powerful soldier who**'d been fighting** all his life.
> Hideyoshi **had been expecting** to see this amazing garden again but instead he found ...

2 **a Complete the folk legend about a famous salt mine in Poland. Use the past simple, past progressive or past perfect progressive.**

"In the south of Poland, in a town called Wieliczka, there's a famous salt mine. According to a traditional story, mining started in Wieliczka because of a Hungarian princess called Kinga.

Kinga ¹_____ (prepare) to marry Bolesław, the Duke of Kraków, so she asked her father, King Bela, for a present which she could give to her husband. Salt was very valuable at the time, so Bela ²_____ (give) her one of his salt mines in Hungary. As she ³_____ (leave) for Poland, Kinga took a gold ring from her finger and threw it into the deepest part of the mine.

After Kinga ⁴_____ (live) in Kraków for some months, she suggested to Bolesław that they should find a place to establish a salt mine. They started their search the next day. They ⁵_____ (travel) for only a few hours when they ⁶_____ (reach) the village of Wieliczka, and Kinga felt sure that this was the right place. The Duke's servants started digging. Almost at once they hit a hard stone and, on lifting it from the earth, saw that it was a block of pure salt and that inside the block, something ⁷_____ (shine). Kinga looked into the block and ⁸_____ (recognise) the ring which she had thrown into the mine in Hungary, hundreds of miles away.

Nowadays the mine at Wieliczka is like a huge underground city, with more than 2000 rooms and 300 kilometres of passages. Not much actual mining happens there, but it's a huge tourist attraction."

**Grammar reference
and practice, p132**

b 🔊 **1.13** **Listen to the story and check your answers.**

SPEAKING

3 **a Work alone. Choose a story from your country which you think would be important or interesting for a visitor to hear about, for example:**

- a traditional fairy tale
- an old legend
- a historical anecdote
- an event from recent history

b Get ready to tell your story.

1 Write down the key words and names to help you remember it.
2 Think about the order of events and decide what verb forms to use.
3 Think of some adverbs you can include.

c Listen to each other's stories and ask questions to find out more about anything which interests you. If you're from the same country, do you think all the details of the stories are correct?

Make a complaint

2.3 goals
- describe events in detail ♻
- explain why you're not satisfied with a service

TASK LISTENING

1 Where you live, what kinds of food can you get delivered to your home? Do you ever order food by phone? What problems can customers experience with this kind of service?

2 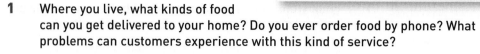 Listen to a phone call from Ian, the manager of a pizza delivery company, to Maureen, an unhappy customer from the previous evening. What's the reason for his call?

   a to find out why Maureen was unhappy
   b to persuade her to pay the rest of the bill
   c to explain the company's mistakes

3 1.14 Listen again. Complete Ian's notes.

> Yesterday evening – problem with order no. 008463 (rec'd. 21:06)
>
> Bill came to £18.45 (2 pizzas XL + 2 salads) Customer paid £10
>
> First order: about ¹_____ pm – lost?
>
> Second order: 8pm
>
> Delivery: ²_____ pm (Barry got lost?)
>
> Food was ³_____. One box was ⁴_____.
>
> (Customer paid ⁵£_____ for a meal from another restaurant.)
>
> ACTION: investigate; send ⁶£_____ refund & discount vouchers.

4 What would you have done in Maureen's position? Would you be satisfied with Ian's offer?

TASK VOCABULARY

Explaining a complaint

5 Look at Maureen's sentences. Which group of highlighted expressions 1–3 can you use to:

   a explain events?
   b explain what was said?
   c explain consequences?

   1 **They said they'd** lost the order. ('d = had)
      They said they'd deliver in about forty minutes. ('d = would)
      Again, **I was told** it would take forty minutes.

   2 **I'd already** ordered **before** that.
      At eight o'clock, the pizzas **still hadn't** arrived.
      By that time, we'd been waiting more than two hours.

   3 **I ended up** ordering some Chinese food instead.
      It cost me another twenty pounds.
      I had to go to the trouble of collecting it myself.

TASK

6 a Work in two groups.

   Group A – look at your situation on p118.
   Group B – look at your situation on p120.

   Think about the questions you need to answer in Situation 1.

  b Get into A/B pairs and talk together to resolve the situation.

  c Go back to your groups and report on your conversations.

   Group A – What did the company representative say to you? Are you satisfied?
   Group B – Why exactly was the customer unhappy? What did you say?

7 Repeat 6a–6c for Situation 2.

8 Do you have any personal experience of this kind of conversation? What happened? How does it compare with the conversations you've just had?

Across cultures Aspects of culture

BRAGA
PORTO
COIMBRA
Portugal
LISBOA
FARO

LISTENING

1 **a** What would you want to know about before you visited or moved to another country? In groups, add to this list.

cost of living   food   regional differences   ...

b Make a class list of all your topics.

2 **1.15** Listen to David talking about Portuguese culture. Which topics on your list does he mention? What other topics does he mention?

3 **a** **1.15** Listen again. Write down one or two details about each of David's topics. Then compare your notes.

b Read the script on pp143–4 to check.

4 If you're from Portugal, do you agree with what David says? If you're from another country, which things are similar to where you live? Is anything very different?

VOCABULARY

Generalising and talking about differences

5 **a** Complete the highlighted expressions with these words.

| can   difference   different   people   speaking   tend   tendency   typically   vary |

Generalising
1 People **have a** _____ to learn languages in the big cities.
2 Apart from some of the young people, **most** _____ won't speak English.
3 **Generally** _____, I think people used to be more open and friendly.
4 People _____ **to** keep to themselves now.
5 In the north, people _____ **be** very opinionated.
6 **You will** _____ have at least three, four coffees a day.

Talking about differences
7 There's a big _____ **between** big cities and the countryside.
8 Traditions _____ **from** city to city, from area to area.
9 In the cities, they **do things in a slightly** _____ **way**.

b Choose five or six expressions from 5a and write sentences about your country.

SPEAKING

6 Prepare a short talk for visitors to your country or another country you know well.

1 Decide who your talk is for. Is it for people who are:
   a coming to live and work in your country?
   b visiting your country for a week on business?
2 Make notes on three or four aspects of culture that are important for them to know about.
3 Mention any important cultural differences between groups of people.

7 Talk in groups. Listen and ask questions about anything that interests you.

8 If you're from the same country, is there anything you disagree with or wish to add? Did you learn anything new about different cities or regions? If you're from different countries, what were the most interesting things you heard?

2 EXPLOREWriting

1 Why do you think people skydive? Have you tried it? Is it something you'd like to try?

2 Read the article about army lieutenant Charlie Williams's skydiving accident. Match the topics a–d with the paragraphs 1–4.

a accepting the situation
b survival and afterwards
c background to the story
d first actions

What it feels like to ... **survive a skydive without a parachute**

¹ I've always had a fear of heights, so one day I volunteered for a jump course. I took part in two jumps that went well. I'd heard that the chances of having a parachute malfunction are about one in 750,000 but on my third jump, I hit the side of the plane. Next thing I knew, I was falling fast, turning over and over.

² When you open your parachute, you need to be in a good position so it comes straight out and opens up, but instead the strings attached to the canopy got tangled around my legs. I tried to untie them but they were too tight. If you can't open your main parachute, you remove it and then open the reserve parachute but that didn't work either.

³ Finally, when I realised that there was nothing more I could do, I thought, "Right, I'm dead." Up till then, this whole process had only taken eight seconds and I was still 900 metres up. I remember feeling incredibly lonely. All the time I was falling and turning, with no control. I briefly saw the ground and a little shack. Then I hit the roof of the shack. I bounced off it, hit a wall and then the ground. I never lost consciousness.

⁴ For the first few minutes, I couldn't feel anything, but then the pain started. I lay there just thinking, "I can't believe I'm alive, this is so bizarre yet amazing." I'd dislocated a finger and slightly fractured three bones in my back. I could have walked away. I haven't jumped since then, but I'm building towards it. I still can't believe how lucky I am.

3 Read the article again. What kind of person do you think Charlie is? Would you dive again if you were Charlie? Compare and explain your ideas.

4 Charlie uses different techniques to make his story exciting to read. In paragraph 3, find:

1 a quotation which shows how Charlie thought and felt.
2 a use of the past progressive to emphasise that an action happened over a period of time.
3 a series of short, dramatic sentences.

5 Which of these expressions are useful:

1 to introduce a story?
2 to finish a story?

> I still can't believe ...   one day
> I've always ...   since then

Look in the article to check.

6 Look at the highlighted expressions in the article. Which does Charlie use to describe:

1 his thoughts and feelings? (x2)
2 a period of time? (x3)
3 the sequence of events? (x3)

7 a Think of a topic for a story with the title 'What it feels like to ...'. The story can be real or made up. Here are some ideas:

* win a competition
* be on television
* see a wild animal close up
* fly in a hot-air balloon

b Think about:

1 how many paragraphs you'll need and what you'll put in each one.
2 which techniques from 4 you'd like to try.
3 what language you'll need:
   * expressions from 5 and 6
   * verb forms to describe the order and duration of events
   * dramatic adverbs: *reluctantly, suddenly, incredibly ...*

8 Write your story.

9 Exchange stories with a partner. Ask questions to find out more. Do you think the story is real or made up?

2 Look again ♻

Review

VOCABULARY Adverbs for describing actions

1 a Think of something:

1 you did accidentally last month. *locked myself out of my flat*
2 you choose carefully when shopping.
3 you reacted furiously to on TV.
4 you've reluctantly agreed to do recently.
5 you find difficult to think about calmly.

b Compare answers. Ask questions to find out more.

GRAMMAR Past verb forms

2 a Read Patti's description of an important day in her life. What is she doing now?

" It sounds unbelievable but one of the most important days in my life was when I went to the park and watched this gardener working in one of the public gardens. It made me realise that that was what I wanted to do – to work outside in the fresh air doing something physical. At the time ᵃI was studying law at university, but I wasn't happy and for a long time ᵇI'd been thinking about giving it up. In fact, the only thing that stopped me was the fact that ᶜI'd already given up a couple of other courses! In the end I did finish my degree, but I've never used it. I went straight on to a course on landscape gardening and now I do it for a living. "

b Which past form a–c describes:

1 an activity in progress at a point in the past?
2 an action which is finished before another action in the past?
3 a period of activity before a point in the past?

c Work alone. Choose two important days from your life and write a few sentences to describe them using a variety of past forms.

d Tell each other about your important days.

CAN YOU REMEMBER? Unit 1 – Routes to success

3 a Complete the questions. Then check on p6.

1 Do you **set specific** g_____ls or just let things happen naturally?
2 Have you **received** any t_____g? Where?
3 Where do you **get** valuable f_____k from?
4 How much p_____e do you **put in**?
5 How were you able to **build up** e_____e?
6 Do you **concentrate on** r_____ts or on technique?
7 How much natural t_____t do you think you **possess**?

b Choose a thing you're good at and think of answers to the questions. Then ask each other the questions.

Extension

SPELLING AND SOUNDS /n/

4 a Underline the letters which make a /n/ sound.

resign canopy reign funniest know
planned sign tendency beginning ground

b Find words in 4a to match these spelling patterns.

1 /n/ is usually spelled **n**.
But there are some important exceptions:
2 You write **nn** between a short vowel and endings like: *-ed -er -ing -ily*
3 A few words begin with **kn**.
4 A few words end with **gn**.

c Spellcheck. Complete the spelling of these words. Then check in a dictionary.

desi__   fu__ier   ceremo__y   __ife
forei__   ru__er   __ee   relucta__tly

NOTICE Verbs with two objects

5 a These sentences from the unit include a **verb** with two objects. Underline the objects. Which comes first, a person or thing?

1 He **sent** me a text.
2 I phoned to **wish** her 'Happy Birthday'.
3 It **cost** me another twenty pounds.
4 I'd like to **give** you some vouchers.

b Put the sentences in order.

1 **get** chocolate me Could some you ?
2 a message **left** I voice mail you your on .
3 euros me fifty **lend** Would you ?
4 seat even me He **offer** didn't a .
5 favour **owe** I a you big .
6 surprise me But a you **promised** !

c In pairs, write a seven- or eight-line conversation between two people. Start with *Could you get me …?* Include three or four verbs with two objects.

d Listen to each other's conversations. Which verbs with two objects did you hear?

3

3.1 goals
- express views about different options
- talk about education and training

Learners and teachers

Doing a course

READING AND LISTENING

1 Talk together.

1 Have you ever done a course in your free time?
2 Is this a common way to spend free time where you live?
3 Why do people do courses in their free time?

2 Read the descriptions of six evening courses in the Markham College brochure. Which courses do you think could help you to:

- communicate more effectively? • entertain guests? • help other people?
- get fit? • understand part of another culture? • save money?
- be more creative? • understand people?

Carrie and Don live in Toronto, Canada. They're considering doing a course at Markham College, which is near their home.

3 ◀ **1.16** Listen to Carrie and Don's conversation.

1 What are their reasons for doing a course together?
2 Which courses do they discuss? Do they manage to choose one together?

4 ◀ **1.16** Listen again. For each course that Carrie and Don decide against:

1 who wants to do it?
2 who doesn't want to do it, or isn't sure? Why?

VOCABULARY

Discussing options

5 Look at sentences 1–8 from the conversation. Find two with similar meanings to each sentence A–D.

1 For me, it's a choice between two or three.
2 I like the sound of this one.
3 There's no way I'm doing that!
4 I can't make up my mind about it.
5 I wouldn't mind doing a course in First Aid.
6 That doesn't really appeal to me.
7 I'd be happy with either Cookery or Psychology.
8 I've got mixed feelings about that one.

A	I'd like to give this one a try. ___ ___
B	This one isn't really my thing. ___ ___
C	I'm in two minds about this one. ___ ___
D	I've narrowed it down to these two. ___ ___

6 In pairs, cover 1–8 above. Look at A–D and try to remember the two expressions with similar meanings.

PRONUNCIATION

Fluent speech 1 – leaving out /t/

7 a ◀ **1.17** Listen to the sentences. Notice how the speakers leave out some /t/ sounds.

I wouldn't mind doing a course in First Aid. That doesn't really appeal to me.

I can't make up my mind about it. This one isn't really my thing.

Now choose the correct explanations. You can often leave out a /t/ sound if:

1 it's at <u>the beginning</u> / <u>the end</u> of a word *and*
2 it's between two <u>consonant</u> / <u>vowel</u> sounds.

b Practise saying the sentences.

MC Markham College
Center for Continuing Education

Bollywood Workout
10 weeks Fridays, 19.00–21.00 $220

Lessons focus on the classic moves of the entertaining and beautiful dance forms seen in Bollywood films, all accompanied by lively traditional music. The classes offer a great full-body workout for those who want to stay in shape and include more exercise in their weekly routine. Comfortable clothes are recommended.

Car Maintenance for Beginners
10 weeks Thursdays, 18.30–21.00 $400

This course provides practical training in basic servicing, replacement of parts and minor repairs. It also includes lectures on car engines, tires and brakes as well as how to buy cars. You will gain a better understanding of how cars work and practical knowledge on how to keep your car in good working order.

Creative writing
8 weeks Mon. and Thu., 19.30–21.00 $265

This course introduces you to the skill and process of creative writing. In-class exercises focus on characterization, dialogue and narrative. Assignments done at home will develop your own ideas. You're encouraged to listen to each other's work and offer critical support. You'll discover your own writing voice while producing both fiction and poetry.

Basic First Aid
8 weeks Tuesdays, 19.30–21.30 $175

We offer hands-on learning of this important life skill so you'll be able to act confidently in various emergency situations requiring first aid. You'll also learn about common medical conditions, along with suitable treatments for people of various ages. Successful participants will receive a certificate in basic first aid.

Malaysian Cookery
6 weeks Wed. and Fri., 19.00–21.30 $440

Our course introduces students to Malaysian cooking – a fantastic blend of cuisines, mainly Malay, Chinese and Indian. The varied dishes guarantee something for everyone's taste. All our tutors are Malaysian-born and fully qualified. Classes are small to ensure good supervision. Students work in individual, fully equipped cooking stations. And no washing up!

An introduction to psychology
12 weeks Tue. and Fri., 17.30–19.30 $495

Psychology is about understanding human behaviour and this course is designed for people who would like to increase their knowledge of this important and fascinating area. The course covers a range of topics, and seminars encourage discussion of past and present theories and case studies. A certificate of completion will be awarded.

SPEAKING

8 **a** You want to do a course with some friends in your free time. Working alone, read the brochure again carefully and decide which courses:

- you definitely don't want to do
- you're not sure about
- you're interested in

b Discuss in groups. Try to find a course you're all happy to do.

Learning choices

VOCABULARY

Education and training

1 Talk together. What's the difference between each expression in the groups a–d?

a distance learning, online learning, face-to-face learning
b postgraduate courses, evening courses, full-time courses
c vocational training, apprenticeships, work experience
d lectures, seminars, coursework, dissertations

2 Cover 1 and complete the statements. Then look at 1 to check.

1 Employees who've done a_____ are better than those with paper qualifications.
2 Schools should focus on academic subjects rather than v_____ _____.
3 S_____ are a waste of time. Students learn much more from l_____.
4 D_____ _____ isn't as effective as f_____ _____ or on-campus learning.
5 Students' grades should be based on c_____ rather than final exams.
6 Students should get some w_____ _____ before going to college.
7 These days you need to do p_____ _____ to get a good job.
8 E_____ _____ for adults should be partly financed by the government.

SPEAKING

3 **a** Work alone. What do you think about the statements in 2? Mark each statement with:

++ totally agree   + mostly agree   ? not sure   – mostly disagree   – – totally disagree

b Talk together. Express your opinions about each statement and give reasons.

Head teacher

3.2 goals
◎ talk about experiences of education and training
◎ describe habits and tendencies in the past and present

Hello, class, I'm the 16-year-old head

Dean Nelson in Delhi

For his classmates, the four o'clock bell means lessons are over, but for 16-year-old Babur Ali, it is time to take off his uniform and start a new school day as probably the youngest head teacher in the world.

READING

1 a Look at the pictures and read the headline and first paragraph of the article about Babur Ali. Tell a partner what you'd like to find out in the rest of the article.

b Read the rest of the article. Did you find out what you wanted to know?

Since he was 11, Babur has been running his own school in Bhabta, a small village in West Bengal, passing on to the children of poor families the knowledge he has acquired at his fee-paying school during the day.

It began when children in his village plagued him with questions about what he learned at the 1,000-rupee-a-year school their parents could not afford.

"It started without much effort," he says. "There were lots of children who had dropped out of school, or never been to school at all. They were always asking questions about my lessons and I would repeat everything for them.

"There used to be just eight pupils, and my friends helped me with the teaching. We worked on the standard of teaching, the word spread to nearby villages, and gradually we took on more and more students."

Five years later, Babur is recognised by district education officials as 'head teacher' of the Anand Shikshya Niketan school, with 10 teachers and 650 pupils. The teachers work unpaid, the children wear their own clothes rather than uniforms, and the books and desks are financed through donations.

Babur works remarkably long hours. On a typical day, he'll rise at 5am for morning prayers, do household chores, then take a bus to school in a village three miles away. From 10am to 4pm, he focuses on his own studies, then he races back to his village to welcome his students at 5pm.

He teaches until 8pm and supervises his colleagues, mainly fellow pupils ranging from 16 to 19 years old. The teaching doesn't make him tired, he says, but gives him more strength to keep up his busy schedule.

His parents are bursting with pride.

His father, Mohammed Nasiruddin, was shocked when he first discovered his son was teaching. "I couldn't believe it. He's always rushing from place to place and I was worried it might affect his studies. So I visited his school. Seeing his determination and dedication to teaching cleared my doubts," he says.

Babur believes he has found his vocation. He's working towards qualifying as a teacher so that he can carry on developing his school. His plan is to sign up for a distance degree so that he won't have to give up teaching classes.

The secret of his success, he says, is commitment. "You have to be dedicated and determined. You need to create a positive learning environment. And there has to be goodwill between teacher and students."

2 Read again. Find out:

1 why children used to ask Babur about his lessons.
2 how many pupils there were at first.
3 how many teachers and pupils Babur's school has now.
4 how the school's able to run without charging fees.
5 how many hours a day Babur teaches.
6 who the other teachers are.
7 what Babur's father felt after visiting the school.
8 why Babur wants to do a distance degree.

3 Talk together.

1 What do you think about Babur? What do you think motivates him?
2 Do you agree with him about what teachers need to be successful?

Work and commitment

4 **a** Complete the expressions with the verbs in the boxes.

| work on <br> work towards | 1 | _____ the standard of teaching / a problem / an essay |
| | 2 | _____ qualifying as a teacher / a solution / a goal |

| carry on <br> keep up | 3 | _____ a busy schedule / a high standard / good grades |
| | 4 | _____ developing / with a task / as normal |

| sign up <br> take on | 5 | _____ new students / a lot of work / a big responsibility |
| | 6 | _____ for a degree / for a course / for lessons |

| drop out <br> give up | 7 | _____ teaching / smoking / rugby |
| | 8 | _____ of school / of a race / of a competition |

b Find the verbs in the article to check.

5 **1.18** Listen to eight instructions which use the verbs in 4. Note down your answers – but don't write them in order.

6 Look at each other's notes from 5 and try to guess what they mean. Ask questions to find out more.

> Swimming ... would you like to sign up for a course?

> No. I'm a good swimmer. It's just that I find it difficult to keep up these days.

They were always asking questions

Habits and tendencies – past and present

1 **a** Which of the sentences 1–7 are about the present? Which are about the past?

A Simple forms	1	My friends **helped** me with the teaching.
	2	From 10am to 4pm, he **focuses on** his own studies.
B will/would + infinitive	3	I **would repeat** everything for them.
	4	On a typical day, he'll **rise** at 5am for morning prayers.
C used to + infinitive	5	There **used to be** just eight pupils.
D be always -ing	6	They **were always asking** questions about my lessons.
	7	He's **always rushing** from place to place.

b Which form A–D can you use:

1 to emphasise that something happens / happened very often?
2 to describe habits or states in the past?
3 to describe habits or typical behaviour, but not states?
4 to describe different things in the present and past: actions, habits, states, etc.?

2 **a** Complete Brianna's description of a writing course. Use the forms in 1a.

Grammar reference and practice, p133

> " Last year, I did this fantastic course in creative writing. We ¹_____ (meet) on Monday evenings to study stories and poems, and then we ²_____ (do) various exercises to develop our own skills. The tutor was quite demanding, which was great. He ³_____ (push) us to try new things, and he ⁴_____ (suggest) really interesting ideas for us to try at home. Nowadays, I ⁵_____ (write) something, even just a few lines of poetry, every day. Sometimes I ⁶_____ (read) my work to my friends and ask them what they think. I ⁷_____ (tell) them they should try the course too! "

b Compare your answers. Did you choose the same forms?

3 **a** Write a few sentences about these topics. Use the forms in 1a.

• an entertaining or useful course you did or are doing
• a fellow student you'll never forget
• what you did during breaks or after school

b Talk about the topics together.

Decide who to nominate for an award

3.3 goals
- express views about different options ♻
- talk about experiences of education and training ♻
- describe habits and tendencies in the past and present ♻
- describe important mentors in your life

TASK LISTENING

1 Read the notice in a local newspaper about the 'Great Mentor' award.
Do you know of any organisations that offer similar awards?

W Westfield Community Association

Nominate Someone for a 'Great Mentor' Award!

Is there someone who's been a great mentor to you? Someone who's taught you important things in any area of your life? If so, why not nominate them for a 'Great Mentor' award?

This award recognises and celebrates the contributions to our lives of mentors of all kinds, from a teacher to a sports coach, from a manager to an older sister or a good friend.

The 'Great Mentor' award is presented quarterly. Winners are featured on our website and will receive a medal, a certificate and a small gift.

2 a Alex is thinking of nominating Bill, his old driving instructor, for a 'Great Mentor' award. What kind of character and skills does someone need to be a good driving instructor?

b ◉ **1.19** Listen to Alex describing Bill. What characteristics and skills does he mention?

3 a ◉ **1.19** Listen again. What does Alex say about:

1 why he started having lessons?
2 how long it took him to get his licence?
3 what kind of driver he was?
4 what happened when he considered giving up?

b Read the script on pp144–5 to check.

TASK VOCABULARY

Describing a mentor

4 a Complete Alex's sentences with the words in the box.

owe	never	always	those	impression	taught	ever	positive	so

1 He made a big _____ on me.
2 I've never met **anybody** _____ patient.
3 He **was the calmest person I've** _____ met!
4 He would _____ shout, never lose his temper.
5 He was one of _____ people who have a lot of inner strength.
6 He'd _____ encourage me to carry on.
7 He was quite a _____ **influence on** me.
8 He _____ me a lot about determination.
9 I _____ him a lot.

b Which sentences describe:

1 Bill's character? 2 his typical behaviour? 3 his effect on Alex?

TASK

5 a Work alone. You're going to talk about someone from your life who you'd like to nominate for the award. Think about:

1 your relationship with the person. 4 what they taught you.
2 their character and skills. 5 how they taught you.
3 their achievements. 6 any other reasons you think they should get the award.

b In A/B pairs, describe your mentors. Ask questions to find out more.

6 a Get into two groups, As and Bs. Tell each other about the mentors your partners talked about in 5b. Then decide who you'd nominate for the award.

b Tell the other group who you'd nominate. Explain your choice.

Keyword *use*

The verb *use*

Karen and Niklas are on a company training course. They've been given a creativity task:
How many ways can you think of to use a tennis ball? You have <u>one minute</u> *to come up with as many ideas as you can.*

1 **a** Look at the picture and caption. How many ideas can *you* think of? Talk together.

   b 🔊 **1.20** Listen. How many ideas do Karen and Niklas have? Are any of them the same as yours?

2 **a** Match 1–3 with a–c to make three sentences from the conversation.

   1 Obviously, you can **use** it **to**
   2 You could cut it in half, **use** it **as**
   3 I suppose you could **use** them **for**

   a a cup.
   b packing things, fragile things.
   c play different ball games.

   b Do you say the verb *use* with a /s/ or a /z/?

3 **a** Look at the pictures. How many more ways can you think of for using a bottle? Brainstorm ideas.

   b Make a class list. Which two ideas are best?

The noun *use*

4 **a** Work alone. Look at the questions about education. Think about your answers.

   1 Do you think **the use of** these things in teaching young children is a good idea? Why? / Why not?
      • games
      • online learning
      • group projects
      • homework
      • exams

   2 How has technology affected education where you live? What kinds of technology and equipment:
      • **are in regular use** nowadays?
      • are starting to **come into use**?
      • have **gone out of use**?

   3 Do you think you **made good use of** your time at school or college? How could you have **made better use of** it?

   b Do you say the noun *use* with a /s/ or a /z/?

5 Ask and answer the questions in 4a.

be used to, get used to

6 Look at the sentence and answer the questions.

> Babur is used to working remarkably long hours.

   1 Is this sentence about the past or present? Which word tells you this?
   2 How does Babur feel about working long hours?
   3 In this sentence, do you say **used** with a /s/ or a /z/?

7 **a** Read the questions and add two or three more of your own.

   Do you know anyone who:
   1 **is used to** a lot of pressure in their daily life?
   2 **isn't used to** getting up early?
   3 **was used to** getting their own way when they were a child?
   4 takes a long time to **get used to** new people?
   5 will have to **get used to** a big change in their life soon?

   b Ask and answer all the questions.

1 a 🔊 1.21 Listen to two conversations and answer the questions.

Conversation 1
1 What does Alan think of Babur Ali?
2 What does his wife suggest?
Conversation 2
3 What accident happened near Mathias's home?
4 Why were his neighbours lucky?

b Read the extracts from the conversations to check.

2 a Match the highlighted expressions in the two conversations with meanings 1–9.

1 "This is strange but ..."
2 "I heard or read this somewhere."
3 "It's clear that ..."
4 "This is my honest opinion."
5 "This is the key information, without details."
6 "I didn't expect this but ..."
7 "This is *my* opinion."
8 "I'm pleased about this."
9 "I'm not joking."

Notice that the expressions often go just before the main message.

b Look at five more expressions. Can you explain their meanings?

| unfortunately hopefully to tell you the truth |
| actually between you and me |

3 Choose expressions from 2a and 2b to complete this conversation. 🔊 1.22 Then listen to one possible answer. Did you have similar ideas?

ERYN Is Dominic coming tonight?
OMAR No, ¹_____ he can't make it. He's still at the office.
ERYN Again? He's always working late these days.
OMAR Well, ²_____, I think his company's in trouble. He may even go out of business.
ERYN I didn't know that. That's terrible!
OMAR Yes, but ³_____ it won't come to that. ⁴_____, I think owning your own business is quite stressful.
ERYN Yeah. ⁵_____, I'd rather be an employee than an employer. What about you?
OMAR Oh, I'd agree with that. But ⁶_____, I'd like to be so rich that I didn't have to work at all.

①

ALAN Yes. Apparently, he goes to quite a good school but it's too expensive for a lot of kids in his area. So basically, after he gets home from school, he teaches them what he's learned.
MIKI But who funds his school and pays for the teachers?
ALAN Surprisingly, he managed on his own at first but nowadays he gets funding from the regional government and from donations. Personally, I think it's amazing.
MIKI Hmm, then perhaps we should send a donation, too.
ALAN Us?
MIKI Yeah. Seriously, I think we should consider it.

②

MATHIAS Well, yesterday evening, one of the branches of that big tree outside my flat broke off and crashed straight through my neighbours' living-room window.
CORRIE Wow! Was anyone hurt?
MATHIAS No. Thankfully, the whole family was out. Funnily enough, they were on their way home at the time of the accident but got stuck in a traffic jam. If they'd arrived back a few minutes earlier ...
CORRIE Obviously, they had a lucky escape. But what's going to happen to the tree now?
MATHIAS Frankly, I think it should be cut down. I don't think it's safe.

4 a In pairs, follow these instructions. Each pair should:

1 Choose one of these lines. Write your line at the top of a piece of paper.
   • Is the bus usually this late?
   • Is Vicki all right? She looks upset.
   • Wow! Where did you get that ring?
   • Did you hear that Danny got fired?
   • Do you mind if we have burgers for dinner?
2 Add the next line of the conversation between two people. Include one of the highlighted expressions.
3 Pass the paper to the pair on your right.
4 Read the conversation on your new paper. Add another line, including another of the highlighted expressions.
5 Repeat steps 3 and 4 four times.

b As a class, listen to all the conversations. Which do you like the most?

A Is the bus usually this late?
B No. Hopefully, it'll come soon.
A Frankly, this is your fault. I wanted to get the earlier bus.
B Actually, ...

3 Look again ♻

Review

VOCABULARY Discussing options

1 a Neil and Jez are choosing a venue for a party. Replace 1–4 with different expressions, keeping the meaning the same. Then check on p22.

> **NEIL** Well, ¹I'd like to give Silks Nightclub a try.
>
> **JEZ** No, ²there's no way I'm going there. It's horrible.
>
> **NEIL** Well, anyway, ³I'd be happy with either Silks or Terence's Café.
>
> **JEZ** Hm. ⁴I'm in two minds about Terence's Café. It's quite expensive.

b You're thinking of having a class party. As a class, make lists of possible venues, things to eat and drink, and things to do.

c Talk about the options in groups and plan a party. Then tell the class what you've decided.

GRAMMAR Habits and tendencies – past and present

2 a Underline the verb forms which describe habits and tendencies.

> When I was 21, I had a Volkswagen camper van. I was extremely proud of it, and I was always polishing it. I used to go travelling in it every summer. Sometimes my friends would come with me, and we'd have a great time. But I'm 'green' nowadays, so I'm always thinking of ways to help the environment. I go most places by bicycle, and for long-distance journeys I'll take the bus or train. But to tell you the truth, I still miss my old van.

b Think of something from your past, for example:

a friend   a pet   a toy   a vehicle   a holiday spot

Tell a partner about what you used to do. Then compare it with what you do or feel now.

CAN YOU REMEMBER? Unit 2 – Misunderstandings

3 Complete the expressions in the conversation between Eva and her sister. Then check on p14.

> **EVA** I ¹th_____ you'd promised to take Marina to the Water Park today.
>
> **RENA** What? But I ²m_____ next Saturday, not today!
>
> **EVA** That's not what you ³s_____. You just said Saturday. I called you but your phone was off.
>
> **RENA** That's because I was in a training session all day.
>
> **EVA** I see – that ⁴e_____ it. Anyway, she was very upset.
>
> **RENA** I'm sorry. Look, what ⁵i_____ I take her tomorrow?
>
> **EVA** No, she's going to the school fair. I guess the logical ⁶th_____ is to take her next Saturday. Or the other ⁷o_____ is to take her to a film tomorrow evening, I suppose.
>
> **RENA** No, she'll like the Water Park better.

Extension

SPELLING AND SOUNDS /ʃ/

4 a Complete the spelling of these words with sh ch che s. Then check in a dictionary.

__out	__ampagne	__ure
mu__room	bro__ure	champion__ip
ru__	cre__	selfi__

b Which spellings can show a /ʃ/ sound:

1 at the start of a word?
2 in the middle?
3 at the end?

Which spelling do you think is the most common?

c ▶ 1.23 Spellcheck. Listen and write ten words. Then check your spelling on p145.

NOTICE provide, include, cover, ...

5 a Match 1–6 with a–f. Then look back at the Markham College brochure on p23 to check.

1 Lessons **focus on** the classic moves
2 We **offer** hands-on learning
3 This course **provides** practical training
4 It also **includes** lectures
5 This course **introduces** you **to** the skill
6 The course **covers** a range

a of this important life skill.
b in basic servicing ... and minor repairs.
c of creative writing.
d of this entertaining and beautiful dance form.
e of topics.
f on car engines, tires and brakes.

b Work in groups.

1 Think of a subject for a course which people in your class might like to do.
2 Write a description of your course for a college brochure. Use some of the **expressions** in 5a.

c Read the other groups' descriptions and decide which course you'd most like to do.

Self-assessment

Can you do these things in English? Circle a number on each line. 1 = I can't do this, 5 = I can do this well.

⊚ express views about different options	1	2	3	4	5
⊚ talk about education and training	1	2	3	4	5
⊚ talk about experiences of education and training	1	2	3	4	5
⊚ describe habits and tendencies in the past and present	1	2	3	4	5
⊚ describe important mentors in your life	1	2	3	4	5
⊚ show different attitudes and feelings	1	2	3	4	5

• For Wordcards, reference and saving your work → e-Portfolio
• For more practice → Self-study Pack, Unit 3

4

Local knowledge

Landmarks

VOCABULARY

Describing landmarks

1 a Look at the pictures of well-known landmarks. Can you guess (or do you know):

1 where they are?   2 how big they are?   3 what they're made of?

❶ *The Millennium Spire* in Dublin, Ireland, was designed by Ian Ritchie Architects. Officially known as 'The Monument of Light', this 120m steel spire is 3m wide at the base but just 15cm wide at the top.

❸ *Saigō Takamori* was a nineteenth-century Japanese warrior and politician, known as 'the last true samurai'. This 3.7m bronze statue of Saigō walking his dog was made by Takamora Kōun and can be seen in Tokyo's Ueno Park.

❷ *The Angel of the North* stands on a hill near the town of Gateshead in the north of England. Designed by Antony Gormley, this steel construction is 20m tall and has a wingspan of 54m.

❹ Joanna Rajkowska's *Greetings from Jerusalem Avenue* is an artificial palm tree in the centre of Warsaw, Poland. It's about 15m high and is made of steel, plastic and natural bark.

b Match the landmarks with the descriptions. Find answers to the questions in 1a.

2 Work as a class. Compare your ideas about these questions.

1 Which of the landmarks A–D might be a **monument**?
2 Which would you describe as **a statue**?
3 Which would you describe as a **sculpture**?
4 Which are **modern**? Which are **traditional**?
5 Which are **abstract**? Which are **realistic**?
6 Which do you think were made:
  a to **commemorate** a past event?
  b to **celebrate** something?
  c in **honour** of somebody?
  d to **signify** an idea?
  e to **amuse** people?
  f to **make people think**?

> Well, it's a kind of abstract sculpture, maybe a monument, ...

3 Work in pairs. Cover 2 and describe the landmarks A–D using the highlighted expressions.

LISTENING

4 ⭐1.24 Listen to Cian, Beryl and Dominika. Which landmark A–D does each person talk about? How do they feel about it?

5 ⭐1.24 Listen again and make notes on these topics for each monument.

1 its location
2 when it was put up
3 its meaning or purpose
4 people's reactions to it

6 What do you think about each of these landmarks? Do you like them? Talk together.

A big impression

1 Do the highlighted expressions in a and b have similar or different meanings?
If they differ, explain how.

	a	b
1	It was erected to celebrate the Millennium.	It was put up during the 1990s.
2	It was unveiled at the very end of 1999.	It was opened to the public in 2006.
3	It was heavily criticised at first.	It was badly received.
4	It caused a lot of controversy.	It made a big impression on people.
5	People didn't know what to make of it.	People were baffled by it.
6	People grew to love it.	People warmed to it after a while.
7	It became a landmark.	It became a tourist attraction.
8	People see it as part of the landscape.	People regard it as an eyesore.

2 a Choose expressions from 1 to complete the description of the Eiffel Tower. In some
cases, more than one answer is possible.

AT 324 METRES HIGH, THE EIFFEL TOWER is the tallest structure in Paris.
It ¹_____ between 1887 and 1889 as the entrance arch for the 1889 Exposition Universelle ('World Fair'). Its designer, Gustave Eiffel, had originally planned to build the tower in Barcelona, but it was decided that his idea would not suit the city. Eiffel therefore took his design to Paris instead, and the Tower ²_____ on 6 May 1889.

The Tower ³_____ when it was first built. The newspapers of the day were filled with angry letters, with many people calling the Tower ⁴_____ . Other people ⁵_____ it, unsure whether the Tower was intended to be a work of art or a demonstration of engineering.

The city planned to allow the Tower to stand for twenty years and then tear it down, but with time people ⁶_____ it and it became both ⁷_____ and ⁸_____ . Today, the Tower is widely regarded as a striking piece of structural art. Since its construction, it's been visited by more than 200 million people.

b Compare your answers in groups.

3 a 🔊 **1.25** Some very common words have weak forms: when they're not stressed,
you can say them with a schwa sound /ə/. Listen and notice the weak forms in this
sentence.

It was erected to celebrate the Millennium.

Practise saying the sentence.

b Words we usually say as weak forms include:

• articles *a*, *an*, *the* • forms of *be* • prepositions *as*, *at*, *for*, *from*, *of*, *to*

Look at the other sentences in 1. Write /ə/ above the words you'd probably say as a
weak form.

c 🔊 **1.26** Listen and look at the script on p146 to check. Practise saying the sentences.

4 a Work alone. Choose two or three landmarks in your region or country. For each
one, think about these questions.

1 What does it look like? How would you describe its style?
2 Why was it built? What do you think it represents?
3 When was it built? Is it popular with local people and tourists?
4 Has its reputation changed over time?
5 What do you think about it? Why?

b Talk in groups. Can you add any more information to each other's descriptions?
Which places would you most like to see?

Two voices

4.2 goals
◉ talk about well-known people where you live
◉ describe someone's life and work

READING

Umm Kulthum (1904–1975) was a singer famous in Egypt and throughout the Arabic-speaking world.

1 a Look at the photos and read the captions.
Which six of these things do you think could be mentioned in an article about: Umm Kulthum? Bohumil Hrabal?

Prague   Cairo   radio concerts   an accident or suicide
real events   a huge funeral   lyrics   an Oscar   records
a single sentence   up to six hours   banned books

b Work in two groups.

Group A – read the article about Umm Kulthum below.
Group B – read the article about Bohumil Hrabal on p119.

Find out which six things are mentioned in your article.

Bohumil Hrabal (1914–1997) was one of the Czech Republic's best-known and best-loved writers.

Article | Discussion   🔍 Log in/create account

Umm Kulthum

Umm Kulthum was probably the most famous singer of the Arab world in the 20th century. Even today, more than three decades after her death, she is known as 'the Voice of Egypt' and 'the Star of the East', and her music can often be heard on radio and television.

She was born in a village in northern Egypt in around 1904 and showed an extraordinary singing talent from an early age. When she was 12 years old, she started performing in a small group directed by her father. Four years later, she was noticed by Zakariyya Ahmad, a famous musician, who invited her to Cairo. There, she was introduced to the poet Ahmad Rami, who went on to write 137 songs for her. She had her first real success when she began performing at the Arabic Theatre Palace.

By 1932, Umm Kulthum had become so popular that she began a long tour of the Middle East, performing in cities such as Damascus, Baghdad, Beirut and Tripoli. Her radio concerts, held on the first Thursday of every month, were famous for emptying the streets of some of the world's busiest cities as people rushed home to listen.

Umm Kulthum's songs are about the universal themes of love and loss. A typical concert would consist of two or three songs performed over a period of up to six hours. The duration of her songs varied from concert to concert and was based on the interaction between singer and audience. One of her techniques was to repeat a single line of a song's lyrics again and again, slightly changing the emphasis each time to bring her listeners into a euphoric state. It is said that she never sang a line the same way twice.

Umm Kulthum gave her last concert in 1973. She died in Cairo on February 3, 1975. Her funeral was attended by one of the largest gatherings in history – over four million people. In Egypt and the Arab world, she is remembered as one of the greatest singers and musicians who ever lived. Since her death, it is estimated that about a million copies of her records have been sold every year.

---

2 a Read again. Note down one or two details about each of the six things in your article.

b In A/B pairs, tell each other about Umm Kulthum and Bohumil Hrabal. What do you find most interesting about each person?

VOCABULARY

Talking about well-known people

3 Match 1–8 with a–h to make sentences from the articles.

1 She was probably the most famous
2 She had her first real success when
3 One of her techniques was to
4 He started out as
5 He had his first breakthrough with
6 One of his most famous works is
7 The movie won an Oscar for
8 The first of his collected writings came out in

a repeat a single line of a song's lyrics.
b Best Foreign Film in 1967.
c a collection of short stories.
d singer of the Arab World.
e 1991.
f a story written in a single sentence.
g she began performing at the Arabic Theatre Palace.
h a poet.

SPEAKING

4 Think of two or three famous writers or performers in your part of the world. Choose expressions from 3 and talk in groups about:

• what they're famous for.
• how and why they became famous.

> Well, Jang Nara is famous in South Korea. She had her first breakthrough with the hit song …

She's known as ...

1 **Read the information about using the passive, and sentences 1–6. Find an example of:**

a present simple passive   c present perfect passive
b past simple passive   d passive after a modal verb

In English, you usually put the person or thing you want to talk about (the **topic**) at the beginning of a sentence. New information (the **comment**) comes after it:

topic	comment
Umm Kulthum	was probably the most famous singer of the Arab world in the 20th century.

Notice how the writer chooses **active** or **passive** to keep Umm Kulthum, and things closely related to her, as the topic:

1	She	**is known as** 'the Voice of Egypt' and 'the Star of the East'.	PASSIVE
2	Her music	**can** often **be heard** on radio and television.	PASSIVE
3	She	**showed** an extraordinary singing talent.	ACTIVE
4	She	**started** performing in a small group directed by her father.	ACTIVE
5	She	**was noticed** by Zakariyya Ahmad, a famous musician.	PASSIVE
6	A million copies of her records	**have been sold** every year.	PASSIVE

Grammar reference and practice, p133

2 **Find and complete five common passive expressions from the last two paragraphs of the Umm Kulthum article.**

1 The duration of her songs was b_____ on
2 It is s_____ that
3 Her funeral was a_____ by
4 She is r_____ as
5 It is e_____ that

3 **a** Read the profile of Jang Nara from a website for people interested in South Korean culture. At the moment, all the sentences are active. Decide which should be active and which passive, and rewrite the profile.

Profile   ## Jang Nara, entertainer (1981 – present)

∗ Jang Nara was born in Seoul in March 1981. People consider her one of the best entertainers in South Korea.

∗ She started out as an actress in her primary school days, when theatre producers invited her to appear in the play *Les Misérables*. Later, in high school, she modelled in a number of television ads.

∗ Jang had her first real success as a singer in 2001, when a record company released her debut album. They sold 300,000 copies of the album, and the Korean music world awarded her Best New Singer of that year.

∗ At the same time, her acting career continued to develop. Korean TV companies hired her to star in popular sitcoms and dramas, and a Chinese television station also invited her to star in the successful drama *My Bratty Princess*. She is very popular in China, where they know her as 'Zhang Na La'.

∗ In addition, people have recognised her for her charity work in different countries. One Chinese charity appointed her a goodwill ambassador, the first foreigner to receive this honour.

---

b ● **1.27** Listen to check. Did you have the same ideas?

4 **a** Choose a person you think should be included on a website for people who are interested in your country, its history and culture, for example:

an artist   *a successful business person*   *a scientist*   *a sportsperson*   *a leader*

Write a profile of the person for the website. Use passive expressions from 1 and 2.

b Read each other's profiles and ask questions to find out more.

Describe well-known sights to a visitor

TASK LISTENING

1 If you were visiting Beijing or another part of China, what would you like to see? Talk together.

2 ◆ 1.28 Conor is visiting his friend Mei in Beijing. Mei is describing some things to see in the Beijing area. Listen to their conversation. Which one of these sights *don't* they talk about?

The 'Bird's Nest'   The Forbidden City   The Great Wall
The Summer Palace   The Temple of Heaven

3 ◆ 1.28 Listen again. According to Mei, which of the sights:

1 were built by the Emperor Yongle?
2 have been restored?
3 took fourteen years to build?
4 is outside Beijing?
5 is made entirely of wood?

TASK VOCABULARY

Recalling details

4 a Complete the sentences 1–6 with the words in the box.

> say   ~~far~~   read   remember   think   heard

1 As _far_ as I can remember, it was in the fifteenth century.
2 They _____ that it took a million workers fourteen years to complete.
3 I _____ I'm right in saying that you can rent an audio tour.
4 I _____ somewhere that it's made completely of wood.
5 I've _____ that they have English-speaking guides there.
6 If I _____ rightly, it's a two- or three-hour trip by bus.

b Read the script on p146 to check.

TASK

5 a Work alone. A friend from abroad is visiting you for a few days. Make a list of interesting things they could see or do during their stay. Think about things:

- in your home town
- in the countryside
- in towns and cities nearby

If the people in your class are from the same place, make a list of things to describe to a friend who's planning to visit another region or country you know about.

b Plan what to say about the things on your list.

1 What are they like? What makes them important or interesting?
2 What can you say about their history or reputation?
3 Are there any interesting people or stories connected with them?

Think of what language you can use from 4a.

c Work in A/B pairs.

A – tell your friend B about the things on your list.
B – you're the visitor. Listen to A and ask questions to find out more.

Then change roles and have another conversation.

6 Which of the things you've just heard about would you definitely like to see or do? Tell your partner.

Across cultures Special occasions

LISTENING

1 What's happening in the pictures? How would you describe the atmosphere?

2 🔊 **1.29** Listen to Beryl and Dominika describing the occasions. Who mentions these topics – Beryl, Dominika or both?

fireworks   food   a kind of doll   borrowed items
government buildings   the community   dancing

3 🔊 **1.29** Listen again. According to the speakers, are these statements true or false?

1 Bonfire Night is now usually organised by local councils.
2 Guy Fawkes saved the king's life.
3 All children love Bonfire Night.
4 Traditionally, Polish weddings are a community occasion.
5 A wedding lasts at least two days.
6 The bride and groom must each wear something borrowed.

Beryl talks about Bonfire Night in England.

Dominika talks about traditional weddings in Poland.

4 Which of these special occasions would you most like to experience? Why?

VOCABULARY
Describing a special occasion

5 a Which of these sentences are about Bonfire Night? Which are about weddings in Poland?

1 **Nowadays,** people celebrate it together.
2 **In the old days,** people used to celebrate it in their back gardens.
3 **Traditionally,** it's a celebration for an entire community.
4 **The reason we** have it **is because** about 400 years ago, a group of …
5 **It's quite normal to** have another celebration the day after.
6 **There's a lot of** laughing, shouting and screaming – and crying as well.
7 **There will be** a huge bonfire, with a guy sitting on the top.
8 **It can be anywhere between** two hundred **and** four hundred people.
9 Almost the whole town or village will **turn out**.
10 They **go on for** days **on end**.

b Read the script on pp146–7 to check.

SPEAKING

6 Choose a special occasion from your own or another culture. Think about how to describe:

1 what happens and why.
2 the atmosphere.
3 how it can vary from place to place.
4 how it's changed over the years.

Write a few sentences about it using the expressions in 5a.

7 Talk about your special occasions in groups.

• If you're from the same country, say if you disagree with anything. Add any information you think is important or interesting.
• If you're from different countries, ask questions to find out more about the things that interest you.

1 Read Gareth's email to a friend. Where are he and his family going? What are they interested in?

Options

Hi Ellie,
Can I get a bit of advice from you? You used to live in Japan and know a lot about it, and we're planning to go there for three weeks in October. Dylan will love Tokyo Disneyland, of course, but Sandrine and I are more interested in culture, history and art. So, can you give us an idea of some of the 'must-see' sights? It would help us a lot with our plans. Thanks!
Best wishes,
Gareth

Goal

- write an email or letter recommending places to see

2 Now read Ellie's reply. Which of the things she recommends would you find most interesting?

3 Which paragraph is about:

a wishes for the future?
b the purpose of the email?
c the countryside?
d the main city?
e other cities?

4 Find and complete these expressions of recommendation:

1 *Be* sure *to*
2 ... advisable ...
3 check ...
4 ... miss
5 ... should
6 ... recommend ...
7 ... sure ...
8 ... forget ...
9 try ...
10 ... worth

5 Find adjectives in the text to match these meanings.

paragraph 2
a extremely large
b pleasant, attractive
c very crowded
d extremely interesting
e having a lot of goods

paragraph 3
f causing you to admire it
g very old
h important in history

paragraph 4
i giving you new energy
j following the customs of long ago

Delete | Reply | Reply All | Forward | Print

Hi Gareth,

¹It's great that you're off to Japan. I know you'll love it. I've put together a few ideas for you. Of course you'll discover lots more things while you're there but this should get you started.

²There's lots to see in Tokyo. Sensoji Temple's great. You go through an enormous red gate, then walk along a row of charming little shops to the temple. It's a busy area, jammed with people. Next, be sure to go to the Kabuki Theatre. It's advisable to get tickets for one act only as the whole thing can last four hours. And check out the food floors in department stores. They're fascinating and give you a good idea of the range of Japanese food. Also, for Dylan's sake, don't miss the well-stocked Hakuhinkan toy store in Tokyo.

³Ideally, you should see the cities of Kyoto, Nara and Kamakura as well. In Kyoto, I recommend you visit Ryoanji (Zen rock garden), Kinkakuji ('Golden Pavilion') and Kiyomizu Temple. Nearby Nara also has some very impressive ancient buildings and statues. As for Kamakura, it's a historic city about an hour south of Tokyo. Make sure you see the Great Buddha there (a huge bronze statue) and don't forget to wash your money at the Zeniarai Benten Shrine. They say if you do, it will double.

⁴If you can, try out a mountain onsen (hot spring). They're wonderfully refreshing. And it's well worth staying at a ryokan, a traditional inn, where meals are brought to your room on trays.

⁵I hope you have a great time! I look forward to hearing all about it later.

Lots of love, Ellie

6 **a** A friend has written to you to ask what to see in a country or city you know well. Make a list of places to recommend. Then think about:

1 how many paragraphs you'll need and what to put in each one.
2 how to begin and end your email or letter.
3 what language you'll need from 4 and 5 to recommend and describe the places.

b Write your email or letter.

7 Exchange emails or letters with a partner. Ask questions about any places that interest you.

4 Look again ♻

Review

VOCABULARY Talking about landmarks

1 **a** Add expressions for talking about landmarks to each group. Then check on pp30–31.

1 TYPE: a **statue**, ...
2 APPEARANCE: **modern**, ...
3 PURPOSE: to **celebrate** something, ...
4 AGE: it was **put up** in, ...
5 REACTIONS: people **warmed to** it, ...
6 REPUTATION: an **eyesore**, ...

b What can you remember about these landmarks?

The Millennium Spire   The Angel of the North
Greetings from Jerusalem Avenue

GRAMMAR Using the passive

2 **a** Read the mini-biography of the Scottish crime writer, Ian Rankin. Choose the correct option.

Born in 1960, Ian Rankin [1]graduated / was graduated from the University of Edinburgh and [2]employed / has been employed as a grape-picker, taxman and journalist. He [3]moved / was moved to France for six years while developing his career as a novelist, and his first Inspector Rebus novel, *Knots and Crosses*, [4]published / was published in 1987. His books [5]have translated / have been translated into 26 languages, and six of them [6]have adapted / have been adapted for television. In 2005, Ian Rankin [7]awarded / was awarded the Grand Prix de Littérature Policière (France). He now [8]lives / is lived in Edinburgh.

b Now write a mini-biography about yourself, including some imaginary details.

c Read each other's mini-biographies. Guess which details are true and which are imaginary.

CAN YOU REMEMBER? Unit 3 – Work and commitment

3 **a** Read about the people's hopes and plans for the next twelve months. Choose the best verbs.

I'd like to [1]carry on / keep up exercising every day. I feel so much fitter and more energetic now.

I really don't want to [2]sign up for / take on any more big responsibilities at work. I'm already far too busy as it is.

I'm going to try to [3]drop out of / give up smoking again. I might try going to a hypnotist.

I've booked a five-day summer break in Paris. I'd like to [4]work on / work towards my French a bit before I go.

b Use the verbs to discuss some of your hopes and plans for next year.

Extension

SPELLING AND SOUNDS /m/

4 **a** <u>Underline</u> the letters which make a /m/ sound.

cli<u>mb</u>   column   common   immediately
millennium   monument   palm   summon

b Find words in 4a to match these spelling patterns.

1 /m/ is usually spelled just m.
2 You write mm in beginnings such as: *imm–* *comm–* and *summ–*
3 A few spellings of /m/ include silent letters: mb lm mn

c 🔊 **1.30** Spellcheck. Listen and write twelve words. Then check your spelling on p147.

NOTICE *very*, *the very*

5 **a** Look at the extract from Cian's talk about the Millennium Spire. In which expressions does *very*:

1 mean: a *really*?   b *exact*?
2 add emphasis to: a an adjective?   b a noun?

> It's situated in [1]the very middle of Dublin on the street called O'Connell Street. It's essentially just [2]a very tall spire or spike that extends above all the buildings that are in Dublin. ... It was erected to celebrate the Millennium so it was unveiled, er, at [3]the very end of 1999.

b Work alone. Choose a word to complete 1–4.

| first/last | beginning/end | top/bottom | best/worst |

1 What were you doing at the very _____ of last year?
2 What's the very _____ thing you remember doing or thinking yesterday?
3 Have you ever come at the very _____ of the class in an exam?
4 Who do you think is the very _____ singer in your country at the moment?

c Ask and answer your questions.

Self-assessment

Can you do these things in English? Circle a number on each line. 1 = I can't do this, 5 = I can do this well.

describe landmarks	1	2	3	4	5
talk about landmarks where you live	1	2	3	4	5
talk about well-known people where you live	1	2	3	4	5
describe someone's life and work	1	2	3	4	5
give information about interesting or important sights	1	2	3	4	5
write an email or letter recommending places to see	1	2	3	4	5

• For Wordcards, reference and saving your work → e-Portfolio
• For more practice → Self-study Pack, Unit 4

37

5.1 goals
◎ describe and give opinions about images
◎ choose something for a room

5 Images

Picture story

1 a Look at the page from an art gallery website. What can you guess about:

1 the people in the painting?
2 the relationships between them?
3 what's happening?

And when did you last see your father?

by William Frederick Yeames (1878)

◀ Click here for an introduction to this painting.   ◀ Click on ❶–❻ in the painting for comments on the people.

b 🔊 2.1 Listen to the audio guide introduction to the painting. Find answers to the questions in 1a.

2 🔊 2.2 Listen to the audio guide commentary about the people in the painting. In what order do you hear about the people 1–6?

3 a 🔊 2.2 Listen again. What does the commentary suggest about:

1 the appearance of the little boy?
2 the fact that the little girl is crying?
3 the soldiers outside the door?
4 the expression on the questioner's face?
5 the soldier standing next to the little girl?
6 the jewel box and open chest?

b Compare your answers, then read the script on p147 to check.

4 What aspects of the painting do you like or dislike? Having listened to the commentary, do you feel differently about the painting? Talk together.

VOCABULARY

Describing an image

5 Look at the sentences from the audio guide. Find five pairs of highlighted expressions with a similar meaning.

shows – portrays

1   This painting **shows** an imaginary scene from a Royalist household.
2   The small size of the boy, his blond hair and blue suit **highlight** his innocence.
3   Two other women, probably the boy's elder sister and mother, **can be seen**.
4   Through a doorway, more soldiers **are visible**.
5   This further **emphasises** the family's helplessness.
6   Yeames **portrays** the Parliamentarian soldiers with some sensitivity.
7   The guard with the sobbing young girl **seems** to be comforting her.
8   This **implies** that he has some sympathy for their situation.
9   The gentleman standing at the table **appears** to be opening the family jewel box.
10   This and the opened chest **suggest** that the soldiers may be searching the house.

SPEAKING

6 a Work alone. Choose a painting A–D on p122, then choose expressions from 5 to describe:

• what it shows   • the most interesting or significant details
• how you interpret the painting.

b In groups, listen to each other's descriptions. Do you agree with the interpretations?

I can imagine it in the kitchen

LISTENING

1   **2.3** Listen to Paloma and James's conversation about the paintings on p122. Which posters do they decide to buy?

2   **2.3** What opinions do they express about each painting? Listen again and make notes, then compare.

Paloma and James have recently redecorated their flat. Now they want to buy a poster of a work of art to go in their living room.

VOCABULARY

Choosing something for a room

3 Complete the sentences from the conversation with the words in the boxes.

| go   look   put   ~~see~~   suit   imagine |

1   I can't __*see*__ it in the living room.
2   We could _____ it in the toilet.
3   It wouldn't _____ the living room.
4   I can _____ it in the kitchen.
5   It could _____ in that corner.
6   It would _____ nice in the living room.

| ~~strong~~   bigger   bright/cheerful
good   sure   wrong |

7   I love the *strong* colours.
8   It's the _____ shape.
9   It's a _____ size.
10   I'm not so _____ about the style.
11   It's nice and _____.
12   It'd make the room feel a lot _____.

4 a Work alone. For each painting A–D on p122, think about these questions.

1   Do you like it?
2   Would it suit any of the rooms in your home or where you work?

Prepare to explain your opinions using the highlighted expressions in 3.

b Tell each other your opinions. Which are the most and least popular paintings?

SPEAKING

5 a In pairs, decide on a picture to go in your classroom, and where exactly it should go. Choose a picture one of you knows well or a picture from this lesson.

b Explain your choice to another pair. As a group of four, decide on one picture.

c Listen to all the groups' ideas. Have a vote to choose a picture for your classroom.

Design classics

5.2 goals
- discuss what makes a good design
- describe designs and designed objects

VOCABULARY

Discussing design

1 a Look at the two products and talk together. When do you think they were made? What could the connection between them be?

b Read to check your ideas.

Dieter Rams, born in 1932, was head of design at Braun for more than three decades from the early 1960s. His simple but modern designs continue to influence generations of younger designers like Jonathan Ive, renowned creator of Apple's iMac, iPod and iPhone. Compare, for instance, the Braun T3 radio of 1958 with the Apple iPod of 2001.

Rams defined his approach to 'good design' in ten key principles:

- Good design is [1]innovative.
- Good design makes a product useful.
- Good design is [2]aesthetic.
- Good design helps us to understand a product.
- Good design is [3]unobtrusive.

- Good design is [4]honest.
- Good design is [5]durable.
- Good design is [6]purposeful in every detail.
- Good design is [7]environmentally friendly.
- Good design is as little design as possible.

2 Match the highlighted expressions 1–7 with a–g that have a similar meaning.

a attractive   c novel   e low-key   g green
b straightforward d long-lasting   f meaningful

3 Talk together.

1 Think of a few things you have that are well designed. How would you describe them?
2 Think of some things that you feel are badly designed. Explain why.

READING

4 Read the article about the paperclip. Do you think it deserves to be regarded as a 'design classic'?

Classics of everyday design No. 3
the paperclip

When I asked for your favourite everyday designs a fortnight ago, someone nominated the paperclip. First patented in Germany in 1899 by Johan Vaaler (1866–1910), a Norwegian inventor, the humble paperclip remains indispensable.

The genius of the paperclip lies in its utter simplicity. Ubiquitous, this little bit of folded metal does its job well enough and, besides, can be used as an all-purpose miniature tool, for shaping desk-top animals, cleaning fingernails, making miniature buildings, or simply as something to fiddle with in times of bureaucratic stress. According to a survey conducted by Lloyds Bank some while ago, of every 100,000 paperclips made in the United States, 19,143 are used as poker chips, 17,200 hold clothing together, 15,556 are dropped and lost, 14,163 are absent-mindedly destroyed during telephone calls, 8,504 clean pipes and nails, while 5,434 serve as stand-in toothpicks.

There are several different types of paperclip but the one many readers will have in mind – and in drawers of desks at home and at work – is the familiar double U-shaped 'Gem' clip, made originally by Gem Manufacturing Ltd. This British company had probably been making paperclips for several years before Johan Vaaler created his version, but it hadn't thought of taking out a patent as the Norwegian did – not that Vaaler made any money out of his invention.

Even so, in recent years a giant paperclip (I promise this is true) has been erected outside Oslo in Vaaler's memory. There is, though, a perfectly serious reason for this seemingly mad moment in the world of public art. During the Second World War, when Norwegians were forbidden to display national symbols, they began to wear paperclips on their clothes. Not only was it, in their minds, a Norwegian invention but it symbolised the idea of holding on together.

From a simple tool to a national symbol of resistance, the paperclip is a small triumph of everyday design. An example of the Gem clip is even held in the collections of New York's Museum of Modern Art.

5 Read again. What information does the article give about:

1 Johan Vaaler?
2 how people use paperclips?
3 the early history of paperclip production?
4 the importance of the paperclip in Norwegian culture?

A survey conducted by …

1 Read the information and examples in the box. Then answer the questions.

> You can describe a <u>noun</u> with a past participle clause.
> • According to <u>a survey</u> **conducted** by Lloyds Bank …
>
> A past participle clause has a similar meaning to a relative clause with the passive:
> • According to <u>a survey</u> **which was conducted** by Lloyds Bank …
>
> There are two kinds of past participle clause:
> 1 **Defining**
> • Of every <u>100,000 paperclips</u> **made in the United States**, 17,200 hold clothing together, …
> 2 **Non-defining**
> • The one many readers will have in mind is <u>the familiar double U-shaped 'Gem' clip</u>, **made originally by Gem Manufacturing Ltd**.
> • **First patented by Johan Vaaler**, <u>the humble paperclip</u> remains indispensable.

1 Which kind of clause, defining or non-defining:
  a identifies which thing or person you're talking about?
  b adds extra details about the thing or person?
2 Which kind of clause:
  a always goes after the noun?　　c is separated from the noun by a comma?
  b can go before or after the noun?

KIKKOMAN
NATURALLY BREWED
Soy Sauce
150 ml ℮

2 Look at the descriptions of more design classics. Use past participle clauses (defining or non-defining) to rewrite each pair of sentences as a single sentence.

1 The famous soy sauce bottle was designed by Kenji Ekuan in 1961. It's made by the Kikkoman company.
2 The Boeing 747 was chosen by architect Norman Foster as his favourite 'building'. It was first flown in 1969.
3 More than five million cigarette lighters are sold every day. They're made by Bic.
4 Zhang Xiaoquan scissors are made in Hangzhou, China. They were first produced in 1663.
5 A Swiss Army knife features 85 tools and weighs a kilo. It's known as The Giant.

3 a 🔊 **2.4** Listen to some answers to 2 above. Notice how the speaker makes the sentences easier to understand by dividing them into groups of words.

// The Boeing 747 // first flown in 1969 // was chosen by architect Norman Foster // as his favourite 'building' //
// More than five million cigarette lighters made by Bic // are sold every day //

Which kind of past participle clause is usually pronounced:

1 in the same group of words as the noun it describes?　　2 as a separate group?

b Practise saying the sentences, paying attention to the groups of words.

4 a In groups, make a list of things for an exhibition of design classics. Consider:

clothes　cars　things for the home/office　electronics　logos　packaging

Use past participle clauses with verbs like:

designed　invented　called　known as　produced　made　built　manufactured

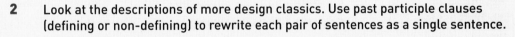

esign classics
'ball' vacuum cleaner made by Dyson
dress designed by Versace (Liz Hurley)

b Get into new groups. Tell each other about your ideas.

Choose a logo

5.3 goals
◎ describe and give opinions about images
◎ describe designs and designed objects
◎ participate in a decision-making discussion

TASK LISTENING

1 Look at three possible logos for a chain of florist's shops. Which do you think is best? Why?

2 **2.5** Listen to three people who work for Forever Flowers discussing the three designs.

1 Which do they choose?
2 What adjustment will they make to it?

3 **2.5** Listen again. Which design is each sentence about?

a It emphasises the idea of 'forever' quite well.
b I'd say the colours are low-key and quite elegant.
c It's pretty colourful but I wouldn't say it was flashy.
d It's too abstract, too cold, too much lettering.
e It's nice and modern.

TASK VOCABULARY

Getting a consensus

4 **a** Which highlighted expressions can you use to:

a ask for opinions or agreement?
b state a decision in favour?
c state a decision against?

1 **What are your thoughts?**
2 **Are we all agreed on that?**
3 **Let's eliminate** this one.
4 **Would that work for you?**
5 These two **are out.**
6 **We're going with** this one.
7 Brett? **It's not too late to change your mind.**
8 So, **we're all in favour of it.**

b **2.6** Listen to check. Practise saying the sentences.

TASK

5 **a** Read and underline the key points in this description.

100% Natural

You run a service called **From Nature To You**. It delivers organic food to people living in your town or city. You get all your products from a large farm, which grows vegetables and fruit. You also get organic nuts, seeds and oil from other sources. When customers send you orders, you gather and package the items, put them in a basket, then send the baskets to the customers' homes by courier. Because it's become quite a popular service, you want a striking new logo.

b Work alone. Look at the logos and think about these questions.

1 How would you describe the style of each logo?
2 What are the good and bad points of each logo?
3 Which logo would best represent *From Nature To You*? Why?
4 Would you make any changes to your chosen logo to improve it? How?

c In groups, compare your ideas and agree on the most suitable logo. Use expressions from 4a to ask for each other's opinions and get agreement. Decide on any changes you might want to make to your chosen design.

6 Tell the class which logo you've chosen and why.

5 EXPLORE

Keyword *as*

as compared with like

1 a Complete these sentences with as, such as or like. In two of the sentences, two answers are possible.

```
1   Of every 100,000 paperclips made in the United States, 19,143 are used _____ poker chips. Unit 5
2   His simple but modern designs continue to influence younger designers _____ Jonathan Ive. Unit 5
3   Ian Rankin has been employed _____ a grape-picker, taxman and journalist. Unit 4
4   She began a long tour of the Middle East, performing in cities _____ Damascus and Baghdad. Unit 4
5   Nowadays the mine at Wieliczka is _____ a huge underground city. Unit 2
```

b Which expression – as, such as or like – can you use:

1 to describe the identity or purpose of a person or thing?
2 to say two things or people are similar?
3 to give examples? (x2)

2 a Work alone. Complete these sentences with as, such as or like and your own ideas. Make four true sentences, and two false.

- I once worked ...
- I really don't enjoy films ...
- I know someone who looks a bit ...
- At school I was known ...
- I think my friends see me ...
- I wouldn't mind a career ...

> Well, I once worked as a zookeeper.

> Right ... when was that, exactly?

b Listen to each other's sentences and ask questions to find out more. Can you guess which sentences are false?

Referring expressions with *as*

3 a Keith and Leona work in different departments of a company. Read their emails and put them in order 1–6.

A
Hi Keith,
As you know, I'm putting together the agenda for Monday's meeting. I was wondering if you had any last-minute points to add?
Leona

B
Not to worry. I'll be there, though I might have to miss the afternoon as you suggested. Are the time and venue still as agreed last time (9.30 in Media Room B)? K.

C
Nothing to add thanks, but as I mentioned last week, Monday's pretty busy for me. I can do some rescheduling but would rather not. Any chance of a different day (Tue or Thu)? K.

D
Sorry Keith: I did ask about changing the date as promised, but half the sales team are on a training course from Tuesday! So it looks like we'll have to go ahead on Monday as planned. Hope you can still make it (even if only the morning part?) L.

E
This all looks fine to me Leona, but I'd put the time and room number at the top. As you probably remember, someone usually goes to the wrong room or turns up late! K.

F
Thanks for your understanding about the date, and yes, the time/venue are unchanged. Here's the agenda. Could you have a quick look through before I send it round? As you'll see, it's pretty full. L.

b Look at eight expressions with as in the emails. Which refer:

1 to the reader's knowledge? (x2)　　2 back to the past? (x5)　　3 forward to the future? (x1)

c Here are more common expressions with as. Which expressions in the emails could they replace?

```
as arranged   as I said   as you proposed   as you're aware
```

4 Work in two groups.

Group A – look at Leona's emails on p120. Write Keith's emails.
Group B – look at Keith's emails on p123. Write Leona's emails.

Your emails don't have to be exactly the same as the originals, but they should have the same meaning. Include one or two expressions with as in each email.

5 EXPLORESpeaking

Goals
- express disagreement in different situations
- make concessions and counter-arguments

1 🔊 **2.7** Listen to extracts from two conversations from this unit. In each conversation:

1 Where are the people?
2 What are they doing?
3 What's the relationship between them?

2 a Use the expressions a–h to complete the two conversations.

Expressing disagreement
a Are you joking?
b I wouldn't exactly say
c I'm not so sure about
d Oh, come on.

Making a concession
e I have to admit that
f I see what you mean.

Making a concession and counter-argument
g It's true that ... but
h But even if that's the case,

b 🔊 **2.7** Listen again to check.

3 a Add more expressions to the groups in 2a.

> Are you serious?
> That may be so, but
> How can you say that?
> I have to disagree with you there.
> I take your point, but
> I wonder about that.
> I'd go along with you there.
> Maybe you're right about that.

b 🔊 **2.8** Listen to check.

4 Which of the expressions for disagreeing:

1 would you probably *not* use in formal or professional situations?
2 could you use in any situation?

5 a Work in two groups, A and B. As read the situations below and your group's opinions. Bs read the situations and your group's opinions on p121. Think of reasons to support your opinions.

b Get into A/B pairs and talk about the topics. Use expressions from 2 and 3.

6 Go back to your group and tell them about your discussions. Did you reach any conclusions?

1

JAMES	Well, how about this one? It's a good size.
PALOMA	¹_____ Ugh ...
JAMES	What? It's nice and cheerful.
PALOMA	Yeah. We could put it in the toilet, perhaps.
JAMES	²_____ The horse is nice.
PALOMA	No, it isn't.
JAMES	OK. Have you got any suggestions?
PALOMA	Yes, how about this? I love the strong colours.
JAMES	Yeah, they're very striking, aren't they?
PALOMA	But?
JAMES	³_____ the style. For the room, I mean.
PALOMA	Hmm, ⁴_____ No, it wouldn't suit the living room, would it?

2

KIM	Alright, well, I think all three designs have their strengths, but I think this one's the weakest.
BRETT	Really? I liked that one.
KIM	Well, ⁵_____ it emphasises the idea of 'forever' quite well – you know, the idea that you can give flowers any time – _____ the colours are a bit weak.
BRETT	Well, ⁶_____ they're weak. I'd say the colours are low-key and, well, quite elegant.
KIM	⁷_____ I don't think they look dynamic enough for our business. I mean, we're all about colour.
BRETT	But too much colour can look flashy if you're not careful.
KIM	Yeah but look at this one – which is my favourite, by the way. It's pretty colourful but I wouldn't say it was flashy.
BRETT	Well, I think it's a bit strong myself, though ⁸_____ the flower image is nice.

Situation 1
You're colleagues deciding where to have the company party. You think it should be in a restaurant in a four-star hotel.

Situation 2
You're friends at university considering if you should have a cleaning rota in your flat. You think it's a good idea.

Situation 3
You're guests on a radio show discussing what kind of books teach you more about life. You believe fiction books do this.

Situation 4
You're a married couple deciding what kind of animal to get as a pet. You'd prefer to have a cat.

Review

VOCABULARY Choosing something for a room

1 a Choose the correct verbs in each expression. Then look back at p39 to check.

1 It would go / look nice in my bedroom.
2 I could feel / put it above the sofa.
3 It could go / put next to the bookcase.
4 I can't look / see it in the kitchen.
5 It wouldn't feel / suit my bathroom.
6 It'll make the room feel / see brighter.

b Think of one or two things you'd like to buy for your home, for example:

a picture or poster   an ornament   a piece of furniture   a lamp   a carpet or rug   ...

Describe the items to a partner. Say where you would and wouldn't put them. Explain why.

GRAMMAR Past participle clauses

2 a In pairs, prepare questions for 1–6. Then add two more questions with past participle clauses.

Find someone who:
1 has lived in a house (build) more than a century ago.
2 eats fruit (grow) in their own garden.
3 still has a present (give) to them when they were very young.
4 recently saw a film (base) on a true story.
5 is wearing shoes (make) in Italy.
6 likes raisins (cover) in chocolate.

b Talk to different people in the class. Ask and answer all the questions.

c Get back into your pairs from 2a and tell each other what you found out.

CAN YOU REMEMBER? Unit 4 – Recalling details

3 a Read the sentences about the artist Vincent Van Gogh. Put the letters in order, then look back at p34 to check.

1 If I beeemmrr ghilrty, he was from Holland.
   If I remember rightly
2 I hinkt I'm ighrt ni aginsy ahtt he spent a lot of his life in Paris.
3 As afr as I acn beeemmrr, he killed himself when he was quite young.
4 I aedr eeehmorsw ahtt he was very close to his brother.
5 I've aedhr ahtt he cut off part of his own ear.
6 They asy ahtt he only ever sold two paintings.

b Choose someone who's very famous at the moment. Get ready to tell each other what you know about them. Choose expressions from 3a.

c Tell each other what you know about the people. What new things did you learn?

Extension

SPELLING AND SOUNDS /g/

4 a <u>Underline</u> the letters which make a /g/ sound.

<u>g</u>uide   ghost   bigger   guard   colleague   fog   degree   hugged   dialogue   blogger   global   digging   guarantee   logo   guest   vague

b Find words in 4a to match these spelling patterns.

1 /g/ is usually spelled g.
2 You write gg between a short vowel and endings like: -ed -er -ing -est
3 /g/ is sometimes spelt gu- at the start of a word, or -gue at the end.
4 A few words start with gh.

c Spellcheck. In pairs, take turns to choose eight words and test your partner's spelling. Then check your spelling together.

NOTICE *the* with times and places

5 a Look at the extracts 1–4 from this unit. Find examples of the before:

a   decades or centuries.
b   important historical events.
c   places in a picture or document.

1 The soldier and the boy's father support different sides in the English Civil War.
2 On the far left of the painting, two other women can be seen.
3 The opened chest in the foreground of the painting suggests that the soldiers may be ...
4 Dieter Rams was head of design at Braun from the early 1960s.

b Think of more possible expressions for a–c.

c Talk in groups. What do you think:

1 are the key events in the history of your region?
2 would have been the best decade to live in?
3 are the best-known paintings in your country?
4 is the most memorable photo you've seen?

Self-assessment

Can you do these things in English? Circle a number on each line. 1 = I can't do this, 5 = I can do this well.

⊚ describe and give opinions about images	1	2	3	4	5
⊚ choose something for a room	1	2	3	4	5
⊚ discuss what makes a good design	1	2	3	4	5
⊚ describe designs and designed objects	1	2	3	4	5
⊚ participate in a decision-making discussion	1	2	3	4	5
⊚ express disagreement in different situations	1	2	3	4	5
⊚ make concessions and counter-arguments	1	2	3	4	5

• For Wordcards, reference and saving your work → e-Portfolio
• For more practice → Self-study Pack, Unit 5

Virtual worlds

Is it a crime?

1 Look at the picture of people playing an online role-playing game together.

1 Have you ever played an online role-playing game?
2 Why do you think people enjoy playing games like this?

2 a Read the headline of the newspaper article. What do you think the article's about? Talk together.

b Read the article to check your ideas. According to the police, what was the woman's crime?

a breaking into someone's computer
b destroying a character from an online game
c killing her husband

It was a virtual murder ... but the sentence is real

ONCE the stuff of low-quality science fiction movies, the crime of virtual murder may become a reality, following the arrest of a middle-aged piano teacher from southern Japan who murdered her virtual husband.

The 43-year-old woman hacked into the computer of the man she married in the online game MapleStory and deleted his carefully constructed virtual character after their relationship turned sour.

Police arrested her this week following a complaint by the man, a 33-year-old office worker who lives on the other side of the country in the northern city of Sapporo, 1000 km away. The two apparently never had a face-to-face meeting and the woman is not suspected of a flesh-and-blood crime, say the police.

She is accused of using her virtual partner's password and ID, which she acquired when

they were a happily married virtual couple, to gain illegal access to his computer. The crime carries a maximum sentence of five years in prison or a fine of about $3,200.

"It sounds like a strange case but obviously it is illegal to hack into someone else's computer," said a spokesman for the Sapporo police. "That is why she has been arrested."

According to investigators, the woman flew into a rage when the relationship was abruptly terminated. "I thought everything was fine, and then I was suddenly divorced without a word of warning. That made me so angry," she was quoted as saying.

The two met while playing a hugely popular role-playing game called MapleStory, which encourages anonymous users to create online characters that explore alternative worlds, fight monsters and engage in virtual relationships. Long-term commitments and marriage are not uncommon among players,

who are sometimes not even living in the same country. Originally from South Korea, MapleStory now reportedly has more than 50 million members worldwide.

The latest case comes amid growing controversy about online crimes. A court in the Netherlands sentenced two teenagers to a total of 360 hours of community service this month for breaking into a classmate's computer and stealing his virtual possessions. "These virtual goods are goods under Dutch law, so this is theft," said the court, which was criticised for going too far.

Online gamers are debating the possible results of the Japanese woman's arrest, with many supporting the 'murdered' husband. "It takes a lot of time and effort to build up a virtual character. This could mean other wronged people may seek real-world justice for people who harm them virtually," wrote one gamer. "I hope she goes to prison."

3 Read again. Correct these sentences.

1 The man and woman were married to each other legally.
2 Though they lived quite close to each other, they never met in real life.
3 The man divorced the woman after a serious argument.
4 *MapleStory* has millions of members but long-term relationships are unusual.
5 In the Netherlands, two young people were sent to prison for virtual theft.

4 Do you think people should be punished for virtual crimes? How?

VOCABULARY
Crimes and justice

5 Use the words in the box to complete the summary of the article.

> accused   arrested   crime   fine   prison   suspected
> law   sentence   sentenced   community

A woman who 'murdered' her virtual ex-husband [1]**has been** _____ for hacking into his computer. She [2]**has been** _____ of using the man's password and ID to delete his online character after he suddenly 'divorced' her. Although deleting online characters may not [3]**be a** _____, breaking into someone's computer certainly is. It [4]**carries a** maximum _____ of five years in prison or [5]**a** _____ of £3,200. Although the woman [6]**is not** _____ of a 'flesh-and-blood' crime, many online gamers feel that she ought to [7]**go to** _____. In a similar case in the Netherlands, two teenagers [8]**were** _____ to 360 hours of [9]_____ **service** for stealing virtual possessions from a classmate's computer. Stealing virtual goods is a crime [10]**under** Dutch _____.

SPEAKING

6 a Using expressions from 5, prepare to talk about a crime, for example:

• a crime that's been in the news recently   • a crime connected with you or someone you know   • a famous crime or criminal from the past

b Talk about the crimes in groups. Do you know what the sentence was? If so, do you agree with it? If not, what do you think it should be?

Consequences

VOCABULARY
Justifying your point of view

1 Read the web postings about the article. Who thinks the woman should go to prison?

> >> Of course they should send her to prison. [1]**Otherwise,** everyone'll start doing this! *Sue756 Oct 26, 7:27*
>
> >> She should pay a fine, OK. But prison? No way. Keep prison for the real criminals. *SpaceMan Oct 26, 22.45*
>
> >> A virtual fine? Ha ha! But seriously, this is a real crime and we need to get tough on it. *Sue756 Oct 26, 23.27*
>
> >> Agreed, but I'd rather she did something like community service. [2]**That way,** she'll be paying something back to society. *Whiz Oct 27, 9:14*
>
> >> Sue756 got it right. This kind of crime is increasingly common and nobody's stopping it. We need tough sentences [3]**or** it'll get totally out of control. *Mortimer Oct 27, 14.14*

2 a Replace expressions 1–3 in the web postings with: a If not,   b or else   c Then

b Choose the correct option.

1 We need to pass new laws against virtual crimes, then / or else they'll continue to increase.
2 Maybe – but if not / then I think we'll end up giving too much importance to this type of crime.
3 We need to be aware of new kinds of crime. That way / Otherwise, criminals always have the advantage.
4 We've got to pay attention to *real* crime. If not / That way, things are going to get a lot worse in *real* life!

SPEAKING

3 In groups, consider each situation in the list on p123. What punishment do you think would be suitable? Use expressions from 1 and 2 to justify your ideas.

Sharing or stealing?

6.2 goals
- talk about media and the Internet
- report different points of view
- describe possible consequences of actions

LISTENING

1 Talk together.

1 How common are these ways of getting music and films, compared with ten years ago?
   - buying or renting CDs, DVDs, Blu-ray discs, etc.
   - paying for downloads from online media stores
   - watching videos on the Internet
   - using unofficial file-sharing websites
   - getting copies of things from friends

2 Which of these things do you do?

3 Where you live, how do people feel about using file-sharing websites? Is it easy to do? Are there any risks?

2 🔊 2.9 Listen to a radio interview about file sharing with a music journalist, Robin Bland. According to the interview, are these statements true or false?

1 The government wants ISPs (Internet service providers) to cut off people for illegal file sharing.
2 Music companies definitely lose a lot of money because of file sharing.
3 ISPs don't want to get involved in the issue of file sharing.
4 There's no way ISPs will agree to the government's idea.

3 a 🔊 2.9 Listen again. Note down two or three:

1 arguments why file sharing should be stopped.
2 arguments why file sharing isn't a problem.
3 reasons why ISPs are unhappy with the government's idea.

b Read the script on p148 to check. Add to your notes.

VOCABULARY

Reporting points of view

4 a Look at your notes for 3a. In pairs, use these expressions from the interview to summarise the arguments for and against file sharing.

The music companies say that …
As far as they're concerned, …
They'll tell you that …
Many musicians will say that …

On the other hand, you have people who say that …
There's also the argument that …
A lot of people think that …
What they say is that …

> The music companies say that they lose a lot of money.

> But a lot of people think that …

b Get into new pairs and summarise the arguments again. Try to use the expressions in 4a without looking at your books.

SPEAKING

5 What do *you* think about the different arguments mentioned in the interview? What are your opinions about file sharing? Talk together.

Making a case

1 a Look at sentences 1–6 from the interview. Why are 1–4 called 'real' conditionals, and 5–6 'unreal' conditionals?

> *Real conditionals*
> 1 If people like a particular album, then they'll go out and buy it legally.
> 2 If you like a band's music, you should really be prepared to pay for it!
> 3 There's a chance the ISPs will take action **as long as they can all agree to act together.**
> 4 **Unless that happens,** they'll just be afraid of losing customers to their rivals.
> *Unreal conditionals*
> 5 **Even if you stopped file sharing completely,** it wouldn't lead to a big increase in sales.
> 6 Most people would be happy to buy the real thing **provided the prices were lower.**

b The highlighted clause in these sentences is the conditional clause and the other clause is the main clause.

1 What verb form is used in the conditional clause of:
  a real conditionals?   b unreal conditionals?
2 What modal verbs can be used in the main clause of:
  a real conditionals?   b unreal conditionals?

2 a Choose the correct options so these conditional clauses mean the same as the clauses in 3–6 above.

Sentence 3: ... but only if / because they can all agree to act together.
Sentence 4: If that doesn't happen / happens, ...
Sentence 5: Whether or not / If you stopped file sharing completely, ...
Sentence 6: ... when / but only if the prices were lower.

b Which two of these expressions have a similar meaning?

| even if   as long as   unless   provided |

3 Work alone. In each sentence, choose one of the underlined expressions and add a conditional clause so it's true for you. Use different linking expressions.

1 I could live / I couldn't live without the Internet ...
2 I'm happy / I'm not happy to copy things for friends ...
3 I'd get / I wouldn't get all my music online ...
4 I'd pay / I wouldn't pay for access to news websites ...
5 I'll replace / I won't replace all my DVDs with Blu-ray discs ...
6 I'd be happy / I wouldn't be happy with more censorship of the Internet ...
7 I'll buy / I won't buy an e-reader ...
8 I'd do / I wouldn't do all my shopping online ...

Grammar reference
and practice, p135

4 a 🔊 **2.10** Remember that speakers say words in groups. There are no strict rules about how to do this, but the groups should be logical and help people understand what you're saying. Listen. Which alternative is more likely?

// If people like a particular album // then they'll go out // and buy it legally //
// If people // like a particular album then // they'll go out and buy it legally //

b Look at the sentences you wrote in 3. Decide how to divide them into groups.

5 Listen to each other's sentences from 3. Compare and explain your ideas.

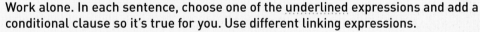

I wouldn't do all my shopping online even if there was free delivery.

Really? I would. It would save me so much time.

Maybe, but I like looking around the shops!

Design a site map

TASK LISTENING

1 Talk together.

1 Which websites do you most often visit? Why?
2 What would you say are the characteristics of a well-designed website?
3 What things about websites really annoy you?

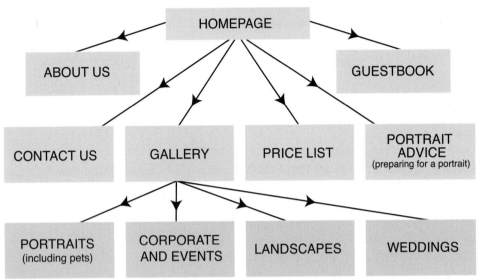

Ben and Ramdas have just started a small photography business. They're discussing a possible site map for their business's website.

2 Read the caption and look at the site map, which shows the proposed structure of the website. Do you think the site map is logically organised? Would you add or change any pages?

3 ● **2.11** Listen to Ben and Ramdas talking about the site map. Which pages do they mention?

4 ● **2.11** Listen again. Look at the site map and mark the changes Ben and Ramdas suggest. Do you think the site map's better now?

TASK VOCABULARY

Describing changes

5 Look at the sentences from Ben and Ramdas's conversation. Which five highlighted verbs could be replaced by a verb from the box?

> switch   connect   add   drop   shift

1 I think we should **link** that page to 'Portraits'.
2 I think we should **cut** the 'About Us' page.
3 If we **leave** it where it is, no one'll see it.
4 It's better to **move** all that information to the homepage.
5 My idea is to **stick** another page here.
6 I think we should **swap** 'Landscapes' and 'Weddings'.

TASK

6 a Work in groups. You're going to plan a website for:

a shop   a band   a gym   a language school   a family   a café   a sports team

Choose one of these ideas or think of your own.

b Now work alone. Think about these questions, then sketch a site map based on your ideas.

1 What pages should your site have (up to 12)? What will be on each page?
2 How should the pages be linked together?
3 Which pages need photographs, animation, music, etc.?

c In your groups, compare your site maps. Discuss your ideas and consider possible changes and consequences. Then design a final site map together.

7 Show the other groups your site map. Can you suggest any improvements to each other's maps?

Across cultures Ways of communicating

LISTENING

1 Talk together.

1 How many ways of communicating can you think of? Make a list. *texting, face-to-face, ...*
2 Which do you use most often to communicate with: friends? family? colleagues?

2 **2.12** Listen to Hugo and Liesbeth. Which three of these situations do they discuss, and in what order?

- applying for a job
- inviting someone to a party
- being offered a job
- thanking someone for a gift

3 a **2.12** Listen again. According to Hugo and Liesbeth, which of these ways of communicating are most appropriate for each situation?

in writing   by phone   by text   online

What reasons do they give for their ideas?

b Read the script on pp148–9 to check.

Hugo from England and Liesbeth from the Netherlands discuss how they communicate in different situations.

4 Where you live, do you think most people would say the same as Hugo and Liesbeth, or would they say something different? Talk together.

VOCABULARY

Habits and customs

5 a Which highlighted expressions from the conversation can you use to describe:

a personal habits?   b general customs?

1 If you receive a job offer, **it's really important that you** get it in writing.
2 **It's increasingly common for** people to call you first.
3 If my uncle sent me a gift, **I wouldn't dream of** phoning him.
4 If it's a mate, **then I'll probably** just call him or text him.
5 If it's my grandparents, **then I'll definitely** send a letter.

b Now add these highlighted expressions to groups a and b above.

6 Writing a letter is considered **the proper thing to do.**
7 **There's no way I'd** just telephone.
8 **It's unheard of** to reply to a job offer by text.
9 **You're expected to** respond pretty quickly.
10 **I'd always** say thank you face to face.

SPEAKING

6 a Work alone. Choose four or five of the situations below and think about these questions. Choose expressions from 5 to help you explain your ideas.

1 Which ways of communicating do you or would you use personally?
2 Which ways do people expect where you live?
3 Are people's expectations changing? How?
4 Which ways wouldn't be acceptable? Why?

- *inviting someone to a wedding*   • *replying to a wedding invitation*
- dismissing an employee   • inviting someone to dinner at your home
- congratulating someone on having a baby   • making a complaint to a company
- responding to a customer's complaint   • *asking someone to marry you*
- making a business proposal   • leaving a boyfriend or girlfriend

b Discuss your answers in groups.

7 Have you ever experienced different customs of communication in other cultures? If so, what happened? How did you feel? Talk together.

Goal

© put forward an argument in a web posting

1 Read a web posting by RealGuy about virtual gaming. Then talk in groups.

    1   Do you agree with RealGuy or not? Why?
    2   Imagine you had to argue against him. What points would you make?

2 Read Merlynda's response to RealGuy's posting. How many of her arguments are the same as the ones you discussed above?

3 Read Merlynda's posting again. In what ways does she think virtual worlds can:

    1   add to people's life experience?
    2   make people equal?
    3   make them stronger?

4 Look at the three paragraphs. What's the main purpose or theme of each one?

5 a Look at the highlighted expressions 1–7 in the posting. Which can you use to:

    a   state your intention?
    b   state your main arguments?
    c   refer to other people's views?
    d   state your conclusion or final thought?

  b Add these expressions to the groups a–d above.

    1   But consider this for a moment.
    2   At the end of the day, ...
    3   What you might not know is that ...
    4   I'd like to reply to ...
    5   Experts say that ...
    6   Don't forget that ...
    7   To sum up, I believe that ...
    8   I'd like to have my say about this.
    9   A lot of people have found that ...

  c Can you think of more expressions for each group?

6 a Read the web postings 1–3 and decide which one you will argue against.

  b Find someone who's chosen the same posting. Plan your responses together. Think about:

    • what arguments to present (facts, your own ideas and experiences, other people's views).
    • how to organise your arguments (starting, ending, grouping ideas into paragraphs).

  Choose the language you'll need to express the things in 5a.

  c Work alone and write your posting.

7 In groups, read each other's postings on the three topics. What are the most convincing arguments in each one? Do you agree? Talk together.

---

www.virtualnewsandgossip.org

Discussions > virtual gaming

posted by RealGuy @ 12.33 pm

Why waste time in a virtual world? If you're trying to escape from problems, they'll still be waiting for you when you turn off the computer. If you're just playing for fun, you could have fun in a much more constructive, creative way in the real world. If you want friends, then get to know the people in your community or join a group with similar interests to yours. Virtual friends are empty. Grow up and start REALLY living!

comments

posted by Merlynda @ 6.01 pm

[1]This is in response to RealGuy's comments that virtual worlds are a waste of time and we should give up our 'empty' friends and start living. I couldn't disagree more. He's not the only one who has that point of view and while I know I can't change his mind, [2]I'd like to present the other side of the story.

[3]Psychologists have long recognised that there are many forms of 'experience'. There's real-life experience, experience through dreams, experience through imagination (like daydreaming) and now experience through virtual reality games. [4]It's important to remember that gamers interact with people from around the world, learn new technological and social skills and work together to build things, fight enemies and tackle challenges. Thinking back, I'm astonished at how much I've learned about myself and others in virtual worlds and all this has had a very positive influence on my real-world life.

[5]Another benefit is you won't be judged on the basis of your real-world age, health, appearance, job or financial status. You present the image you want and people will respond to that. Maybe they'll like you, maybe they won't, but at least your image is your own choice. [6]Many gamers have claimed that because of this, they've felt free to express themselves better, make decisions more confidently and become more independent. [7]All in all, you have to admit that's not a bad result!

+ Add comment   Print

1 'There's nothing wrong with file sharing. Everyone does it – and if everyone does it and the police haven't stopped it, then it must be OK.' **JayC posted 23.16**

2 'Live concerts are awful. They're too crowded, you can't see anything and the audience is incredibly noisy. It's better to buy CDs or download albums of music produced in the studio.' **SeoulMan posted 14.10**

3 'The government's just spent half a million dollars on a sculpture for the park. What's it good for? Nothing! Basically, public art is a waste of taxpayers' money.' **ModelCitizen posted 16.43**

Review

1 a 🔊 **2.13** Listen to some extracts from the interview with Robin Bland. Complete the expressions.

1 As f_____ a_____ they're c_____, ...
2 You h_____ p_____ w_____ s_____ that ...
3 There's also t_____ a_____ that ...
4 The music companies w_____ t_____ y_____ that ...
5 A l_____ o_____ p_____ t_____ that ...
6 What t_____ s_____ i_____ that ...
7 Many musicians w_____ s_____ that ...

b In pairs, think of arguments for and against. Use the expressions in 1a.

* Is the world a better place than 100 years ago?
* Is community service a useful punishment?
* Does global warming really exist?
* Do all students need Internet access?

c Change pairs. Tell each other your points from 1b and give your personal opinion.

2 a Choose the most likely expressions.

1 I don't mind Thai food *as long as / unless* it's not too spicy.
2 *If / Unless* the weather's bad this weekend, we could go camping.
3 It wouldn't matter if we were late *provided / unless* we got there by nine.
4 *If / Even if* it's raining, Michael goes for a run every morning.

b Do you think it's ever OK to do these things? In what circumstances? Talk together.

* keep money you found on the street
* lie to your parents
* buy a gift for a business customer
* open someone else's mail

3 a Read five of Dieter Rams's principles. Think of synonyms for 1–5. Can you remember his other five principles? Check on p40.

* Good design is [1]innovative.
* Good design is [2]aesthetic.
* Good design is [3]unobtrusive.
* Good design is [4]honest.
* Good design is [5]durable.

b In pairs, choose two or three objects in your classroom. Do they meet Dieter Rams's principles of good design? Talk together. Do you agree?

Extension

4 a Underline the letters which make an /ʌ/ sound. Then complete the spelling patterns 1–3.

otherwise   abrupt   onion   luxury   discuss   government   husband   justice   punishment   sometimes   hunt   suddenly

1 /ʌ/ can be spelled _____ or _____.
2 _____ is the most common spelling.
3 _____ is most often found before the letters *m, n, th* and *v*.

b /ʌ/ is also spelled **ou** in some very common words, for example:

couple   trouble   enough   rough   country   touch

c Spellcheck. Complete the spelling of these words. Then check in a dictionary.

t__gh   sp__nge   p__zzled   d__ble
m__scle   y__ngster   gl__ve   h__mble
c__sin   am__ng   s__thern   st__mach

5 a Combine the compound adjectives with 1–8 to make expressions from the article *It was a virtual murder*. Then check in the article on p46.

~~33-year-old~~   face-to-face   flesh-and-blood   long-term   low-quality   middle-aged   real-world   role-playing

1 an office worker   5 a crime
2 science-fiction movies   6 a game
3 a piano teacher   7 commitments
4 a meeting   8 justice

1 a 33-year-old office worker

b Test each other. Take turns to say 1–8 and remember the compound adjectives.

> a meeting

> a face-to-face meeting

Self-assessment

Can you do these things in English? Circle a number on each line. 1 = I can't do this, 5 = I can do this well.

talk about crimes and justice	1 2 3 4 5
justify your point of view	1 2 3 4 5
talk about media and the Internet	1 2 3 4 5
report different points of view	1 2 3 4 5
describe possible consequences of actions	1 2 3 4 5
suggest changes to a plan or document	1 2 3 4 5
put forward an argument in a web posting	1 2 3 4 5

* For Wordcards, reference and saving your work → e-Portfolio
* For more practice → Self-study Pack, Unit 6

7

7.1 goals
⦿ talk about how you deal with problems
⦿ describe experiences of problem solving

Inspiration

Working it out

READING

1 Which of these things help you when you're thinking about a problem? Do you do anything else? Talk together.

having a coffee
walking around the room
listening to music
meditating
going out for a walk

having a bath
getting some sleep
thinking about something else for a while
doing housework
talking to yourself

2 Read the article. Which things in 1 can improve your ability to solve problems, according to the article?

NEWSONLINE

Distracted genius

TOO many distractions? Good. We're constantly experiencing interruptions from mobile phones, emails and all the head-noise of modern life, but, oddly, this may make us far better at finding answers to problems, says new research in the journal *Psychological Science*.

Tests on 130 volunteers have shown that if you're distracted while trying to concentrate on a tough problem, it may help you solve it later on.

A team of psychologists, led by Northwestern University, say their tests show that creative problem solving requires a two-stage process of unconscious thought. And it works better if you get a break between the stages.

Their experiments involved asking two groups of volunteers to perform a series of tricky word-association tests. One group was told to stop work on the tests halfway through and to try some other tests instead. When they returned to the first tests, their performance was much better.

Professor Adam Galinsky, who led the study, says this two-step unconscious system explains a phenomenon that many of us have noticed – if you give up on a problem, somehow it sorts itself out in your head a little later.

It also helps to explain an earlier study by Dutch investigators in the journal *Science*, which reports that the mind can be much better at coming up with solutions if we switch off our conscious thoughts by relaxing in the tub, taking a walk or meditating.

The report in *Science* also suggests that creativity-based companies might well profit from encouraging their staff to build some slack into their days, rather than staying glued to their desks.

---

3 Read again. According to the article:

1 why can interruptions from phones, emails and so on be helpful?
2 what did each group of volunteers at Northwestern University have to do?
3 which group got better results?
4 why might things like meditating help us solve problems?
5 what should some businesses consider doing?

4 What do you think about the ideas in the article? Do they match your own experiences of thinking about problems?

VOCABULARY

Problems and solutions

5 a Decide if these pairs of expressions from the article are similar or different in meaning. If they differ, explain how.

1 **concentrate on** a problem / **sort out** a problem
2 **solve** a problem / **find the answer to** a problem
3 **give up on** a problem / **come up with** a solution

b Now do the same with these expressions.

4 mull over a problem / tackle a problem
5 ignore a problem / put off dealing with a problem
6 figure out what to do / work out what to do

6 Cover 5 and complete these questions about problem solving. Then look at 5 to check.

1 Would you say your work or home life involves s _olving_ lots of problems?
2 At what time of day do you find it easiest to f_____ o_____ answers to problems?
3 Do you prefer to c_____ o_____ one problem at a time or t_____ several at once?
4 Do you tend to p_____ o_____ dealing with problems or s_____ them o_____ straight away?
5 Where do you c_____ u_____ w_____ your best or most original ideas?
6 Are there any situations where you think it's best just to i_____ problems?

SPEAKING

7 Discuss the questions in groups. Give examples to explain your answers.

What we decided to do was ...

LISTENING

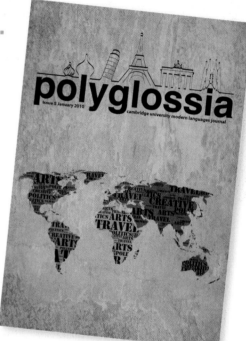

Hugo is the founder of a magazine called *Polyglossia*.

1 a Look at the cover of *Polyglossia* magazine. What kind of magazine do you think it is?

b ◖2.14◗ Listen to part of an interview with Hugo about the problems he had in setting up *Polyglossia*. Check your ideas from 1a. What's unusual about *Polyglossia*?

2 ◖2.14◗ Listen again.

1 Which of these problems does Hugo talk about? How did he solve them?
   a finding people to work with him
   b finding places to sell the magazine
   c finding a way to make it appeal to more people

2 Which of these skills does Hugo say he learned from his experience?
   a being well organised
   b seeing things from other people's point of view
   c being ready to think in new and creative ways

3 What do you think about the idea of *Polyglossia*? Who might buy it?

VOCABULARY

Problem-solving experiences

4 Put the highlighted words in the right order to make sentences from the interview.

1 The that problem biggest was it was just an idea.
2 I it difficult to found select different people.
3 It us a because with presented problem what do you do with a casual reader?
4 What was do decided to we (to) include English summaries.
5 My problem to way was solving of this include English summaries.
6 What was to learned I put myself in other people's shoes.

SPEAKING

5 You're completing an application for a job when you come to these questions:

Please describe two or three problems you've solved successfully in your work, studies or other areas of your life. How did you solve them? What did you learn from your experiences?

Work alone. Think about how you'd answer the questions, using expressions from 4.

6 a In groups, tell each other about the problems you had and how you solved them.

b What were the most original solutions you heard about?

Dreamers

7.2 goals
- talk about where you get ideas
- describe a scene

LISTENING

1 Talk together.

1 Do you usually remember your dreams? Do you tend to dream in colour or black and white?
2 Do you think it's possible for dreams to do any of these things?
- give you new ideas
- tell you what's happening in other places
- show you the future
- help you understand your thoughts and feelings

VINTAGE **SHELLEY**

FRANKENSTEIN

Mary Shelley wrote the novel Frankenstein in 1816.

Srinivasa Ramanujan (1887–1920) proved over 3000 mathematical theorems.

$$\frac{50_a(q^{25})}{\theta_a(q)} = 1 + r_1^{1/5} + r_2^{1/5}$$

August Kekulé discovered the chemical structure of benzene in 1865.

2 Dreams played an important part in the work of these three people. Which of the people have you heard of before? What do you know about them?

3 ● 2.15 Listen to a radio programme about these people's dreams. Do the descriptions of the dreams mention images, sounds, or both images and sounds?

4 a ● 2.15 Listen again and match five of these things to each story. Write M (Mary), S (Srinivasa) or A (August).

M Switzerland	___ a fire	___ atoms	___ a hand	___ a circle
___ a chair	___ Byron	___ blood	___ ghost stories	___ equations
___ Namagiri	___ a screen	___ storms	___ a snake	___ a monster

b In groups, use the things in 4a to help you retell each story.

VOCABULARY

Inspiration

5 a Work in groups. Can you complete the sentences from the radio programme?

1 The image of the famous monster _____ to the author in her sleep.
2 Mary _____ the idea for *Frankenstein* from a dream.
3 Srinivasa Ramanujan was _____ by dreams.
4 Scientists and engineers _____ a lot of **inspiration** from dreams.
5 Kekulé _____ that benzene molecules have the shape of a ring.
6 A dream could _____ you **the idea for** a great work of art.

b Read the script on pp149–50 to check.

PRONUNCIATION

Fluent speech 2 – the with linking /j/

6 a ● 2.16 Listen to these expressions. In 3, notice the long vowel /iː/ and the linking sound /j/. Why's the pronunciation in 3 different?

/ə/	/ə/	/iː/
1 the famous monster	2 the shape of a circle	3 the‿idea for *Frankenstein*
		/j/

b Practise saying these pairs of expressions. Make sure you use the correct pronunciation of **the**.

1 the eighties, the nineties
2 the east, the west
3 the beginning, the end
4 the English, the Japanese
5 the solution, the inspiration
6 the writer, the artist

I decided to go to Dubai to learn Arabic a few years ago. I got the idea from reading a newspaper article about Arabic courses in universities.

7 a Think of some good ideas you've come up with in your life. Think about your work, home, studies or an interest. Where did the idea or inspiration come from? E.g.:

dreams   reading   brainstorming with colleagues   talking to experts
TV   the Internet   chatting to friends and family   watching what other people do

b Talk in groups about your ideas. Ask questions to find out more.

I saw atoms dancing ...

GRAMMAR

Describing scenes – present and past participle clauses

1 Read the information and examples in the box. Then answer the questions.

> You can use participle clauses after <u>nouns</u> to help you describe a scene.
> • I saw <u>atoms</u> **dancing before my eyes**.
>
> A participle clause is similar to a relative clause:
> • I saw <u>atoms</u> **which were dancing before my eyes**.
>
> Here are more examples from the radio programme:
> 1 I saw a pale student **kneeling beside the monster he had put together**.
> 2 There was a red screen **formed by flowing blood**.
> 3 I could see long rows of atoms **twisting like a snake**.
> 4 Benzene molecules, like the snake **made of atoms**, have the shape of a ring.

1 Which **clauses** in 1–4 are made with:
   a present participles (-*ing*)?   b past participles (often -*ed*)?
2 Which kind of participle has:
   a an active meaning?   b a passive meaning?

2 a Read about the poet Coleridge and his poem *Kubla Khan*. Do you believe his story?

Grammar reference and practice, p136

> *Kubla Khan* is an unfinished poem [1]inspiring / inspired by a dream which Samuel Taylor Coleridge had in about 1797. It's well known for its beautiful imagery, and for a mystery [2]connecting / connected with its composition.
>
> According to a story [3]telling / told by Coleridge himself in his introduction to the poem, he was staying at a cottage in the countryside when he fell into a deep sleep and saw the entire poem [4]writing / written out for him in a dream. When he awoke, he found that he could still see the text in his mind and immediately started writing it down. Unfortunately, Coleridge had written just the first 54 lines when he was interrupted by someone [5]visiting / visited on urgent business from the nearby village of Porlock. Although Coleridge and his visitor had a conversation [6]lasting / lasted more than an hour, to this day nobody knows who he (or she?) was, or what they spoke about. But when Coleridge returned to his desk, he found that the rest of the poem had vanished from his memory.
>
> For a long time this story was generally accepted as true, but scholars and poets [7]writing / written more recently have suggested that it was a fiction or perhaps even a kind of joke. Whatever the truth of Coleridge's story, nowadays a 'Person from Porlock' is a humorous term [8]using / used to describe an unwelcome interruption to creative work!

b Read again and choose the correct participles.

3 a Work in pairs. A – look at the pictures on p121. B – look at the pictures on p124.

- Imagine these are scenes from dreams.
- Think about how to describe them. What can you see and hear?
- Think of participle clauses to use in your descriptions.

flying	lying	pointing	standing	wearing
buried in	connected to	covered in	made of	surrounded by

b Describe the dream scenes to each other.

4 Look at each other's pictures. Are they what you expected from your partner's description? What do you think the pictures might 'mean'? Do you like them?

Target activity

Come up with solutions

7.3 goals
◎ describe experiences of problem solving
◎ describe a scene
◎ participate in a problem-solving discussion

TASK LISTENING

1 Read Case study 1 from a training course on problem solving.
What's Chen's problem? Why hasn't he taken any action?

> ### CASE STUDY 1: CHEN
> ✱ Chen is a lab assistant in an environmental science company.
> ✱ He's noticed that equipment is disappearing – usually minor things, but last week an expensive digital microscope.
> ✱ He suspects two male office workers, though many people use the lab.
> ✱ He saw them quietly leaving the lab two days ago, carrying something.
> ✱ He heard them talking yesterday about selling something – but what?
> ✱ He doesn't want to accuse them until he's sure – it could be someone else.
> ✱ He can't risk losing any more equipment as he's responsible for it.

2 *2.17* Listen to three students on the course discussing Chen's problem. Which of these possible solutions do they decide would be best?

a lock the lab door when he's away
b tell his boss about the missing items
c get someone to supervise the lab when he's out
d set up a camera to film the thieves
e tell his boss who he thinks is doing it
f speak directly to the two office workers
g hide in the lab and wait for the thieves

3 *2.17* Listen again. Why do they reject the other ideas in 2?

4 Do you agree with their solution? Why? / Why not?

TASK VOCABULARY

Discussing possible solutions

5 Complete the sentences from the conversation. Then check the script on p150.

Proposing ideas
1 It might be w_____h speaking to the two workers privately.
2 Al_____y, he could hide somewhere and wait.
3 Another o_____n would be to lock the lab door.
4 A different a_____h would be to inform the head of the lab.

Reacting positively
5 There's s_____g in that.
6 That's quite f_____e.
7 That's worth c_____g.

Reacting negatively
8 That would be t_____y.
9 That's not really p_____l.
10 I wouldn't r_____d that.

TASK

6 **a Work in groups. Read Case study 2 on p123.**

1 Brainstorm a number of possible solutions.
2 Consider the pros and cons of each one.
3 Decide on the best solution.

Use language from 5 to propose and react to ideas.

b Now do the same for Case study 3 on p123.

7 **a Plan how to tell another group about your discussions.**

1 What possible solutions did you consider?
2 Which did you choose? Why?
3 What were your reasons for rejecting the other options?

b Tell the other group about your discussions. Did you have similar ideas?

> We thought it might be worth going to the police but that wasn't really practical because ...

Keyword *come*

Expressions with *come*

1 Look at the extracts A–C. Where do you think each one could be from?

A

In this month's issue ...

- **Curious about Moroccan food?** *Our wonderful recipes will come in useful for parties or quiet dinners for two.*
- **Planning a trip to Hong Kong?** *This month's World Food Guide has tips on all the best places to eat.*

B

Early results from yesterday's poll suggest that a second round of voting will be required in two weeks' time. The president, who is seeking a third term in office, polled 47% of the vote, while former justice minister Laurence Taylor came second with 31%. The results have come as a shock to the ruling party, which has won every election since independence without the need for a second round of voting.

C

Discussions here are coming along slowly as there are a few problems with the draft contract which we hadn't anticipated. However, I'm pretty confident we'll be able to sort things out and come to an agreement by the end of tomorrow. I'll keep you posted.

2 a Find expressions with come in the extracts. Complete 1–5.

1 come in _____   4 coming along _____
2 came _____   5 come to _____
3 come as _____

b Match these words to 1–5 above to make more expressions with come.

a conclusion   a decision   a disappointment
an end   first   handy   last   nicely   quickly
a relief   a surprise   well

come in useful, come in handy

3 a Work alone. Choose four or five expressions from 2 which you could use to describe your life now or in the past. Write sentences.

When I was eight, I came first in an art competition.

b Listen to each other's sentences. Ask questions to find out more.

Multi-word verbs with *come*

4 Can you guess the meaning of the multi-word verbs from the context?

> The first of Hrabal's collected writings – in nineteen volumes – [1]came out in 1991.

> The bill [2]came to £18.45.

> You have one minute to [3]come up with an idea.

> Sorry, but I'm going to be late again tonight. Something's [4]come up at work.

> We were walking through the woods when we [5]came across a strange little house.

> Enrico [6]comes across as very serious at first, but actually he's got a lovely sense of humour.

> Would you like to [7]come round for dinner this weekend? I'm making couscous.

> Marta's always been well off. Her uncle died when she was a baby and she [8]came into a lot of money.

> Kieran's going to be off work all week. I'm afraid he's [9]come down with a cold.

5 a Use verbs from 4 to complete the questions. Then write two more questions with multi-word verbs for the people in your class.

1 Have you ever _____ something you thought you'd lost a long time ago?
2 What are your favourite books, records and films? When did they _____?
3 Do you know anyone who's _____ a lot of money?
4 Where you live, is it normal for friends to _____ without calling first?
5 What would you do if a restaurant bill _____ a lot less than you expected?

b Ask and answer the questions.

Goal
◉ speak tactfully in different situations

1 a ◖2.18◗ Listen to three short conversations.

Conversation 1
What's Jan noticed about Kelly?
What's the reason?

Conversation 2
Why's Harold worried about Rajeev?
What kind of problem is it?

Conversation 3
What does Lucia ask Hee-Sun?
What won't Lucia explain?

b Read the conversations to check.

2 Which expressions 1–8 in the conversations have a similar purpose to a–c?

a   Maybe it's none of my business but …
b   It's a difficult situation.
c   I'd prefer not to answer that.

3 a Choose expressions from 2 to complete these conversations. Different answers are possible.

1   A   _____ but I heard your brother's company just closed down.
    B   Yes, but _____.
2   A   Well, happy birthday! _____ how old are you?
    B   _____. It's a secret!
3   A   Alistair told me you're not speaking. _____ what's the problem?
    B   Well, _____. It's just that he's sometimes so opinionated.
4   A   Do you know why Jerry was fired?
    B   I do, but _____. I promised not to gossip about it.

b ◖2.19◗ Listen to some possible answers. Were yours similar?

4 a Work in two groups.

Group A – read the six situations on p122.
Group B – read the six situations on p126.

In your groups, plan what to say for each situation. Think of what language you can use from 2.

b Get into A/B pairs. Have your conversations.

5 Go back to your groups. What answers did you get from the people you talked to?

①

JAN	Max, have you got a moment?
MAX	Sure.
JAN	I'm slightly worried about Kelly.
MAX	OK … erm, how do you mean?
JAN	Well I can see that she's not happy in Finance, but she won't say why. [1]I don't want to be nosy but do you know what's going on? You know her better than I do.
MAX	Well, [2]it's a bit delicate. Erm … She has to work with Ken but, erm, they used to be in a relationship.
JAN	Oh, I see. I didn't know that.

②

HAROLD	So, how are things?
RAJEEV	Oh, not too bad, you know. Getting along.
HAROLD	Rajeev, [3]I don't mean to pry, but is something wrong? You've been looking really tired recently.
RAJEEV	Erm, yeah, [4]I'd rather not say. Sorry.
HAROLD	No, no, that's fine.
RAJEEV	It's just, erm … [5]it's just a personal thing.
HAROLD	OK, no problem. So, did you see the game last night?

③

LUCIA	Hee-Sun! I'm so glad to see you! I'm a bit confused. What's the quickest way to get to Paul's from here?
HEE-SUN	Oh, well, er, you go down 125th Street, then left into White Avenue, then turn right into Orchard Street.
LUCIA	Right into Orchard … OK, sorry I can't stop. Bye.
HEE-SUN	Er, [6]if you don't mind me asking, what is the big hurry?
LUCIA	Erm, [7]I can't really talk about it right now. [8]It's kind of complicated.
HEE-SUN	Ah. OK.
LUCIA	But don't worry. I'll be fine. See you.
HEE-SUN	Bye.

7 Look again ♻

Review

VOCABULARY Problems and solutions

1 a Add the missing words to these comments.

on (x2)   out (x2)   ~~with~~   over   off

with

1 I came up /\ a brilliant solution.
2 I spent a long time mulling it.
3 I couldn't figure what to do.
4 I couldn't concentrate my work.
5 I thought it was best to put the decision till later.
6 It was so frustrating that I just gave up it.
7 They promised to sort the problem straight away.

b Choose two comments which remind you of experiences you've had yourself. Make brief notes, then talk about your experiences together.

GRAMMAR Describing scenes – present and past participle clauses

2 a Circle the correct participle in each description.

1 There's part of an application form asking / asked about your experiences.
2 There's a magazine designing / designed for people who speak different languages.
3 There's a molecule discovering / discovered by August Kekulé.
4 There are two people leaving / left a lab and carrying / carried something.

b In this unit, find the pictures or text described in 1–4.

c Work in three teams. In your team, write four descriptions of pictures from anywhere in the book. Use participle clauses.

d Take turns to read a sentence to the other teams. Whichever team finds the picture in the book first gets a point.

CAN YOU REMEMBER? Unit 6 – Describing consequences

3 a Complete the sentences about health and fitness with your own ideas.

1 I have to get at least ... hours of sleep a night or else ...
2 Eating good food, such as ..., is important. Otherwise, ...
3 You really need to ... or ...
4 You also need to have ... . If not, ...
5 It's a good idea to ... . That way, ...
6 It's an advantage to have ... . Then ...

b Do you agree with each other's ideas about health and fitness? Say why / why not.

Extension

SPELLING AND SOUNDS /ɒ/

4 a Underline the letters which make an /ɒ/ sound.

Australia because cauliflower conscious problem psychology quality solve squash swap volunteer watch

b Find words in 4a to match these spelling patterns.

1 /ɒ/ is usually spelled o.
2 After *qu* or *w*, /ɒ/ is spelled a.
3 In a few words, /ɒ/ is spelled au.

c 🔊 2.20 Spellcheck. Listen and write ten words. Then check your spelling on p150.

NOTICE *he*, *she* and *they*

5 a Read the extract from the interview with Hugo. Say which words could go in the gap. Then check on p149 to see what he actually said.

"
My way of solving this problem was to include English summaries of all of the foreign-language articles and this meant that at least the reader would feel that _____ had an idea of what was going on in each article ...
"

b Complete the explanation about the use of *he*, *she* and *they* with these words.

He   He or she   He/she   s(he)   They

[1]_____ is traditionally correct when gender is unknown or unimportant but is increasingly unusual in modern English as it is felt by many people to be sexist. [2]_____ is also correct, but rather long and clumsy. [3]_____ is very common in modern English, although some people regard it as incorrect because it is plural. [4]_____ and [5]_____ are, of course, only possible in writing.

c Talk together. Which expressions would you prefer to use in speech and in writing? Are there similar choices in your first language(s)?

Self-assessment

Can you do these things in English? (Circle) a number on each line. 1 = I can't do this, 5 = I can do this well.

◎ talk about how you deal with problems	1	2	3	4	5
◎ describe experiences of problem solving	1	2	3	4	5
◎ talk about where you get ideas	1	2	3	4	5
◎ describe a scene	1	2	3	4	5
◎ participate in a problem-solving discussion	1	2	3	4	5
◎ speak tactfully in different situations	1	2	3	4	5

• For Wordcards, reference and saving your work → e-Portfolio
• For more practice → Self-study Pack, Unit 7

8.1 goals
⊚ make deductions about the past
⊚ describe strong feelings

8

Critical incidents

One side of the story ...

LISTENING

1 ⏵ **2.21** Listen to the stories. Which person in each picture is telling the story?

2 ⏵ **2.21** Listen again.

Picture 1 1 Why did Vic and his wife take Neil to dinner?
2 How did the evening suddenly change?
Picture 2 3 What was the party like?
4 What did Daniela do at the party?
Picture 3 5 How did Haneul act when Virginia greeted her?
6 How did she act later at home?

GRAMMAR

Making deductions about the past

3 a Read the sentences from the stories, then add the highlighted expressions to the diagram.

- It **can't have been** because I paid. He knew I was going to.
- He **might have** been a bit angry. It's hard to say.
- I think she **must have** felt homesick.
- She **may well have** forgotten what I looked like.

I'm sure it's not true.	It's possible.	It's very possible.	I'm sure it's true.
1 _____	3 _____	6 _____	7 _____
2 _____	4 _____		
	5 _____		

b Now add these expressions to the diagram.

- may have   • could have   • couldn't have

c What form of the verb is used after have?

4 Read the sentences about Vic's story. Rewrite the <u>underlined</u> part of each sentence using an expression from 3 which has the same meaning.

1 <u>There's no way that Neil was</u> unhappy with the meal. He really enjoyed it.
2 <u>Maybe he felt</u> a bit ill after eating too much.
3 <u>It's possible the waiter made</u> a mistake in the bill, and Neil noticed it.
4 <u>Or perhaps Vic said</u> something that upset Neil.
5 <u>But obviously the waiter was</u> upset about something, too.
6 <u>There's a good chance Neil was</u> embarrassed by the waiter's strange expression.

Grammar reference and practice, p136

5 a In pairs, talk about the other two situations. Use expressions from 3 to speculate about why Daniela and Haneul acted as they did.

b Compare your ideas. How many different ideas did you get?

... and the other

1 Read the postings on the web page *Cross-cultural misunderstandings*. What were the real reasons that Neil, Daniela and Haneul acted and felt as they did?

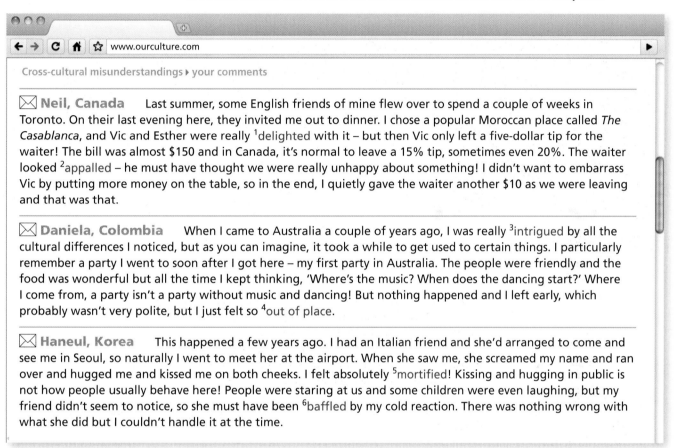

Cross-cultural misunderstandings ▸ your comments

✉ **Neil, Canada**   Last summer, some English friends of mine flew over to spend a couple of weeks in Toronto. On their last evening here, they invited me out to dinner. I chose a popular Moroccan place called *The Casablanca*, and Vic and Esther were really ¹delighted with it – but then Vic only left a five-dollar tip for the waiter! The bill was almost $150 and in Canada, it's normal to leave a 15% tip, sometimes even 20%. The waiter looked ²appalled – he must have thought we were really unhappy about something! I didn't want to embarrass Vic by putting more money on the table, so in the end, I quietly gave the waiter another $10 as we were leaving and that was that.

✉ **Daniela, Colombia**   When I came to Australia a couple of years ago, I was really ³intrigued by all the cultural differences I noticed, but as you can imagine, it took a while to get used to certain things. I particularly remember a party I went to soon after I got here – my first party in Australia. The people were friendly and the food was wonderful but all the time I kept thinking, 'Where's the music? When does the dancing start?' Where I come from, a party isn't a party without music and dancing! But nothing happened and I left early, which probably wasn't very polite, but I just felt so ⁴out of place.

✉ **Haneul, Korea**   This happened a few years ago. I had an Italian friend and she'd arranged to come and see me in Seoul, so naturally I went to meet her at the airport. When she saw me, she screamed my name and ran over and hugged me and kissed me on both cheeks. I felt absolutely ⁵mortified! Kissing and hugging in public is not how people usually behave here! People were staring at us and some children were even laughing, but my friend didn't seem to notice, so she must have been ⁶baffled by my cold reaction. There was nothing wrong with what she did but I couldn't handle it at the time.

2 How would you have felt in these situations? What would you have done?

3 a Which of the highlighted expressions in the postings have a similar meaning to a–f?

a   alone, not part of a group?
b   very pleased?
c   very confused?
d   extremely embarrassed?
e   very interested?
f   extremely shocked and upset?

b Now match more words with the meanings in 3a.

1   fascinated
2   horrified
3   humiliated
4   isolated
5   mystified
6   thrilled

4 a Think of one or two incidents from your life when there was a misunderstanding, for example when you were:

on holiday   travelling   at work   with family or friends
in a relationship   shopping   eating

Think about how to:

• describe what happened.
• speculate about why it happened.
• describe your feelings.

b Listen to each other's stories. Do you agree with each other's speculations? Can you suggest any other explanations?

Turning points

8.2 goals
◎ say how you feel about past events in your life
◎ speculate about consequences of past actions

Jeanette from the USA

Fernando from Argentina

Tristan from Wales

LISTENING

1 Do you know anyone who's done any of these things in the past year? How did it make them feel? Talk together.

got engaged or married   had a baby   emigrated   started university
bought a home   moved home   started a new career   changed jobs

2 ◖◗ **2.22** Look at the pictures and listen to Jeanette, Fernando and Tristan. What important moment in each person's life do the pictures represent?

3 ◖◗ **2.22** Listen again. Answer the questions for each person.

1   What happened before the moment in the picture?
2   What happened afterwards?
3   How do they feel now about what happened?

4 Do you know anyone who's had a similar important moment in their life?

VOCABULARY

Reflecting on the past

5 a Look at the sentences. Which three are from the recording? Who said them?

1 I **regret** telling that lie. 2 I **don't regret** a thing.	+ noun or *-ing* form
3 **I'm sorry** I didn't say yes. 4 **I'm not sorry** I changed jobs. 5 **I'm glad** things turned out the way they did. 6 **It's a good thing** I didn't send that email.	+ past simple
7 **I wish** I'd thought about it more carefully. 8 **If only** I'd asked for some advice.	+ past perfect

b Which highlighted expressions can you use for:

1   a   positive feelings?   b   negative feelings?
2   a   things that really happened?   b   imaginary situations?

6 Think of three or four things you did recently, for example:

buying something   meeting someone   saying something
going to an event   giving advice   throwing something away

Write a sentence saying how you feel now about each thing. Use expressions from 5a.

SPEAKING

7 Talk in groups. Tell each other about the things you did recently and how you feel about them now. Ask questions to find out more.

> I bought a new car last month. I'm completely broke now but I don't regret it at all!

> Oh, right. What kind of car is it?

Speculation

GRAMMAR

Conditionals –
past and present

1 Look at sentences a–d in the table and answer the questions.

1 In each sentence, are the speakers describing things that really happened, or are they imagining them?

2 Look at the two parts of each sentence. Which parts are about the past? Which are about the present?

3 Complete the forms with these terms: *infinitive*, *-ing form* or *past participle*.

if + had + _____,	*modal verb + have + _____*
a If I'**d married** Juli, b If I **hadn't seen** the head teacher,	we **could've had** kids. I **wouldn't have gone** to China.
c If I **hadn't seen** the head teacher,	*modal verb + _____* my life **would be** completely different.
d If my company **hadn't decided** to move,	*modal verb + be + _____* I'd probably still **be doing** the same job.

2 a Work alone. Use your own ideas to complete the sentences about the people.

Jeanette
1 If she hadn't looked in that newspaper, ...
2 She might not have gone to college if ...
Fernando
3 He'd probably have asked Juli to marry him if ...
4 If he'd asked her to marry him, ...
Tristan
5 If he'd been away from school that day, ...
6 He probably wouldn't be married if ...

Grammar reference
and practice, p137

b Compare your ideas.

PRONUNCIATION

Prominent
words 1

3 a (•2.23) Listen to the groups of words in these sentences. Notice how in each group, the speaker chooses one word to have extra-strong stress. This word is PROMINENT.

1 // If I'd married JULi // we could've had KIDS //
2 // If I hadn't seen the head TEAcher // I wouldn't have gone to CHIna //
3 // If I hadn't seen the head TEAcher // my life would be completely DIFFerent //
4 // If my company hadn't decided to MOVE // I'd probably still be doing the same JOB //

The prominent word is often the last important word in a group of words.

b Practise saying the sentences.

SPEAKING

4 a Choose a turning point in your life you'd like to talk about. It could involve, for example:

someone important in your life   a job or career decision   moving to a different place
buying or selling something   an idea you had   advice someone gave you

b Think about these questions. Think of some conditional sentences you could use.

1 When did it happen? What were you doing at the time?
2 Was it your choice or did it just happen?
3 What happened afterwards? How has it affected your life now?
4 What if something different had happened?
5 How do you feel about it now?

c Talk about your turning points in groups. Have any of you had similar experiences?

Work out what happened

8.3 goals
⊙ make deductions about the past ♻
⊙ speculate about consequences of past actions ♻
⊙ disagree with speculations about the past

Jo and Angela are cousins. They're looking after their aunt's flat while she's on holiday. They've just realised they've got a serious problem.

TASK LISTENING

1 a **2.24** Look at the picture and read the caption. Then listen to the first part of Jo and Angela's conversation. Can you guess what the problem is? Compare your ideas.

b **2.25** Listen to the rest of the conversation to check.

2 a Listen to the whole conversation again. Why are these facts significant?

1   The flat's on the fourth floor.
2   It took Jo and Angela a while to bring their shopping into the flat.
3   The neighbours are friendly.
4   There's an empty bowl in the kitchen.
5   Angela takes a long time to wake up in the morning.

b Compare your answers, then look at the script on p151 to check.

TASK VOCABULARY

Disagreeing with past speculations

3 Put the second line of each extract in order.

1 ANGELA It might have jumped out the window, or fallen.
    JO No, _____ . (have / it / outside / seen / we'd)
2 JO It must have gone out the front door.
    ANGELA Yeah, but _____ . (it / on / seen / somebody / the stairs / would've)

Notice that would have can explain why an idea about the past is unlikely or impossible.

4 a Think of some arguments with would have to complete these conversations.

1 A She might have got stuck in traffic.
   B No, ...
2 A My wallet must have been stolen last night.
   B No, ...
3 A They might have cancelled the party.
   B But ...
4 A You must have left your keys at Eric's.
   B But ...

b Compare your ideas.

TASK

5 a Work in pairs and prepare to talk together. Read Situation 1 on your card.

Student A – look at your situation cards on p124.
Student B – look at your situation cards on p126.

b Talk together and try to decide:

1   what probably happened.   2   what to do next.

6 Now repeat 5a and 5b for Situation 2.

7 Compare your conclusions with another pair, then look at the suggested explanations on p128. Did you have the same ideas?

Across cultures Languages

SPEAKING

1 **a** More than half the words of modern English have been adopted from other languages. In groups, guess which language each of these words came from.

> alphabet boss cotton hamburger ketchup
> marriage opera plaza robot sauna
> shampoo ski tsunami yoghurt

> Arabic Cantonese Czech Dutch Finnish
> French German Greek Hindi Italian
> Japanese Norwegian Spanish Turkish

Sahana from India

b Check your ideas on p121, then talk together.

1 Do you know if your language has given any words to English? Which words?
2 What languages have given words to your first language? Give examples.

Liesbeth from the Netherlands

LISTENING

2 **a** You're going to listen to Sahana and Liesbeth talking about languages in India and the Netherlands. What do you know about languages in these countries?

b 2.26 Listen to Sahana and Liesbeth. What do they say about these questions?

1 What languages are spoken? Where?
2 What about language learning in schools?

3 **a** 2.27 Listen to Sahana and Liesbeth saying more about their languages. Which three of these questions do they answer?

1 How has the language changed in the last fifty years?
2 How do people feel about: gestures? volume? silence? interrupting?
3 How do people feel about changes in the language?
4 How have languages been important in the history of the country?
5 What are or were the most popular languages for people to learn?
6 How would you describe the character of the language?

b 2.27 Listen again. Note down two or three details about the answers to each of the three questions. Compare your notes. Read the scripts on pp151–2 to check.

VOCABULARY

Languages

4 How do the expressions in each group 1–4 differ in meaning? Do any have the same meaning?

1	2	3	4
a language	an official language	a mother tongue	monolingual
a dialect	a regional language	a first language	bilingual
an accent	a common language	a second language	multilingual

SPEAKING

5 **a** Prepare to talk about languages where you live or in another place you know.

1 Choose questions to talk about from 2b and 3a.
2 Plan what to say about each topic, using language from 4 to help you.

b Listen to each other's talks.

• If you're from the same place, do you agree with each other's ideas?
• If you're from different places, which facts do you think would be the most interesting or significant for a visitor?

8 EXPLOREWriting

1   Have you ever had a problem at a hotel? Did you complain, and if so, was there any solution?

2   Read the complaint from a hotel guest.

   1   What error did he find on his bill?
   2   How did the clerk react?
   3   What action did the manager take?
   4   What does the guest want the hotel directors to do?

Identification   User name or email address: **a.al-jabiri@spacenet.com**

Message category   [Complaint ⬍]   Please state your message clearly and briefly.

¹I'd like to make a complaint about the extremely rude and unprofessional behaviour of one of your staff towards me. I stayed at your hotel in Maybury from 10 to 14 May. The incident occurred when I was checking my bill at the Front Desk and found I'd been charged £75 for use of the gym. However, I'd been told when I checked in that if I used the gym, it would be complimentary. When I pointed this out, the clerk (Will Marley) said, "Don't cause trouble. Use of the gym is not complimentary and there's no problem with this bill." I was appalled by his words and refused to pay. The manager came out and immediately cancelled the charge but Mr Marley did not apologise nor did the manager tell him to. If this had happened in my country, he would have been fired on the spot. I regret I didn't insist on seeing a director but I was in a hurry to catch my flight. ²I would like to receive a formal apology from the directors of the hotel and an assurance that the employee has been disciplined. ³I also suggest you take steps to ensure that such an incident doesn't happen again. I look forward to your response and ⁴I hope that you will be able to restore my confidence in your hotel.

---

3   What would you have done in the guest's position?

4   The complaint could be improved by dividing it into paragraphs. In pairs, decide where you'd put the divisions. Then compare your ideas with another pair.

5   Which expressions a–f could you use in place of the highlighted expressions 1–4?

   a   I strongly recommend
   b   I'm writing to express my dissatisfaction with
   c   I trust that
   d   I expect
   e   This is to inform you of
   f   I think you should know about

6   In pairs, try to complete these expressions. Then read the complaint to check.

Describing the incident
   1   The incident o_____ when ...
   2   I'd been t_____ that ...
   3   When I p_____ this out ...
   4   I w_____ appalled by ...
   5   I r_____ I didn't insist on ...

Saying what you want
   6   receive a formal a_____
   7   receive an a_____ that
   8   take s_____ to ensure that
   9   restore my c_____ in

7   **a** You're going to write a complaint. Read this situation, or think of your own.

   At a cashier's desk in a department store, you couldn't find your wallet. You were checking your bags and pockets when the clerk told you to move aside so he could take the next customer. You suddenly found your wallet but the clerk told you to go to the back of the queue. He then served the next customer.

   b Decide how many paragraphs you need. Choose expressions from 5 and 6 to:

   • state your reason for writing.
   • describe the incident, using your own ideas to add more details.
   • state the solution you want and end the message.

   c Write your complaint.

8   Read each other's complaints. Are the incidents described clearly? What do you think of the solutions the writers suggest?

Review

VOCABULARY Reflecting on the past

1 a In each pair of sentences, complete b so that it has the same meaning as a.

   1 a I don't regret getting married.
       b I'm glad ...
   2 a It's a good thing I left college.
       b I'm not sorry about ...
   3 a I'm sorry I never knew my grandfather.
       b I wish ...
   4 a I really regret changing jobs.
       b If only ...

b Work alone. Imagine you're a well-known person in your country, now or in the past. Write five or six sentences using the expressions in 1a.

c Listen to each other's sentences and guess who the people are. Tell each other more about them.

GRAMMAR Conditionals – past and present

2 a ⬥ **2.28** Listen to six situations. Pause after each one and write a conditional sentence for it.

If my alarm clock had rung, ...

b Compare your sentences. Are they similar?

c Think of one or two similar situations that you've experienced. Describe your situations in groups using conditional sentences.

CAN YOU REMEMBER? Unit 7 – Problem-solving experiences

3 a Complete the paragraph about Ian's language-learning experience with these expressions.

   a My way of solving this problem was to
   b What I learned was
   c My biggest problem was that
   d What we decided to do was
   e I found it really difficult to

When I first started learning Korean, I made lots of progress fast. But when I got to Intermediate level, [1]_____ improve my fluency. [2]_____ I kept translating from English and not thinking in Korean. [3]_____ arrange a language exchange with two Korean students at my college, who were keen to improve their English. [4]_____ meet every few days for two hours and speak in either English or Korean. It helped us all hugely. [5]_____ that working with other people gives you more motivation and enjoyment.

b Think of problems you have had with:

learning a language   completing a project
managing a busy schedule   taking care of someone

c In groups, tell each other about the problems and how you solved them.

Extension

SPELLING AND SOUNDS /e/

4 a These words show the two most common ways of spelling the /e/ sound. Underline the letters which make an /e/ sound. Then complete 1 and 2.

speculate dialect education weapon regret
emigrate head instead investigate gesture

   1 Only _____ is used at the start of words.
   2 _____ or _____ is used in the middle of words.

b There are a few less common ways of spelling /e/. How many can you find in these words?

again against any bury friendly leisure
leopard many said says

c Spellcheck. In pairs, take turns to choose ten words and test your partner's spelling. Then check your spelling together.

NOTICE Expressions with *and* and *or*

5 a Read the sentences from listenings in this unit. Complete the expressions with and or or.

   1 It just never happened for one reason _____ another.
   2 Neil took us here _____ there sightseeing.
   3 People were wandering in _____ out.
   4 We really need to find it. Dead _____ alive.

b Complete 1–8 with more and and or expressions.

> sooner or later more or less trial and error
> odds and ends black and blue sick and tired
> rain or shine clean and tidy

   1 I'm _____ of watching TV. It's boring!
   2 You'll have to tell him _____. Why not now?
   3 I'm going for a long walk today, _____.
   4 Wow! The kitchen's so _____. Nice work!
   5 I taught myself to paint, learning by _____.
   6 Just a minute. I've _____ finished this report.
   7 Look! Here's a box of _____ from our old flat.
   8 I fell and hurt my knee. It was _____ for ages.

Self-assessment

Can you do these things in English? Circle a number on each line. 1 = I can't do this, 5 = I can do this well.

◉ make deductions about the past	1 2 3 4 5
◉ describe strong feelings	1 2 3 4 5
◉ say how you feel about past events in your life	1 2 3 4 5
◉ speculate about consequences of past actions	1 2 3 4 5
◉ disagree with speculations about the past	1 2 3 4 5
◉ write a complaint about a service	1 2 3 4 5

• For Wordcards, reference and saving your work → e-Portfolio
• For more practice → Self-study Pack, Unit 8

9

How it's done

9.1 goals
◉ explain how something is made
◉ organise a description

Printing press

LISTENING

1 **Look carefully at the top edge of your coursebook.**

1 How many folded sections is the book made of?
2 How many pages does each section have?
3 What holds the sections together? What holds the cover on?
4 Why do you think it's made in sections?

2 a Look at the pictures and read the captions. Can you put the stages of making a book in order, 1–5?

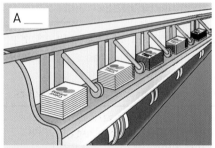

A ___

The sections are collected together to make a 'book block'.

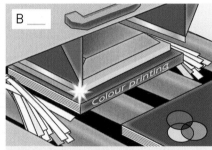

B ___

The book is trimmed down to its final size.

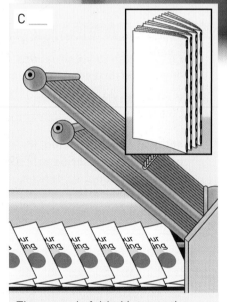

C ___

The paper is folded into sections and notches are cut into the spine.

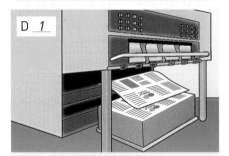

D _1_

A number of pages are printed onto a large sheet of paper.

E ___

The sections and cover are all glued together.

b ◖3.1◗ Listen to a printer, Brian, giving a tour of a printing press. Check the order of the stages.

3 a ◖3.1◗ Listen again. Answer the questions about each part of the tour.

Stage 1   How many pages can the press print at once?
How fast can it go?
Stage 2   How many times is the paper folded?
How do they get the pages in the right order?
Stage 3   What exactly is a 'book block'?
Stage 4   Why are the notches in the spine important?
Stage 5   What temperature is the glue?

b Read the script on pp152 to check.

4 Have you ever been on a tour where you learned about a process? What can you remember about it?

GRAMMAR

Verbs with adverbs and prepositions 1

5 a Use the words in the box to complete the summary of the book-making process.

along   from   into   off   onto   through   to   up

The operator ¹pours ink _____ the printing press. Large sheets of paper go into the press and the press ²prints 16 pages _____ the paper, turns the paper over, and prints another 16 pages on the other side. The printed sections then ³emerge _____ the press and the operator puts the sheets into the folding machine. As the sections ⁴pass _____ the folding machine, the paper is folded and the machine cuts a little notch into the spine to hold the glue later on. The different sections are then carried to the gathering machine, which ⁵picks an 'A' section _____, then a 'B' section and so on, and puts a complete set together to make a 'book block'. Another machine ⁶attaches the cover _____ the book block, using hot glue to hold everything together. The book ⁷moves _____ a conveyor belt and finally drops into the three-knife trimmer, which ⁸cuts the edges of the paper _____, giving the book its final size.

b Look at sentences 1–3. Can you explain why into in 1 and 2 is a preposition, and over in 3 is an adverb? In which sentence can you change the word order?

1	Sheets of paper **go into** the printing press.	*verb preposition* object
2	The operator **pours** ink **into** the printing press.	*verb* object *preposition* object
3	The press **turns** the paper **over**.	*verb* object *adverb*

Grammar reference and practice, p137

c Put the highlighted verbs in the summary in 5a into three lists. Are they like 1, 2 or 3? You should have five verbs in each list.

PRONUNCIATION

Stress in verbs with adverbs and prepositions

6 a ◉ 3.2 **Listen to sentences 1–3 in 5b. Choose the correct words in these descriptions.**

1   In a verb with a preposition, the verb / preposition usually has the main stress.
2   In a verb with an adverb, the verb / adverb usually has the main stress.

b Practise saying the sentences with the correct stress.

SPEAKING

7 Cover the summary in 5a. In pairs, use your lists of verbs and the pictures in 2a to help you explain the book-making process.

First of all, …

VOCABULARY

Organising a description

1 Look at the expressions Brian uses to organise his description of the book-making process. Then add the expressions in the box to the correct groups 1–5.

1	*Opening*	First of all, …
2	*Linking*	The next step is … What happens next is …
3	*Referring forward*	I'll come back to that later.
4	*Referring back*	You remember I told you about …?
5	*Closing*	And that's the whole process.

To start off, …   After that, …   And that's it.   Earlier I mentioned …   To begin with, …
Following that, …   I'll explain that in a minute.   Once that's done, …   The first thing is, …

SPEAKING

2 Look at the pictures. How do you think these things might be made?

3 a Work in two groups. Read the information and follow the instructions.

Group A – read about making Maldon salt on p127.
Group B – read about making glass bottles on p125.

b Get into A/B pairs and give each other your tours. Ask questions to make sure you understand the process.

4 Go back to your group. How much can you remember about the process you heard about?

Maldon salt

glass bottles

Responsibilities

9.2 goals
- describe responsibilities and roles in different situations
- explain how a team or organisation works

READING

1 a Look at the picture in the article about the crew of a film set. Using the picture and job titles to help you, can you guess what the main responsibilities of each job might be?

b Read the article to check.

LIFE ON SET
The Camera Crew

focus puller · clapper loader · camera operator · director · director of photography

At the heart of the creative process, the **director** is responsible for interpreting the screenplay and transforming it into a film with its own distinctive style. The director must be able to communicate their vision not only to the actors but to all the technical departments – lighting, sound, special effects, and so on. On a film set, everybody is accountable to the director. Off set, the director is accountable to nobody except the producer – the person with the money! If the film is a big success, the director will get most of the credit. But look through any film guide and notice how many directors' names appear just once, because they were never invited to direct again.

The **director of photography** (DP) is in charge of the camera and lighting crew. The director will talk to the DP in detail about how they 'see' particular shots. Then it's up to the DP to make sure the team delivers exactly what the director wants. Despite their relatively low profile with the public, creative and reliable DPs are highly regarded in the film industry. A DP on big-budget films will experience many of the things a director does – the travel, the top hotels, the respect – but without taking the blame if it all goes wrong. That's the director's job!

The **camera operator** starts and stops the camera as instructed by the DP. It's the camera operator's responsibility to make sure the camera moves smoothly and to be aware of where the boom – the long pole that holds the microphone – is located, so that it doesn't get into shot. Sometimes the director or DP will take on the role of camera operator too.

The **focus puller**'s main task is to focus the camera so that the images being recorded are completely clear at all times. As the focus puller *doesn't* look through the camera, this requires a high level of expertise, especially if both actors and camera are moving at once. The focus puller also 'builds' the camera before shooting and puts it away at the end of the day. While the camera operator is free to go off and talk to the director or DP about upcoming shots, the focus puller rarely leaves the camera. During shooting, the camera 'belongs' to the focus puller.

The **clapper loader**'s duties include loading film into the camera, unloading used film – carefully! – and making sure it's delivered safely to the developers. As the clapper loader literally holds the results of everyone's hard work in their hands every day, this can be one of the most stressful jobs on set. They also operate the clapper board, the small chalk board filmed at the beginning of every take so that the correct pieces of film can be found later on.

2 a Read again and decide how you'd answer these questions for each job.

1 What are the good and bad things about it?
2 What kind of skills and personality would you need to be successful?

b Compare your ideas, giving reasons from the article.

3 Which information in the article was new for you?

Describing
responsibilities

4 **a** Match 1–5 with a–e to make five sentences from the article.

1   The director is **responsible for**
2   **It's up to** the DP to
3   It's the camera operator's **responsibility to**
4   The focus puller's **main task is to**
5   The clapper loader's **duties include**

a   focus the camera.
b   make sure the camera moves smoothly.
c   make sure the team delivers what the director wants.
d   interpreting the screenplay.
e   loading film into the camera.

b Cover 1–5. In pairs, look at a–e and say who's responsible for each thing, using the highlighted expressions from 4a.

5   Look at two more sentences from the article. Which expressions in the box can replace the highlighted expressions in each sentence?

| manages   answers to   oversees   reports to   supervises |

• On a film set, everybody **is accountable to** the director.
• The director of photography **is in charge of** the camera and lighting crew.

SPEAKING

6 **a** Think of a team or organisation you belong to or know about, for example:

your department at work   a club or society   a small company   your government

Think about how to describe it using the language in 4 and 5.

1   What are the responsibilities of the different people? How are they related?
2   Do you think the team or organisation always works well? How could it be made to work better?

b Listen to each other's descriptions. Which roles within each team or organisation sound the most challenging?

Roles

LISTENING

Josette

1   **3.3** Listen to Josette talking about the different roles she has in her life.

1   What's her connection with the film industry?
2   What other life roles does she mention?

2   **3.3** What details did Josette give about each role? Talk together, then listen again to check.

VOCABULARY

Describing roles

3 **a** Here are some expressions from Josette's talk. What's the next word?

1   I work …
2   I've taken on the role …
3   I'm a member …
4   I play an active part …
5   I act …
6   I belong …
7   I do voluntary work …
8   I'm a supporter …

b Look at the script on p152 to check.

SPEAKING

4 **a** Work alone. Think about these questions.

1   What different roles do you have in your life? Make a short list.
2   What does each role involve? How much of your time or energy does it take up?
3   Would you like to change the roles you have in your life? Why? / Why not?

Choose language from 3a to help you talk about your roles.

b Tell each other about your roles in life. What new information did you find out about each other?

Target activity

Give a factual talk

9.3 goals

- organise a description ♻
- explain how a team or organisation works ♻
- give a detailed presentation on a familiar topic ♻

TASK LISTENING

Adam is a freelance travel writer, originally from Poland.

1 Look at the photo and read the caption. What do you think it's like being a travel writer? Is it a job you'd like to do?

2 a You're going to listen to Adam giving a talk for students of journalism who are interested in travel writing. If you were interested in a career as a travel writer, what questions would you ask Adam?

b 🔊 3.4 Listen to Adam's introduction to his talk. What four things does he plan to talk about?

3 a 🔊 3.5 Listen to the next part of Adam's talk and find out:

1 how he summarises a travel writer's job.
2 how he describes a typical day.
3 two ways to make a living by travel writing.
4 how publishers pay writers of guidebooks.
5 how much a travel writer might make per hour.
6 how most people get into travel writing.

b Compare your notes, then read the script on p153 to check.

TASK VOCABULARY

Organising a talk

4 a Which of the highlighted expressions a–f from Adam's talk does he use to:

1 outline the structure of his talk at the beginning?
2 open a topic?
3 close a topic?

a **I'd like to talk about** four main things: first, what it's like to …
b **Let's begin with** the lifestyle.
c **OK, that's** the lifestyle.
d **The next thing is** money.
e **That's all I wanted to say about** money for now.
f **Let's move on to** how you can get into the business.

b Add the expressions in the box to 1–3 above.

I'll be looking at … main areas.	Next, I'd like to say something about …
So, we've talked about …	That's it as far as … is concerned.
I've divided my talk into … parts.	Now let's take a look at …

TASK

5 a Choose one of these situations or think of your own subject to talk about.

You've been invited to give a brief presentation at a conference. The aim of the presentation is to give people a simple introduction to your company or the organisation you work for: its history, its structure, its main activities, and so on.

You're a member of a small club of people with a common interest or hobby (e.g. hiking, dancing, old films). You're keen to attract new members, so you've arranged to give a brief talk about the club at your workplace or college for people who might be interested in joining.

Your friend is a teacher at an international school and they've asked you to come and give their class a short talk about an aspect of your culture you're enthusiastic about (e.g. the local cuisine, the national football league, the music scene).

b Prepare your talk. Make notes to help you remember what you want to say.

- Decide on three or four main topics to include in your talk.
- Plan the introduction to your talk, including a brief outline of its structure.
- Decide what you want to say about each topic.
- Choose expressions for opening and closing each topic.

c Practise your talks in small groups.

6 Change groups and listen to each other's talks. Ask questions about anything you don't understand or want to know more about.

Keyword *way*

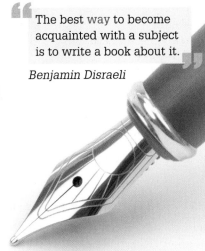

> There's no way to be a perfect mother and a million ways to be a good one.
>
> *Jill Churchill*

> The best way to become acquainted with a subject is to write a book about it.
>
> *Benjamin Disraeli*

> Silence is a way of saying: we do not have to entertain each other; we are okay as we are.
>
> *Martha Grimes*

> Advertising is the easiest way of selling goods, especially if the goods are worthless.
>
> *Sinclair Lewis*

> There are lots of ways of being miserable, but there's only one way of being comfortable, and that is to stop running around after happiness.
>
> *Edith Wharton*

> The only way to keep your health is to eat what you don't want, drink what you don't like, and do what you'd rather not.
>
> *Mark Twain*

way = method

1 **a** Read the quotations from different writers. Which are your favourites? Are there any you disagree with? Why?

b In the quotations:

1 what two grammar patterns are used after way? Are they different in meaning?
2 what expressions are used before way? *there's no way ...*

c Complete the questions with your own ideas, then discuss them in groups.

1 What's the best way to travel around your country?
2 What's the easiest way of giving up smoking?
3 What's the best way ...?
4 What's the cheapest way ...?
5 What's an interesting way ...?
6 What's ... way ...?

way = style

2 **a** Complete the sentences with these words:

different   fastest   imaginative   quiet

```
1   Your job is to collect information in the
    _____ way possible. Unit 9
2   I quite like the idea of using the city
    space in an _____ way. Unit 4
3   He'd always encourage me to carry on in
    that _____ way of his. Unit 3
4   In the cities, people do things in a
    slightly _____ way. Unit 2
```

b Think of more words you could use to complete each sentence.

c ⟨ 3.6 ⟩ Listen and follow the six instructions. Then tell each other about the people and things you wrote down.

way = route

3 **a** way can mean *route*, *path* or *direction*. In which of these examples does way have a more:
a physical meaning? b abstract meaning?

1 Can you move your car, please? It's in the way.
2 Spencer wants to be the next President, but Gomez is in the way.

b Which highlighted expression in each of these pairs is more physical in meaning? Which is more abstract?

1 a We can drive or take the train. Either way takes about an hour.
  b We can cut salaries or employ fewer people. Either way, it's going to be difficult.

2 a Ignoring the dark clouds, the group slowly worked their way up the mountain.
  b Stella worked her way up from shop assistant to regional manager.

3 a Everyone went out of their way to make us feel welcome. It was lovely.
  b Do we have to visit Jon today? His place is really out of our way.

4 a Alan just called to say he's on the way. He'll be here before ten.
  b It's chilly, isn't it? Winter's definitely on the way.

c In your language, do you have similar expressions to those in 3a and 3b? Do they have both physical and abstract meanings?

9 EXPLORE Speaking

1 **Look at the picture and talk together.**

    1   What different fillings do chocolates like this have inside?

    2   Do you know – or can you guess – how chocolate makers get the fillings inside?

2 **a** ▶ **3.7** Listen to a professional chocolate maker, Valeria, telling Sergio about how chocolates are made. Which of these things does Sergio *not* understand at first?

    1   why caramel is refrigerated
    2   what the special ingredient is
    3   why the special ingredient is used
    4   what putty is
    5   why the special ingredient liquefies
    6   how sugar affects other flavours

  b Read the conversation to check and <u>underline</u> the explanations.

3 **a** Add the expressions 1–8 in the conversation to the correct groups.

Checking your listener understands
Do you get what I mean?

Adding more detail
To be precise, …

Asking for clarification or repetition
What do you mean by …?

  b Now add more expressions to each group.

Am I making any sense?	Is that clear?
Can you go over that again?	In fact, …
Can you run that past me again?	Do you follow me?
To be more specific, …	Do you see?

4 **a** Work alone. Choose one of these situations or think of one of your own. Think about what to say.

- A colleague has promised to make dinner for someone but is a bit worried because he/she is not a very experienced cook. He/She asks you for a recipe – not too complicated! – for a dish you like.

- You're watching sport on TV when a neighbour drops by. He/She is interested in the game but doesn't really understand what's going on. He/She asks you to explain the rules.

- A colleague is thinking about buying his/her own house or flat and asks for your advice on how to do it and what's involved. What's the procedure? Is there a lot of paperwork?

  b In pairs, listen to each other's explanations. Talk together to make sure all the details are clear, using the expressions in 3a and 3b.

5 **Change pairs. Tell each other what you learned from your first partner.**

Goals
- check that people understand
- add more detail
- ask people to clarify or repeat things

SERGIO	You know, I always wanted to know how you get the filling inside the chocolate bit.
VALERIA	The chocolate shell, we call it. Well, if it's a caramel, not too soft, refrigeration makes it hard enough so you can just dip it in chocolate by hand. [1]Do you get what I mean? It works as long as you're quick.
SERGIO	Yeah, but what if it's one of those really soft centres?
VALERIA	Well, you add a special ingredient to the filling along with the flavouring and so on.
SERGIO	[2]What do you mean by 'special ingredient'?
VALERIA	Sorry, it's a secret! But it makes the filling a bit harder, so it's like, erm, well, we say it's like soft putty.
SERGIO	And, er [3]what's putty exactly?
VALERIA	It's that stuff they use to hold glass in windows, you know?
SERGIO	Ah, OK.
VALERIA	So obviously, when the filling's like putty, you can easily make it into balls. [4]Does that make sense?
SERGIO	Sure. So then what happens?
VALERIA	Well, once the filling is covered with chocolate, the secret ingredient starts to liquefy.
SERGIO	[5]When you say it liquefies, do you mean it's some kind of chemical reaction?
VALERIA	Yes. [6]To be precise, the chocolate seals off the filling from the oxygen in the air and, because of that, it turns back into a liquid. So you end up with a soft centre inside the chocolate shell.
SERGIO	Hm, clever. So tell me, is it possible to make chocolate less fattening?
VALERIA	Yeah, you just use less sugar. In fact, that can improve chocolate a lot because you can taste flavours that are usually hidden by the sugar. And if you –
SERGIO	[7]Sorry, did you say the sugar *hides* other flavours?
VALERIA	Er, yeah. [8]What I mean is, sugar's so strong, it often dominates other flavours so you just can't taste them.

Review

VOCABULARY Describing responsibilities

1 a Complete the sentences describing people's responsibilities. Different answers are possible.

1 The director ... interpreting the screenplay.
2 On a film set, everybody ... the director.
3 The director of photography ... the camera and lighting crew.
4 It's ... the DP to make sure the team delivers what the director wants.
5 The focus puller's main ... is to control the focus of the camera.
6 The clapper loader's ... include loading film into the camera.

b In pairs, describe the responsibilities of one of these occupations.

police officer   psychiatrist   teacher   journalist

c Listen to each other's ideas. Do you agree?

GRAMMAR Verbs with adverbs and prepositions 1

2 a Add the words in brackets to each extract. If the word can go in two places, show both.

1 Please don't turn the page until I tell you to. (over)

2 NOTE: attach a recent photograph your completed application in the space provided. (to)

3 The prime minister has put a new team to prepare for government reforms due in January. (together)

4 Have you seen Neil today? He's cut all his hair! (off)

5 Pour the water a saucepan. Add the tomatoes, green peppers and garlic. (into)

6 Stacey, will you put the milk the fridge, please? (in)

b Where do you think you could read or hear each extract? Compare with the suggestions on p121.

CAN YOU REMEMBER? Unit 8 – Strong feelings

3 a Choose words to complete the questions.

appalled   baffled   delighted   fascinated
horrified   humiliated   intrigued   isolated
mortified   mystified   out of place   thrilled

Can you tell me about:
1 a story in the news which _____ you?
2 a subject at school which always _____ you?
3 a party where you felt a bit _____ ?
4 a day in your life when you felt really _____ ?
5 a film which _____ you the first time you saw it?

b Ask each other your questions.

Extension

SPELLING AND SOUNDS /ʊ/

4 a Say the words. Underline the letters which make an /ʊ/ sound.

cookery   could   fully   goods   guidebook
likelihood   pull   push   should   would

b What spelling of /ʊ/:

1 usually goes before d or k?
2 usually goes before ll and sh?
3 is used in three modal verbs?

c ◉ 3.8 Spellcheck. Listen and write ten words. Then check your spelling on p153.

NOTICE big and high

5 a Look at the sentences from the article The Camera Crew on p72. Choose big or high, then check in the article.

1 If the film is a big / high success, the director will get most of the credit.
2 A DP on big- / high-budget films will experience many of the things a director does.
3 A focus puller ... requires a big / high level of expertise.

b Complete 1–6 with big or high.

1 a _____ problem you had to deal with
2 a _____-pressure situation in your work or studies
3 an organisation which you feel has _____ standards
4 someone from your country with a _____ profile internationally
5 someone you know with a really _____ personality
6 something which is a _____ priority in your life at the moment

c Talk in pairs. Ask each other about the topics in 5b.

Self-assessment

Can you do these things in English? Circle a number on each line. 1 = I can't do this, 5 = I can do this well.

◉ explain how something is made	1	2	3	4	5
◉ organise a description	1	2	3	4	5
◉ describe responsibilities and roles in different situations	1	2	3	4	5
◉ explain how a team or organisation works	1	2	3	4	5
◉ give a detailed presentation on a familiar topic	1	2	3	4	5
◉ check that people understand	1	2	3	4	5
◉ add more detail	1	2	3	4	5
◉ ask people to clarify or repeat things	1	2	3	4	5

• For Wordcards, reference and saving your work → e-Portfolio
• For more practice → Self-study Pack, Unit 9

10 Discovery

10.1 goals
- talk about exploration and discovery
- explain the benefits of something

a deep-sea submersible

a planetary rover

a research ship

a space probe

Frontiers

VOCABULARY

Exploration and discovery

1 In the pictures, what do you think people are trying to find or find out?

2 a Match 1–10 with the most likely ending, a or b.

1	explore	a	a new species	7	search for	a	climate change
2	discover	b	the sea	8	do research into	b	treasure
3	scan	a	the night sky	9	find evidence of	a	extraterrestrial life
4	detect	b	a radio signal	10	reach	b	the bottom of the sea
5	map	a	a new source of oil			
6	locate	b	an unexplored area			

> Maybe they're searching for new kinds of life.

> Or trying to locate a shipwreck.

b Can you explain how the highlighted expressions in each pair differ in meaning?

3 Now look at the pictures again. Make sentences about each picture, using expressions in 2a.

READING

4 a Do you think these statements are true or false? Talk together.

1 There's no light 200 metres below the sea's surface.
2 Submarines usually travel at depths of more than 1km.
3 No one's ever been to the deepest part of the ocean.
4 Whales are the largest living things in the sea.
5 We've explored less than 5% of the ocean floor.
6 Exploration of the sea is cheaper than ever before.

b Read the article to check.

Forget space travel. The ocean is our final frontier

Beneath the surface of the sea lie untold mysteries and opportunities

Frank Pope

It seems we can't get off the planet fast enough. Two thirds of Nasa's annual budget is devoted to manned space exploration, and that figure will grow with the USA's decision to send a man to Mars in 2037. We've seen all there is to see on Earth, right? Wrong. The final frontier is here, beneath the surface of the sea.

Heading down into the ocean, human limits are quickly reached. At 200 metres, the water is as black as a moonless night. Most nuclear submarines would implode before they reach 1km down. At 3km – still less than the average depth of the ocean – there's a good chance that

you'll discover a species completely new to science. The deepest-diving whales go no further. At the very bottom, more than 11km down, lie the Challenger Deeps. Twelve humans have walked on the Moon. None has set foot in the Deeps, and only two have seen them with their own eyes.

Yet things live down there. Big things. Microphones throughout the sea listen for enemy submarines, but no one has explained the undersea roar that occasionally startles listeners. The sound appears biological in origin, and its wavelength suggests that it is produced

5 Read again. In the writer's opinion:

1 why do we know so little about the oceans?
2 what are the benefits of space exploration?
3 what are the benefits of deep-sea exploration?

6 Talk together. Give your opinions.

1 Why is so much money spent on exploring space? Is this justified?
2 If you could travel into the deep sea or into space, which would you choose? Why?

They're absolutely vital for …

VOCABULARY
Describing benefits

1 Which words and expressions in the box can you use to complete sentences 1–3?

> allow us   benefit   crucial   enable us   essential   improve   vital
> be of (considerable) benefit to   give us the ability   have a positive effect on

1 Satellites _____ to look at our planet with a global perspective.
2 They're absolutely _____ for doing ocean research too.
3 The cost of marine expeditions is rising, but the results would _____ all our lives.

More nuclear power would allow us to use less coal and gas. It would have a positive effect on the environment.

2 Choose four things you think are the most important for the human race to do in the next 50 years. Write sentences to explain each choice, using the language in 1.

- start a colony on the moon
- explore the deep ocean
- locate new sources of oil and gas
- discover a vaccine against AIDS
- produce cheaper medicines
- stop population growth
- send people to explore Mars
- build more nuclear power stations
- find sources of alternative energy
- find a cure for heart disease
- find better ways of farming
- stop eating meat

PRONUNCIATION
Stress in compounds

3 a ◖ 3.9 ◗ Listen. In each of these compounds, decide which word has the main stress.

space probes   the deep ocean   nuclear power   power stations

b On which word, first or second, does the main stress usually go:

1 in noun + noun compounds?   2 in adjective + noun compounds?

c Decide where the main stress goes in these compounds.

heart disease   global warming   climate change   alternative energy

d ◖ 3.10 ◗ Listen to check. Practise saying all eight compounds with the correct stress.

SPEAKING

4 Get into pairs and tell each other which four things you chose in 2. Explain your choices. Try to agree on a list of four things, then tell the class.

---

by an animal bigger than a blue whale, the largest creature known on the planet.

In the late 1990s, a deep-water submersible was dropped in the Southern Ocean, and passing 4,000 metres – well beyond the diving depth of any whale – it detected something enormous passing beneath it. Surprised? Don't be. The ocean covers 70% of the planet's surface and we've investigated less than 5% of it. We know more about the dark side of the Moon than about the bottom of the sea.

One reason that we explore space is to find evidence of other life forms. The search for extraterrestrial life is

important, but robots can look beneath the dry rocks of Mars better than humans. The idea of landing on an alien world to greet alien life is fantasy. For the real thing, I suggest heading down in a deep-diving research submarine.

Satellites and unmanned space probes allow us to look at our planet with a global perspective and stare into the history of the universe. They're absolutely vital for doing ocean research too, but they can't look under the sea, the only place where we can search for clues to the origin of life itself. To do that, we need ships and submersibles, manned and robotic. The

cost of fuel-intensive marine expeditions is rising, but the results would benefit all our lives. Understanding the oceans will give us access to new sources of food, drugs and energy.

It's now more than 50 years since explorers Jacques Piccard and Don Walsh made their pioneering descent into the Challenger Deeps. After that, the focus of our imagination turned to the heavens, but perhaps it's time to begin a new era of sea exploration. Manned exploration of space is science fiction. The adventure of the deep sea is science fact.

Priorities

10.2 goals
◎ describe important issues and priorities
◎ talk about dedicated people and their achievements

READING

1 What words and ideas do you associate with the giant panda? Talk together.

2 a Which of these things do you think are, or have been, a problem for the panda? How?

farming   government policies   logging
tree planting   road building   tourism

b Read the interview with Lu Zhi. What does she say or imply about the things in 2a?

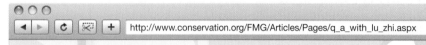

http://www.conservation.org/FMG/Articles/Pages/q_a_with_lu_zhi.aspx

Home > Features & Media > **Articles**

Dr Lu Zhi – saving pandas

By Carol Lane

Like many children, Lu Zhi was always curious about the natural world around her. But unlike most kids, she was to make preserving that world – and one of its most precious species – her life's work. Dr Lu, director of the Shanshui Conservation Center in China, is one of the world's top experts on panda conservation. After years of laboratory work and field research, she has won international acclaim and too many awards to count.

Q: How did you come to dedicate yourself to saving the panda?

Lu Zhi: Initially I studied biology but I was attracted to field work and wanted to work outside of the lab. As an undergrad, I began [1]studying with a professor who was focused on pandas. The more I learned, the more I wanted to learn. And once I began to understand the danger they faced as a species – man's destruction of their habitat – I just felt I had to do something. I wanted to take all the knowledge and training I'd built up and use it to benefit the environment.

Q: What's the biggest challenge you face?

Lu Zhi: The hardest thing is to change people's minds and behaviour, whether it's the government, business or everyday people. Farmers are worried about [2]paying their bills, local governments are concerned about jobs and education, and conservation isn't everyone's top priority.

Q: How do you change minds?

Lu Zhi: It's always a struggle. But the most important thing is to understand and appreciate why people feel the way they do. Everybody likes pandas but their everyday issues take precedence. You have to put yourself in their shoes and when you do, you realise you'd feel the same. That helps you come up with solutions. [3]Complaining and scolding don't work.

Q: What is your experience of working with the Chinese government?

Lu Zhi: There's a lot of cooperation. Years ago, while [4]doing research in an area the logging companies worked in, my professor worked with the government to turn the area into a reserve, and showed people things could change. I was really encouraged. Four years after that, the government actually stopped all commercial logging in western China and this benefited the panda a great deal. The [5]logging companies, subsidised by the government, became tree planters. They became our ally.

Q: Is logging still a threat to the panda?

Lu Zhi: No. But habitat destruction continues in other ways because they're [6]building roads and more tourists are coming. But tourism can be managed in a non-invasive, low-impact way. That's the challenge for that industry.

Q: You seem so positive. Do you ever get discouraged?

Lu Zhi: Sure. But I get strength from the people I work with, my friends. What we're doing is part of human nature so I can always find allies.

Q: What do you hope will be your life's greatest accomplishment?

Lu Zhi: That's easy! I hope one day my work won't be needed any more.

3 Read the article again. Find out:

1 Lu Zhi's reasons for getting involved in panda conservation.
2 what she thinks is the best way of dealing with people, and why.
3 why she feels positive about working with the government.

4 **Talk together.**

1 What do you think of Lu Zhi's work? Is the panda worth saving? Why? / Why not?
2 What other important environmental or conservation issues can you think of? Which are the most urgent?

GRAMMAR

Using the *-ing* form

5 **Read the information. Match a–f with the highlighted *-ing* forms 1–6 in the interview.**

You can use the *-ing* form of a verb in different ways:
a as the subject in a sentence
b after prepositions (*at, by, of, than, without*, etc.)
c after certain verbs (*begin, finish, involve, practise, enjoy*, etc.)
d as part of a progressive verb form
e as an adjective
f after time linkers (*after, before, since, when, while*, etc.)

6 **Work alone. Complete these sentences about issues and priorities with your own ideas, using *-ing* forms where you can.**

Your country
1 A lot of people are concerned about ...
2 The government's focused on ...
3 I think ... should be the top priority

Your personal life
7 I spend a lot of time ...
8 ... usually takes precedence over ...
9 I'm happiest when ...

Your work or studies
4 ... is my main focus at the moment.
5 ... can sometimes be a problem.
6 ... takes up too much of my time.

Grammar reference and practice, p138

SPEAKING

7 **Listen to each other's sentences. How similar are your ideas about priorities?**

Life's work

VOCABULARY

Achievements

1 **Use the words in the box to complete these sentences describing achievements.**

changed   dedicated   faced   made   showed
used   won   worked   greatest   top

1 Lu Zhi's a _____ expert on panda conservation.
2 She's _____ preserving the natural world **her life's work.**
3 She's _____ international **acclaim** and **awards.**
4 She's _____ **herself** to saving the panda.
5 She's _____ her **knowledge** and **training to benefit** the environment.
6 She's _____ some hard **challenges.**
7 She's _____ people's **minds** and **behaviour.**
8 Her professor _____ with the government to improve things ...
9 ... and _____ people that things can change.
10 Her _____ **accomplishment** would be if, one day, her work wasn't needed!

2 **Work alone. Think of somebody you'd describe as particularly dedicated, for example:**

• someone you know or have met   • someone you're interested in or admire
• someone important in your country   • someone well known around the world

Write four or five sentences describing their achievements. Use expressions from 1.

SPEAKING

3 **In groups, tell each other about your people and ask questions to find out more.**

1 Decide what each person's greatest accomplishment probably was.
2 Decide who seems to have had the biggest impact on people's lives today.

Choose a subject for a documentary

10.3 goals
- talk about exploration and discovery ♻
- talk about dedicated people and their achievements ♻
- summarise information from different sources

Naomi Uemura

Valentina Tereshkova

Orlando Villas Boas

Leif Eriksson

A team of researchers for a TV production company is choosing a subject for a documentary.

TASK LISTENING

1 Look at the pictures of the four explorers. Do you know, or can you guess:

a where they were from?   c anything else about them?
b where they explored?

2 ◄ 3.11 Listen to the researcher's talk about Leif Eriksson. In what order did Eriksson visit these places?

Labrador ___   Baffin Island ___   Vinland ___   Norway ___

3 ◄ 3.11 Listen again.

1 When was Eriksson born?
2 How did he arrive in North America?
3 How many men travelled with him?
4 What was Vinland like?
5 When did Eriksson die?
6 Where might Vinland have been?

TASK VOCABULARY

Giving and comparing sources

4 Replace each underlined part in 1–7 with an expression from the box which has a similar meaning. Then read the script on p153 to check.

> claim   mentions   vary   According to   who you ask
> are in agreement   make no mention of

1 Depending on where you look, he was born around 970 or 975.
2 In one version, he was blown off course by bad weather.
3 Other sources state that he was following the route of an earlier explorer.
4 In one article, it says that he sailed with thirty-five men.
5 Interestingly, several sites say nothing about any companions.
6 Most sources agree that Leif Eriksson died in about 1020.
7 Where exactly was Vinland? Sources differ on this question.

TASK

5 a You're going to do some research on the other three explorers to decide which would make the best subject for a documentary. Work in groups of three.

Student A – read the articles about Naomi Uemura on p125.
Student B – read the articles about Valentina Tereshkova on p127.
Student C – read the articles about Orlando Villas Boas on p128.

Make notes of key points from your articles, including any important differences between the sources.

b Plan to give a brief summary of the information about your explorer. Choose language from 4.

c In your groups, listen to each other's summaries. Then decide which of the explorers would make the best subject for a documentary, and why.

6 Tell the class who you chose, and explain why.

Across cultures Rights and obligations

Gavin from England

Hikari from Japan

Ryan from Australia

LISTENING

1 🔊 **3.12** Listen to Gavin, Hikari and Ryan talking about things they do in their countries.

1 What activity does each person talk about?
2 Who talks about an activity: a they have to do? b they have the right to do?

2 🔊 **3.12** Listen again and answer the questions.

Gavin
1 What's 'the right to roam'?
2 Where can't people walk?
3 What's the countryside code?

Hikari
4 What areas do the families clean?
5 What's the money collected for?
6 Why don't they mind this duty?

Ryan
7 What's the voting rate now?
8 What happens if you don't vote?
9 Why does Ryan like this system?

3 What do you think about the things these people describe? Are you surprised by anything they say?

VOCABULARY

Rights and obligations

4 Which of these sentences describe rights or freedom to do something? Which describe obligations?

1 Hikers **have the right to** walk on public or privately owned land.
2 Landowners **are obliged to** let us walk on their land.
3 Walkers **are expected to** obey the countryside code.
4 They're **free to** pass through people's land.
5 It's **our duty to** organise this in turn.
6 We **have the option of** hiring someone to do the cleaning.
7 It's **compulsory to** vote here.
8 My brother thinks we should **have the freedom to** vote or not, as we choose.

5 Choose four or five of these topics. Where you live, what rights do people have in each case? What obligations do they have? Make notes about your ideas, choosing expressions from 4.

- the family   • the workplace   • the neighbourhood   • the countryside
- public places   • school and university education   • driving   • advertising
- demonstrations or public meetings   • animals   • documents   • licences

SPEAKING

6 a Talk in groups and compare your ideas.

b To what extent do people take these rights and obligations seriously?

> People have the right to go on strike if the majority of them vote for it.

> I don't think police officers have the right to strike.

7 Think of other countries and cultures you know of. How similar are the rights and obligations there?

1   Read the information about SETI. Do you think there's life on other planets? Is SETI a worthwhile activity?

2 a You're going to read part of an interview with a director of the SETI Institute in California, Dr Jill Tarter. How do you think she might answer these questions?

   1   If you think you've detected an alien signal, what will you do?
   2   Will you send a message in reply?

b Read the interview to check.

> SETI, the Search for Extra-Terrestrial Intelligence, is the science of using radio telescopes to search the skies for signals from alien civilisations. This is a huge task. In our galaxy alone, there are an estimated 100 billion stars, and radio signals can be sent on millions of different frequencies. The first search was conducted in 1960 but no alien signals have been detected so far.

If you detect an alien signal, or even a specific message, what then?

JT: If we detect a signal, we'll do everything that we can at this site to make sure that it isn't our own technology that's fooling us or that it isn't a deliberate hoax. One of the things that we'll do to rule out a hoax is to call up another telescope and try to get an independent confirmation. Once we've informed the astronomical community, we'll tell the world. We'll tell the world because a signal isn't being sent to us in California – it's being sent to the planet Earth, and the planet Earth deserves to know about it.

If you got a signal, would you send a reply?

JT: That's a big question. Should we reply and if so, who's going to speak for Earth? What would we say? That's not a decision for me. So, most of the people that are working on SETI have agreed that if we receive a signal, we won't transmit back until there's some global consensus about these questions – because some people have a fear of the unknown, the different, and would not want to transmit, while many other people would say, "Yes, we should transmit, and you should tell my story, or describe my religion, or my view of the world, or my country." So there's a lot to be discussed.

Do you really think the world could reach an agreement on what to do?

JT: Well, Freeman Dyson, the physicist, every time he hears me say this, he just laughs and says, "Jill, if you ever announce that you've detected a signal, and say where it's coming from, anybody with a transmitter is going to shout whatever they want! And wouldn't that be just about the best characterisation of twenty-first century Earth?"

---

3 a Read two summaries of the interview with Jill. Which do you think is best? Why?

A

If the SETI Institute detects a signal, they'll do everything they can to make sure it isn't a hoax. They'll tell the world, because the signal isn't only being sent to California. They won't transmit back until there's been some kind of global consensus. But some people have a fear of the unknown and others would want their story to be told. Freeman Dyson says anybody with a transmitter will send whatever signal they want - typical of our twenty-first century world.

B

If the SETI Institute receives a signal, they'll first check with another telescope to make sure it's genuine. They'll then inform other astronomers and the world in general. They won't send a signal back until there's a worldwide agreement about what to say. However, it will take time to reach an agreement, and many people may decide to send their own signals independently.

b How do the summaries above match (or fail to match) these points?

A summary should:
1   be easy to understand.
2   include all the main points of the original, without unnecessary details.
3   not include your own opinions or reactions.
4   not include any unnecessary words and expressions.
5   be written in your own words, without copying sections of the original.
6   be written in complete sentences, linked to make a paragraph.

4 a Now prepare to write a summary of the article *Forget space travel ...* on pp78–9.

   • Read it again to make sure you understand each paragraph.
   • Make notes of the main points.
   • Compare with a partner to see if you agree on the main points.

b Work alone and write your summary. Aim for about 100 words.

5   In pairs, look at each other's summaries and check them. Have they followed the points in 3b? Work together to improve them.

6   Compare with the example summary on p121. Did you include the same points?

Review

VOCABULARY Exploration and discovery

1 a Complete the underlined expressions with vowels.

1 Who has dn_rsrch_nt their family history?
2 Who loves xplrng new towns and cities?
3 Who has srchd_fr_ a job or flat online?
4 Who finds it difficult to lct places on a map?
5 Who has dscvrd a new club or café recently?
6 Who has rchd the end of a marathon?

b Ask and answer the questions in groups.

c Choose your group's top three most interesting answers. Tell the class.

GRAMMAR Uses of the -ing form

2 a Read the facts about giant pandas. Find nine words that should be -ing forms and correct them.

Today, only about 1600 giant pandas are still live in the wild, in central China. Farm, log and other changes have driven them out of the lowlands where they once lived.

Giant pandas weigh up to 115kg and can be almost a metre high at the shoulder. Although people think these slow-move, black and white animals are charm, they can be dangerous.

Pandas usually eat while sit up. Their large teeth and strong jaws are perfect for crush the tough bamboo stems. To get enough nutrition, pandas must eat between 9 and 18kg of bamboo every day. This means that more than half their day involves search for food and eat.

b What uses of the -ing form can you remember? Look on p81 to check. Match the -ing forms in 2a with the uses on p81.

CAN YOU REMEMBER? UNIT 9 – Describing roles

3 a Complete the paragraph with these words.

| as (x2)   for   in   of (x3)   to |

Martine's a full-time chemistry student, though at weekends she works [1]_____ an assistant in the university bookshop. She's a member [2]_____ the Students' Union, and acts [3]_____ one of four student representatives in the Physical Sciences department. In her free time, she plays an active part [4]_____ quite a few different clubs and societies: for example, she belongs [5]_____ the drama society, helping out with the lighting and sound effects. She also does voluntary work once a week [6]_____ the Student Women's Association, and she's an avid supporter [7]_____ the university rugby team. In fact, she's recently taken on the role [8]_____ their minibus driver, and takes them to matches all over the country!

b Write a paragraph describing the roles of someone you know or know about.

Extension

SPELLING AND SOUNDS /eɪ/

4 a Underline the letters in these words which make an /eɪ/ sound.

alien   complain   obey   failure   they
yesterday   exploration   runway

b Find words in 4a to match these spelling patterns.

1 /eɪ/ is usually spelled a at the beginning of words (but notice: *aim*, *eight*).
2 It's usually spelled a or ai in the middle of words (but notice: *straight*, *weight*, *great*).
3 It's spelled ay or ey at the end of words.

c Spellcheck. Complete the spelling of these words. Then check in a dictionary.

__ncient   av__lable   educ__tion   surv__
br__k   f__thful   __d   n__bour
ashtr__   br__n   ess__   r__lw__

NOTICE Adjectives with *something*, *anybody*, etc.

5 a Look at the sentence from the article *Forget space travel*.

In the late 1990s, a deep-water submersible was dropped in the Southern Ocean, and passing 4,000 metres – well beyond the diving depth of any whale – it detected something enormous passing beneath it.

1 Complete the explanation with *before* and *after*: In English, adjectives usually go _____ nouns. But they go _____ words like *something* etc.
2 How many more words like *something* and *anybody* can you think of?

b Work alone. Change the underlined words to make three more questions.

Can you tell me about:
1 somewhere nice in your home town?
2 somebody special in your life?
3 something interesting in your home?

c Talk together. Ask and answer all six questions.

Self-assessment

Can you do these things in English? Circle a number on each line. 1 = I can't do this, 5 = I can do this well.

talk about exploration and discovery	1	2	3	4	5
explain the benefits of something	1	2	3	4	5
describe important issues and priorities	1	2	3	4	5
talk about dedicated people and their achievements	1	2	3	4	5
summarise information from different sources	1	2	3	4	5
write a summary of a text	1	2	3	4	5

• For Wordcards, reference and saving your work → e-Portfolio
• For more practice → Self-study Pack, Unit 10

11

Questions, questions

11.1 goals
- describe people skills
- carry out an interview

Interview with an interviewer

LISTENING

1 Talk together.

1 Where you live, who are the best-known interviewers on TV and radio?
2 How would you describe the style of these interviewers?
3 Which interviewers do you like? Are there any you dislike? Why?
4 What makes a good interviewer, in your opinion?

2 a You're going to listen to Antonia interviewing Andie about his career in radio. Think of some possible answers to these questions.

1 As a young man, why did Andie refuse an offer to work for a 'pirate' radio station?
2 How did his work as a teacher prepare him for being a radio presenter?
3 What kinds of people does he interview?
4 Why does he enjoy his work so much?
5 How does he prepare for an interview?
6 What does he do when guests are reluctant to talk?
7 What's the role of the producer in the interview?

b ◄ **3.13** Listen to the interview and make notes on the questions 1–7.

Andie Harper and Antonia Brickell are presenters at a local BBC radio station.

3 a ◄ **3.13** Compare your notes, then listen again to check or add details.

b Read the script on p154 to check.

4 Talk together.

1 Do you know anyone who'd make a good radio interviewer? Why do you think so?
2 Have you ever considered a big career change like Andie's?

VOCABULARY

Expressions with **people**

5 In the interview, does Andie say a or b? How do the expressions in each pair differ in meaning?

1 He knows how to: a **handle people**. b **manipulate people**.
2 He can: a **get the best out of people**. b **bring out the worst in people**.
3 The first question should: a **put people on edge**. b **put people at ease**.
4 It should also: a **get people talking**. b **make people clam up**.

SPEAKING

6 a Talk in pairs. Think of three or four jobs and professions where you need good people skills. Explain why.

b Compare your ideas with other pairs.

> Well, to be a successful journalist, you need to be able to get people talking ...

Is that right?

¹You say 'people like you'. Is it the person you are that you bring to air?

²So you love this aspect far more. Your eyes are lighting up!

³What do you mean? How did you do that?

You have a producer. ⁴Is that right?

1 a Look at the highlighted expressions Antonia uses. Which does she use to:

    a   pick up something said earlier?   c   summarise or interpret?

    b   ask for more detail?   d   check that something's true?

  b Match more expressions with a–d.

⁵You mentioned that being a sports producer was 'repetitive'. ⁶In what sense?

⁷You seem to be saying that it's best not to plan too much. ⁸Have I got that right?

⁹Basically, the producer isn't very involved in the interview. ¹⁰Am I right?

¹¹You said something about being offered a job on pirate radio. ¹²Tell me more about that.

2 a Work alone. Choose one of these topics and prepare to tell a partner about it.

    • why you'd make a good radio presenter   • why you should get a pay rise

    • your feelings about the media in your country   • how you learned English

    • how to reduce crime where you live   • how to have a good time in your home town

  b In pairs, have conversations about your chosen topics. Listen carefully to what your partner says and choose expressions from 1 to develop the conversation.

3 a 🔊 **3.14** Listen to these sentences. Practise saying them.

    // What do you MEAN? // How did you DO that? //

    // You have a proDUcer. // Is that RIGHT? //

  Remember how:

  1   you speak in groups of words to help people understand you.

  2   in each group, you choose a key word to have prominence (extra-strong stress).

  b In pairs, look at the sentences in 1b and practise saying them. Decide:

  1   how to divide them into groups of words.

  2   which word in each group should be prominent.

  c Compare your ideas with another pair.

4 a On a piece of paper, write down a topic you'd like to be interviewed about and three questions you'd like to be asked about it.

  b Exchange papers with a partner. Add to your partner's paper:

  1   a question to open the interview.

  2   one other question you'd like to ask.

5   Interview your partner. Use expressions from 1 to develop the interview and get further details.

6   Change pairs. Tell your new partner what you learned about the person you interviewed. Do you think you got the best out of the person you interviewed? How?

Unusual behaviour

READING

1 a What advice would you give to someone who's attending their first job interview? Make a list of 'dos and don'ts'.

b Compare your lists. Do you agree with all the advice?

2 Read the introduction to the article. What do you imagine 'unusual behaviour' might include?

3 Now read the rest of the article. Which stories 1–16 do you find difficult to believe?

The job interview: things *not* to say and do

We've all been interviewed for jobs. And we've all spent most of those interviews thinking about what not to do. Don't bite your nails. Don't fidget. Don't interrupt. But some job applicants go a long way beyond this. We surveyed the top personnel executives of a hundred major corporations and asked for stories of unusual behaviour by job applicants.

¹An applicant said he was so well qualified that if he didn't get the job, it would prove the management was incompetent.

²She wore a Walkman but told me she could listen to the music and me at the same time.

³A balding candidate abruptly left the room and returned a few minutes later wearing a hairpiece.

⁴He challenged me to an arm wrestle.

⁵She asked to see my résumé to check if I was qualified to judge her.

⁶She complained that she hadn't had lunch and proceeded to eat a hamburger and fries in my office.

⁷He promised to demonstrate his loyalty by having the corporate logo tattooed on his forearm if he were hired.

⁸He stopped the interview to phone his therapist, who advised him to ignore the question I'd just asked.

⁹She refused to get out of the chair and threatened to stay in my office until I hired her. I had to call the police.

¹⁰When I asked him about his hobbies, he stood up and started tap dancing around my office.

¹¹She pulled out a camera, snapped a picture of me and said she collected photos of everyone who interviewed her.

¹²He asked me to put on a suit jacket to ensure that my job offer was for real.

¹³An alarm clock went off in the candidate's briefcase. He took it out, turned it off, apologised for the interruption and said he had to leave for another interview.

¹⁴She came in wearing only one shoe. She said the other shoe had been stolen on the bus.

¹⁵She came to the interview with a moped and left it in the reception area. She said she didn't want it to get stolen and announced that she would require indoor parking for the moped.

¹⁶A candidate thanked me for seeing him but admitted he didn't want a job. He'd only come because the unemployment office needed proof that he was looking for one.

---

4 a Read again. Which of the applicants would you describe as:

   1 desperate to get the job?   2 over-confident?   3 aggressive?

b Compare and explain your answers.

SPEAKING

5 Talk about your own experiences of interviews for jobs, courses and so on.

   1 Which interviews can you remember most clearly? Why?
   2 Do you think you're good at being interviewed? Why? / Why not?
   3 Do you have any experience of being an interviewer?
   4 Do you think interviews are a good way of choosing people?

He challenged me to ...

1 Replace the underlined part of each sentence using a verb from the box. When necessary, make changes to the form. Then look in the article to check.

> admitted   advised   ~~announced~~   apologised   ~~challenged~~
> complained   promised   refused   thanked   threatened

1 She said she'd require indoor parking for her moped. *announced that*
2 He asked me for an arm wrestle. *challenged me to*
3 She said she hadn't had lunch.
4 He said he'd have the corporate logo tattooed on his forearm.
5 The therapist told him he should ignore the question I'd just asked.
6 She said she wouldn't get out of the chair.
7 She said she'd stay in my office until I hired her.
8 He said sorry for the interruption.
9 A candidate said thank you to me for seeing him.
10 He said he didn't want a job.

2 Test each other in pairs. Take turns to say a sentence from 1 and give the equivalent sentence using a verb from the box.

3 Read the information. Match your sentences from 1 with a pattern in the box.

> There's no simple rule saying which patterns a verb can have, but you can learn verb patterns by noticing them in things you read or checking them in a dictionary. Here are some common patterns:
>
> a   verb + (that) clause
>   He said (that) he had to leave
>
> b   verb + object + (that) clause
>   She told me (that) she could listen ...
>
> c   verb + *to* infinitive
>   She asked to see my résumé
>
> d   verb + object + *to* infinitive
>   He asked me to put on a jacket
>
> e   verb + preposition
>   She asked about the job
>
> f   verb + object + preposition
>   I asked him about his hobbies

4 a Find two more patterns with admit in this dictionary entry.

b Choose three other verbs from 1. What patterns do you think are possible? Give examples.

c Check your ideas in a dictionary.

> **admit** /əd'mɪt/ *verb* **admitting**, *past* **admitted**
> **1** [I, T] to agree that you did something bad, or that something bad is true [+ doing sth] *Both men admitted taking illegal drugs.* • [+ to + doing sth] *She **admitted to** stealing the keys.* • *I was wrong – I admit it.* • [+ (that)] *He finally admitted that he couldn't cope.*

5 a In pairs, choose four of these questions to complete with your own ideas.

1 Do you know anyone who admits ...
2 Has anyone ever challenged ...
3 Do you ever complain ...
4 Have you ever refused ...
5 When was the last time you promised ...
6 Has anyone ever threatened ...
7 What would you advise ...

Grammar reference and practice, p138

b Get into new pairs. Ask and answer your questions.

6 a Think about memorable experiences involving yourself or other people. Choose three or four situations and prepare to talk about them.

a broken promise   a strange excuse   an unfair complaint   a startling admission
bad advice   a polite refusal   a surprising announcement   a reluctant apology

Think about:

• what the situation was.   • how you felt.
• what you or the other person said.   • what you did.

> I remember when a friend at university suddenly announced that he was getting married ...

b Talk about your experiences in groups. Decide which is the most interesting and tell the class.

Carry out a survey

Vicki is one of the owners of a small family bakery. In an effort to improve business, she's done a survey of local people and companies.

11.3 goals
◎ carry out an interview
◎ report what people say
◎ give statistics

SURVEY RESULTS – SUMMARY

Just over [1]_____ people were surveyed, including 40 from local businesses

LOCAL PEOPLE
Buy their **bread** from:
- supermarkets: 80% (because [2]_____ and more convenient)
- other places: 10%
- us: 10%

Need for **cakes** on special occasions:
- never: 15%
- once a year: 10%
- [3]_____ or more times a year: 75%

Nearly everyone was interested in using us but they didn't know we offer this service.

OFFICE WORKERS
Get their lunches from us: 18 people
Reasons why people don't come to us:
- prefer lunch from home: [4]_____ people
- wrong kind of food: [5]_____ people
- too far from work: [6]_____ people

Most people said they would use us if we deliver.

TASK LISTENING

1 Look at the picture of Vicki and the summary of her survey. Who did she talk to? What questions did she ask?

2 🔊 **3.15** Listen to Vicki telling her colleagues about the results of her survey. In what order does she talk about these things?

   a   cakes for special occasions
   b   lunches for company workers
   c   bread for local people
   d   deliveries
   e   healthy food

3 🔊 **3.15** Listen again and complete the summary of the survey.

4 What do you think Vicki and her colleagues should do in response to these results?

TASK VOCABULARY

Giving statistics

5 **a** Which five expressions from the box could go in each sentence?

> about   all   almost   almost none   exactly
> half   just under   most   nearly   none

   1   I spoke to _____ 150 people.
   2   _____ of them were interested in buying from us.

b Look at two more things Vicki says.

- About **eight out of ten** people said they usually got their bread at the supermarket.
- **Three quarters** of local people said they need cakes for special occasions.

How could you say these numbers in the same style? $\frac{1}{4}$ $\frac{1}{3}$ $\frac{2}{3}$ $\frac{2}{5}$ $\frac{7}{10}$

TASK

6 Imagine you all live in the same area. In groups, choose one of these business ideas or think of your own. Make sure each group chooses a different idea.

- You're opening a local shop which sells, e.g. computer hardware, fruit and veg.
- You're starting a service for local people, e.g. a hairdresser's, a dry cleaner's.

Design a survey to find out what people do now and if they'd use your business.

7 Get into new groups. Ask each other questions to complete your surveys.

8 **a** Go back to your original group and prepare to present your survey results.

- Summarise the results of your survey.
- Decide what order to present the results in.
- Decide who will do each part of the presentation.

b Tell the class about your survey and its results.

11 EXPLORE

Keyword *up* and *down*

Meanings

1 **a** Choose **up** or **down** in the sentences from earlier units.

> 1   She decides what day and time we should meet to clean up / down the area. Unit 10
> 2   The bottle-makers crush the ingredients to a powder and mix them up / down. Unit 9
> 3   How about if we ask LogoForum to tone up / down the colours a little? Unit 5
> 4   I like the way the sunlight comes up / down through the clouds. Unit 5
> 5   He saw that Rikyu had deliberately cut up / down all the flowers! Unit 2
> 6   Students should follow their interests earlier to build up / down experience. Unit 1

b Read the information about **up** and **down**. Then match each sentence from 1a with a meaning a–c.

> a   **up** and **down** are often opposites. You use them to talk about movement to a higher or lower place:
> *She **ran up** the stairs.*
> *We **climbed down** the mountain.*
>
> b   You can also use **up** and **down** to talk about things increasing and decreasing:
> *Will you **turn up** the TV? I can't hear.*
> *I don't understand what you're saying. Please **slow down**.*
>
> c   **up** is also used to emphasise that something is finished or done completely:
> *I've **used up** all the milk. Can you buy some more?*
> Compare with: *I **use** a lot of olive oil in my cooking.*

Verbs with *up* and *down*

2 **a** Many verbs with **up/down** have an idiomatic meaning. Replace the underlined parts in 1–8 with an expression about life changes from the box. Use the correct form.

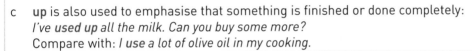

> break up   close down   cut down on   end up   give up   set up   take up   turn down

> 1   To improve my health, I've decided to eat less salty and fatty food …
> 2   … and stop smoking completely.
> 3   We ended our relationship after two years. I think we were too young.
> 4   When I was at university, I started a table tennis club.
> 5   After a lot of problems with the bank, we had to shut the factory.
> 6   My company moved to Alabama, so that's how I came to be living here.
> 7   I started sailing when I was living in Brazil.
> 8   They wanted me to be company director but I refused their offer.

b Use the verbs to make sentences about things which you, or people you know, have done in the last five years. Talk together.

Verbs and adjectives

3 **a** The words **up** and **down** can be used as verbs and adjectives. What do you think they mean in these sentences?

> 1   The news of the takeover **upped** the company's share price by 6%.
> 2   Brenda quickly **downed** her coffee and ran out of the office.
> 3   OK everyone, your time's **up**. Please put your pens down.
> 4   Could you fax the contract? Our network's been **down** all day.
> 5   Sales are **up** by 15% but profits are **down**.
> 6   A: You look a bit **down** today. Are you OK?   B: Yes, I'm just tired. I was **up** all night writing an essay.

b Complete the questions with **up** or **down**. Then discuss them in groups.

> 1   What time are you usually _____ on weekdays? What about on weekends and holidays?
> 2   What kind of weather makes you feel _____? What else affects your mood?
> 3   What do you think's the best way to _____ the level of your English?
> 4   What do you do when your Internet connection is _____?
> 5   Do you follow the stock market? Is it _____ or _____ at the moment?

Goal

⊚ give emphasis to different kinds of information

1 Read the definition and discuss the questions.

1 Do schools and colleges organise work experience where you live?
2 Have you ever done work experience? What did it involve? Did you enjoy it?
3 Do you think it's a good idea? Why? / Why not?

work experience *noun* a period of time in which someone does unpaid work to gain experience: *Many firms understand that giving work experience to students from colleges and schools will benefit everyone in the long term.*

Shawna's on her first day of work experience at a library.

2 a ● 3.16 Listen to a conversation between Shawna and Ruben, the head librarian. What does Ruben tell Shawna to do with:

1 fiction books that people return to the library?
2 non-fiction books that they return?
3 audio books, DVDs and CDs?
4 items that people want to renew?
5 fines paid for items returned late?

b Compare your answers, then read the conversation to check.

3 a Find sentences in the conversation which mean the same as these.

You put fiction books on the right.

1 _____ _____ _____ _____ _____ _____ .

You put non-fiction on the left.

2 _____ _____ _____ _____ _____ _____
_____ .

Where do audio books go?

3 _____ _____ , _____ _____ _____ _____ ?

Do I have to handle fines too?

4 _____ , _____ _____ _____ _____
_____ _____ ?

b Which sentences:

a introduce a new topic before asking about it?
b emphasise the object by moving it to the front?

4 a Rewrite these sentences in the same style. Move the underlined expressions and make any other necessary changes.

1 You can use the TV but the DVD player's not working.
2 You'll find milk in the fridge and the sugar's on the shelf.
3 You open this door with the big key and you open that door with the small key.
4 What did you do with yesterday's newspaper?
5 Can you tell me how this coffee machine works?
6 Where do you want me to put these chairs?

b ● 3.17 Listen to check. Practise saying the sentences.

5 a Work in pairs.

A, you're going to stay in B's home while B's away. You need to find out what things are in the kitchen, where they are and how to use them. Think of five or six things you want to ask about.

B, person A is going to stay in your home while you're away. You need to tell A what things are in your kitchen, where they are and how to use them. Think of five or six things you need to tell A about.

RUBEN	So Shawna, all the books, DVDs and so on have a barcode on them – see? So you just scan the barcodes like this ... and then put the items on these trolleys.
SHAWNA	OK.
RUBEN	These are the book trolleys. Fiction you put on the right, and non-fiction you put on the left.
SHAWNA	Yeah, OK, and audio books, where do they go?
RUBEN	On a third trolley, the silver one over there – along with DVDs, CDs and computer games.
SHAWNA	All right. Erm, what do I do if someone wants to take out the same item again?
RUBEN	Er, if they want to renew, just give it back to them and they can take it out again at the other counter.
SHAWNA	OK, that's easy. Erm ... fines, do I have to handle them too?
RUBEN	Good question. Yes. As you know, readers can only borrow items for three weeks, so if they return something late, the computer'll display a message saying they have to pay a fine.
SHAWNA	Oh, good, so it's automatic.
RUBEN	Yes. People usually pay right away so just click on the 'Paid' option, then take the receipt from this printer and give it to them. If they don't pay, click on 'Pay later' and they can pay next time.
SHAWNA	All right. And what do I do with the money?
RUBEN	Er, the money we put in the cash drawer, which is right here.
SHAWNA	OK, that seems straightforward. What else do I have to do?
RUBEN	Well, I think that's enough to get you started. Any other procedures we'll deal with as they come up.

b Have your conversation. Try to use sentences like the ones in 3.

The oven, is it easy to use?

c Change roles. This time, B will ask about things in A's living room. Follow steps 5a and 5b.

6 Get into new pairs and tell each other what you learned about your first partner's home.

Review

GRAMMAR Patterns after verbs

1 a Read the newspaper article. Then complete it using these reporting verbs in the correct form.

challenge	admit	complain	promise
announce	apologise	refuse	threaten

CULTURE MINISTER TEDDY WALTON has [1]_____ that he has resigned following allegations in *The Correspondent* newspaper that he used his position to obtain free tickets to concerts for family and friends.

In a short speech, Mr Walton [2]_____ that he had received ten tickets to a popular musical as a gift from a friend in the entertainment industry. However, he said that he had done nothing wrong and [3]_____ that he was the victim of a politically motivated campaign. He [4]_____ *The Correspondent* to provide evidence of corruption and [5]_____ to take legal action against the newspaper if it failed to do so. He also publicly [6]_____ to the Prime Minister for the inconvenience caused by his resignation.

The minister has [7]_____ to make a donation to charity equal in value to the cost of the tickets. He is [8]_____ to say whether he expects to return to a ministerial position in the near future.

b <u>Underline</u> the patterns that come after each verb.

c Cover the article. In pairs, can you remember what the minister said? Use the verbs in 1a.

VOCABULARY Expressions with *people*

2 a Work alone. Think about someone you know who:

1 is very good at handling people in a professional context.
2 tends to manipulate people to get their own way.
3 knows how to put people at their ease.
4 sometimes puts people on edge.
5 can get people of any age talking.
6 gets the best out of people in any situation.

b Tell each other about the people. Decide who you'd most like to meet.

CAN YOU REMEMBER? Unit 10 – Describing benefits

3 a What's the next word in these expressions?

1 It allows us / enables us / gives us the ability ...
2 It is crucial / vital / essential ...
3 It has a positive effect ...

b Work alone. What do you think is the most significant invention of the last fifty years? Write reasons using the expressions in 3a.

c Talk with a few people and find out what they think. Ask questions to find out more.

Extension

SPELLING AND SOUNDS Stressed /ɪ/

4 a Say these words. Which three spellings make an /ɪ/ sound?

interviewer   syllable   admit   build   manipulate
mystery   fiction   system   gym   guilty

b A few common words use different spellings. Which letters make an /ɪ/ sound in these words?

busy   business   England   pretty   women

c ● 3.18 Spellcheck. Listen and write ten words. Then check your spelling on p155.

NOTICE Verbs with *off*

5 a Look at the verbs with *off* from the article about job interviews on p88. Which has the meaning of something: **a** starting? **b** finishing?

An alarm clock [1]went off in the candidate's briefcase. He took it out, [2]turned it off, apologised for the interruption and said ...

b Use verbs from the box in the correct form to complete the questions.

break	call	cut	go	kick	round
set	switch/turn				

1 Do you always hear your alarm clock when it _____ off?
2 Do you ever _____ off your phone? When?
3 What time do football matches in your country usually _____ off?
4 Do you like to _____ off a big meal with a coffee or something sweet?
5 What should you do if you get _____ off during a phone call?
6 Do you know anyone who's _____ off an engagement?
7 When was the last time you had to _____ off a meeting?
8 Have you ever _____ off a car or burglar alarm by accident?

c Ask and answer the questions.

Self-assessment

Can you do these things in English? Circle a number on each line. 1 = I can't do this, 5 = I can do this well.

⊙ describe people skills	1	2	3	4	5
⊙ carry out an interview	1	2	3	4	5
⊙ report what people say	1	2	3	4	5
⊙ give statistics	1	2	3	4	5
⊙ give emphasis to different kinds of information	1	2	3	4	5

• For Wordcards, reference and saving your work → e-Portfolio
• For more practice → Self-study Pack, Unit 11

Alternatives

12.1 goals
- talk about health treatments
- express belief and scepticism

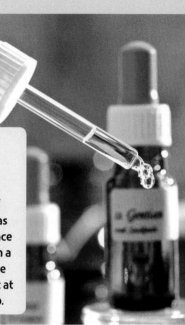

Placebo?

1 What is homeopathy? What do you know about it? Talk together, then read to check your ideas.

> Homeopathy is based on the idea of 'like cures like'. Homeopaths will treat an illness using substances that, in a healthy person, would produce similar symptoms to those of the illness. For example, the herb arnica is used to treat bruising because, when rubbed onto the skin of a healthy person, it turns the skin purple. Another principle of homeopathy is that the more you dilute a substance in a liquid such as water, the more effective it is – so a treatment of one drop of substance in a thousand drops of water would be less effective as a remedy than a treatment of one drop in a million. These treatments are not addictive and have no side effects. Critics, however, believe they have no effect at all and that a homeopathic 'medicine' is nothing more than a placebo.

2 How do these expressions from the paragraph differ in meaning? Can you give examples?

1 an illness / symptoms
2 a treatment / a remedy
3 effect / side effects
4 a medicine / a placebo

3 Discuss these questions about the treatments in the box.

1 What kind of health problems can each treatment be used for?
2 Which would you describe as 'conventional' medicine? Which are 'alternative'?
3 Which do you think:
   a can be effective?
   b can have serious side effects?
   c are probably just a placebo? Why?
   d are probably used too much?
   e should be used more?

> acupuncture
> antibiotics
> hypnosis
> massage
> painkillers
> physiotherapy
> surgery
> vaccinations

4 Work in two groups, A and B.

Group A – read the article against homeopathy below.
Group B – read the article in favour of homeopathy on p129.

Identify the main arguments for or against homeopathy in your article, then compare with someone in your group. Do you agree on what the main arguments are?

Homeopathy – does it work?

Homeopathy: Ben Goldacre says it's nonsense, Jeanette Winterson believes in it – but what do you think?

THE SCEPTIC: BEN GOLDACRE

Homeopaths claim that their pills make people get better. This is a very easy claim to test, and it has been tested thoroughly. The pills perform no better than ordinary everyday sugar pills which have never been given the magical treatment by a homeopath: they're nothing more than placebos.

The placebo effect is far more powerful than most people realise. It's fascinating, and it has been studied extensively by medical science. We know that four placebo sugar pills a day will clear up an illness quicker than two sugar pills, we know that an injection is a more effective treatment for pain than a pill, we know that green pills are more effective for stress than red pills, and we know that brand packaging on painkillers increases pain relief.

5 Group A – read again. What examples does Ben give of:

1 'the placebo effect'?
2 health problems which placebos may be suitable for?
3 the bad practices of some homeopaths?

6 Get into A/B pairs and tell each other about your articles. Which writer do you agree with more? Why?

It works for me

1 Which of these sentences express a belief in something and which express scepticism?

1 It works for me.
2 It offers no benefit.
3 It's tried and tested.
4 It's worthless.
5 It's nonsense.
6 I trust it.
7 I believe in it.
8 It has no scientific basis.
9 There's no proof that it works.
10 It's nothing more than a placebo.
11 You can see its effects.
12 It's no better than a sugar pill.

2 Read the quotations about what people do to feel better. Write sentences expressing your reactions to each idea, using highlighted expressions from 1.

I don't believe in astrology at all. There's no proof that it works.

" I tend to worry about the future so I use astrology to find out what might happen. "

 I've found that meditation's great for reducing stress. "

" Whenever I have problems – personal problems – I go to a counsellor. "

" I like using colours to change my mood. When I wear red, I feel more energetic. Pale blue is calming, so I've done my living room in pale blue. "

 Prayer really helps me when I don't know what to do. "

" I think the reason I'm so healthy is that I only eat organic food. "

3 a 🔊 **3.19** Listen to these expressions from 1 and practise saying them.

I̶t's tried and tested.   I̶t's worthless.   I̶t's nonsense.

At the beginning of a sentence, people often leave out the It in It's.

b In pairs, practise these short conversations without It.

1 A What's the weather like?
  B It's warm and sunny.
2 A Should I call him now?
  B No. It's not a good idea.
3 A What time is it?
  B It's half past nine.
4 A You're looking tired.
  B Yeah. It's time to go.

4 Tell three or four people what you think about the ideas in 2. Find someone who shares most of your opinions.

> I don't do meditation myself but I think it works for a lot of people. It's OK, I guess.

But if homeopathy users are being deceived by the placebo effect, is that so bad? Maybe not. There are often situations where people want treatment but where medicine has little to offer – back pain, stress at work, medically unexplained fatigue, and most common colds. Trying every known medication will give you only side effects. A sugar pill in these circumstances seems a very sensible option.

But there are ethical problems. Modern doctors are very open and honest with their patients. But when someone prescribes a homeopathy pill that they know is no more effective than a placebo, without telling their patient, then they show no respect for some very important ideas, such as getting consent from your patient and respecting their right to make decisions.

There are also more concrete harms. It's routine marketing practice for homeopaths to attack conventional medicine. Homeopaths have been caught giving patients sugar pills to protect them against fatal diseases like malaria while not even giving basic advice on prevention, and giving dangerous advice on vaccines. Was there any action against these homeopaths? None.

This is shamefully foolish, and to point this out should not be considered an 'attack' on homeopathy. It's simple common sense.

Ben Goldacre is a science writer and doctor.

A school with a difference

12.2 goals
- persuade someone of your point of view
- tell people what to expect
- support an argument

1 Read the descriptions a–g, then discuss the questions.

Fay is a teacher at Southglen, a school for 12- to 18-year-olds in Winnipeg, Canada.

a Students and teachers call each other by their first names.
b The school is managed by a headteacher.
c All students have to help out in the school kitchens.
d All students have to wear a uniform.
e Lessons mainly involve listening and note-taking.
f Students choose which subjects they want to study.
g Students are expected to do regular homework.

1 How true are a–g for the schools you went to?
2 Which do you think are good ideas? Which are bad ideas? Why?

2 ● 3.20 Listen to the beginning of Fay's talk about Southglen school. Who's she talking to? What's the occasion?

3 ● 3.21 Listen to the main part of Fay's talk. Which of the descriptions a–g in 1 are true for Southglen? Which are false?

4 a ● 3.21 Listen again.

1 How often are 'parliaments' held? How do they work?
2 What examples does Fay give of things the parliament decides about?
3 Why does she think the parliament system is successful?
4 What are students encouraged to do when they start at Southglen? Why?
5 What are students expected to do if they're not in class?

b Read the script on p155 to check.

5 Talk together. Imagine:

1 you were a member of Fay's audience. What would you want to ask?
2 you could send a child to Southglen or a conventional school. Which would you choose?

6 Read the information in the box.

> At the beginning of her talk, Fay uses **will be -ing** to let people know what to expect:
> • I'**ll be taking** you on a tour of the school.
> • We'**ll be coming back** here to talk about the application process.
>
> This form gives the impression that a future event is a simple, natural fact or is part of a plan or schedule. Compare:
> • I'**ll take** you on a tour ... (sounds like Fay's wish or decision)
> • I'**ll be taking** you on a tour ... (sounds like a fact)

Now match the examples 1–4 with the speakers a–d.

1   I'll **be talking about** three topics. First, ...
2   We'll **be flying** at an altitude of 9,000 metres.
3   Alison from marketing **will be joining** us later on.
4   Today we'll **be looking at** how to write a letter of complaint.

a   a teacher at the beginning of a lesson
b   a presenter at the beginning of a talk
c   a chairperson at the beginning of a meeting
d   a pilot talking to passengers at the beginning of a flight

Grammar reference and practice, p139

7   **a** Write another possible sentence using will be -ing for each of the situations a–d in 6.

b Compare your ideas.

SPEAKING

8   **a** Choose one of these situations.

1   Some important clients from overseas have come to find out about the place where you work.
2   Some exchange students have come to find out about the place where you study.
3   Some tour operators have come to find out about your town or city.

b You're going to give the people a tour. Think about what you'd include and plan a short talk welcoming your guests and giving an outline of the tour. Use will be -ing.

c Listen to each other's talks. Which part of each tour sounds the most interesting?

My experience is that ...

VOCABULARY

Supporting an argument

1   In her talk, Fay supports the idea that Southglen has a successful approach to education by:

1	referring to her personal experience.	To some people this is a strange – even frightening – idea, but **my experience is that** rights and responsibilities go hand in hand.
2	referring to other evidence.	**There's a lot of evidence that** people learn in different ways, so we use a variety of different techniques in lessons.
3	giving specific examples.	People are sometimes surprised at the kinds of ideas our students have. **For example,** any student who has a cooked lunch here in school is expected to help with the washing up afterwards.

Which of these expressions could replace the highlighted expressions in 1–3?

> experts have shown that   for instance   in my experience
> research suggests that   to give you an example   I've always found that

SPEAKING

2   **a** In pairs, find a statement below that one of you agrees with and the other disagrees with, or make up your own.

- computer games have a bad effect on young people
- we should all become vegetarians
- everyone should learn foreign languages at school
- air travel for leisure purposes should be banned
- doing lots of sport and exercise is bad for you

b Working alone, prepare a short talk presenting and explaining your point of view.

- Think about how to outline at the beginning what you'll be talking about.
- Decide what points to make and what order to make them in.
- Try to use expressions from 1.

c Practise your talks in your pairs.

3   Listen to talks from other pairs. Whose arguments do you find the most persuasive?

Present a proposal

12.3 goals
◎ persuade someone of your point of view ♻
◎ make and justify recommendations

TASK LISTENING

Ji-Sun's been asked to research weekend activities that encourage employee team-building.

1 Read the caption. What activities can you think of that would be suitable for team-building?

2 ◖3.22◗ Listen to Ji-Sun making her proposal to her manager, Bryn. Which of these options does she discuss? Which does she recommend?

a camping weekend   an acting workshop   mountain climbing   a treasure hunt
learning ballroom dancing   cooking a dinner together

3 ◖3.22◗ Listen again. Make a list of the pros and cons of each option.

4 ◖3.23◗ Listen to Bryn's decision later that day. Do you agree with him?

TASK VOCABULARY

Recommending and justifying

5 a Read Ji-Sun's recommendations. Which are in favour of an option? Which are against?

   1   I'd **rule** it **out** since it might not involve everyone equally.
   2   I'd **advise against** it because it's not really what we're looking for.
   3   I'd **strongly recommend** it.
   4   I'd **reject** the first on the grounds that it could be too cold.
   5   If I were you, I'd **go for** the second as it offers value for money.

b Underline the expressions that introduce the four reasons for the recommendations.

TASK

6 Read the situation and underline the key points. Then read about each venue.

> You work for a theatre company. You've been asked to research exciting locations for a week's performance of a murder mystery play, then recommend one. You expect an audience of about 250. These venues are the best you've found.

The Warehouse

▸ $1000 a night
▸ Up to 400 people
▸ 30 min from city centre
▸ Full facilities, amenities

Atmospheric, dramatic, flexible event space with beautiful flooring and classic windows. Seating provided. A 10% discount for groups over 200.

Marquee Events

• **$800 a night. Holds 300.** • **Food catered, full bar**
• **1 km outside city on bus and underground routes.**
Bright, modern, reasonably priced events marquee in quiet, attractive setting. Adaptable to any kind of event. Seating, tables provided. Friendly staff.

CITY RIVER BOAT

$1500 per night
Capacity: 250 adults
City centre (River Dock)
Food, full bar, toilets
Want to hold a conference, dinner or theatrical event in a unique venue? Book a historical river boat. Space is adaptable for your needs. A wonderful atmosphere.

Helm's Cavern

✴ $750 / night, full facilities

✴ Up to 275 guests

✴ 2 km from city centre: easy access by train, bus, car.

A fantastic underground venue in very high demand. Comfortable seating, excellent heating / lighting. For an experience you'll never forget, book now!

7 In groups, discuss the pros and cons of each venue and decide which one you'd recommend, noting your reasons. Consider, for example:

size   price   location and access   facilities   novelty value   atmosphere

8 a Prepare to present your proposal to other groups. Think about:

   • what language you'll need to explain why you rejected three of the options.
   • what language you'll need to recommend and justify your final choice.
   • which member(s) of your group will present your proposal.

b Listen to each other's proposals. Which is the most popular venue?

Across cultures Health and healthcare

LISTENING

Liesbeth from the Netherlands

1 **a** In pairs, make a list of five things you think are important for good health.

b Compare with other pairs. How many of your ideas are the same?

2 ◄ 3.24 Listen to four people talking about health and healthcare in their countries. Match each statement 1–8 to one of the speakers.

Hugo from England

Reginald from Nigeria

1 People are more health-conscious now than twenty years ago.
2 People go to hospitals for minor illnesses, not to family doctors.
3 We worry too much about our health and this stress damages our health.
4 Many people who live in the countryside prefer traditional or alternative medicine to modern treatments.
5 People pay for their own healthcare. It's not paid for by the state.
6 The media include too much negative coverage of health issues.
7 People's lifestyles are not as active or healthy as they used to be.
8 Few people in the countryside have seen a medical doctor.

Sahana from India

3 Talk in groups. Do you think the statements in 2 are true where you live?

VOCABULARY
Healthcare

4 Use the verbs in the boxes to complete the questions.

A Healthcare systems
1 Does everyone _____ health insurance?
2 Does it _____ every kind of **treatment**?
3 _____ medicines **free of charge**?
4 Are people encouraged to _____ regular **check-ups**?
5 How easy is it to _____ **an appointment** at a clinic or with a doctor?

> Are
> cover
> have (x2)
> make

B Doctors and patients
6 Would you say that doctors and nurses _____ **a high status**?
7 _____ people **entitled to** choose or change doctors as they wish?
8 Do doctors tend to _____ a formal or informal **manner towards** patients?
9 Are patients _____ **access to** their own medical records?
10 Do doctors _____ medical treatments **openly with** their patients?

> Are
> discuss
> given
> have (x2)

C Hospitals
11 Do patients _____ **a choice between** public and private hospitals?
12 Do hospitals _____ **people** immediately or are there waiting lists?
13 Do patients usually _____ in rooms or wards? How many people share the wards?
14 Are families expected to _____ with patient care?
15 Do hospitals _____ **information about** the success rates of their surgeons?

> help out
> provide
> stay
> treat
> have

SPEAKING

5 Work in three groups, A, B and C. Ask and answer your set of questions (A, B or C) in 4 about healthcare where you live.

6 Tell the other groups about your discussion. Can they add any more information?

7 Have you ever experienced – or do you know about – healthcare in other countries? Describe any similarities or differences compared with healthcare where you live.

Goal
◉ write a proposal

1 Talk together. Which of these things do you think are most important to have in a company café? Why?

a good choice of food   helpful staff
wireless Internet   plants   free tea and coffee
music   comfortable chairs   big tables   paintings

2 Read the proposal and answer the questions.

1 Who's it for? Who wrote it? What's its purpose?
2 What proposals has the Board made? How do the staff feel about them?
3 What proposals do the staff make? Which are the most important?

To: Li Ming Chen, Managing Director   From: Constanza Brookes, Staff Representative
Subject: ᵃ _____

....

ᵇ _____

¹As you know, money was recently allocated for improvements to the café, and the Board has made some suggestions about how to spend it. ²The purpose of this proposal is to summarise the reaction of the staff to your ideas and ³to present some suggestions of our own.

ᶜ _____

⁴As we understand it, the Board has three main suggestions:
• to repaint the walls and hang curtains
• to buy longer tables and more chairs
• to brighten up the café with plants

We are very happy with the idea of repainting and curtains. ⁵This would certainly make the café more attractive. ⁶We also propose that the company buy several poster-size prints to brighten up the walls even more.

However, ⁷we do not feel that there is any need for new tables and chairs. The present furniture is in good condition and because the tables are small, they encourage a friendlier feeling than long tables would. As for plants, we feel the money could be better spent on other things.

ᵈ _____

⁸We believe that the money should be spent in four areas. ⁹Our proposals are:
• to invest in a new dishwashing machine. According to our café staff, the present machine is of poor quality and doesn't always clean the dishes and cutlery thoroughly.
• to purchase a new coffee machine. The present machine breaks down constantly and takes a long time to get repaired.
  Also, ¹⁰would it be possible to change our servicing company?
• to buy more salt and pepper sets so we have one for every table.
• to buy new uniforms for the café staff, as they find their present uniforms are uncomfortable and unattractive.

¹¹We hope that our proposals will be given serious consideration, particularly those related to the two machines. ¹²We look forward to discussing them with you at a convenient time.

Constanza Brookes

---

3 Read again. What reasons does Constanza give for what the staff want and don't want?

4 It's important for a proposal to have a clear title and useful headings. In pairs, decide on a title and headings a–d. Then compare your ideas with another pair.

5 Look at the highlighted expressions in the proposal. Which:

1 state the aim? (x2)   3 give opinions and reactions? (x3)   5 conclude? (x2)
2 introduce background information? (x2)   4 introduce proposals? (x3)

6 a Work as a class. Choose a place in the building where you all work or study and make a list of ways in which it could be improved. Think about, for example:

the reception area   a classroom   a meeting or conference room   a computer room   a games room

b In pairs, choose the best ideas from your list in 6a. Then plan and write a proposal on behalf of the class.

7 Read two or three other proposals. Do you agree with each other's ideas?

12 Look again ♻

Review

VOCABULARY Health and treatments

1 a Complete the conversation between a doctor and patient. Then look at p94 Vocabulary to check.

DOCTOR So, what exactly are your [1]s_____?

PATIENT Well, just a really painful sore throat. I bought a natural [2]r_____ at the chemist's, but it doesn't seem to be having any [3]e_____.

DOCTOR Right. Have you had this kind of [4]i_____ before?

PATIENT No. Well, not as far as I can remember.

DOCTOR Do you know if you're allergic to any [5]m_____?

PATIENT No, I don't think so.

DOCTOR OK. I'm going to give you a couple of prescriptions. One of them's an [6]a_____, the other's a [7]p_____.

PATIENT OK. Do they have any [8]s_____ _____?

DOCTOR Well, you might feel a bit sleepy. But apart from that, no.

b Write down one or two words to help you remember each line of the conversation. Then cover 1a and practise the conversation in pairs. Take turns to be the doctor and patient.

GRAMMAR will be -ing

2 a Complete the conversations with your own ideas. Use *will be -ing*.

1 A Are you working late tonight?
  B No, not tonight, but ...
2 A Are you free this weekend?
  B Sorry, no. I ...
3 A Congratulations! How are you going to celebrate?
  B Well, we ...
4 A Can I have a sandwich? I'm hungry.
  B Can you wait a bit? We ...

b Compare your ideas.

CAN YOU REMEMBER? Unit 11 – Giving statistics

3 a Match the expressions and percentages.

about two-thirds of them   23%
almost none of them   97%   exactly half of them
60%   just over half of them   65%
just under a quarter of them   50%
most of them   2%   nearly all of them
80%   six out of ten   51%

b Talk in pairs. How many people in your class:

1 have dark eyes?   4 are tall?
2 are male?   5 have brown shoes?
3 are wearing jewellery?

Use expressions from 3a.

c Compare your answers with another pair. Do you agree?

Extension

SPELLING AND SOUNDS /eə/

4 a Complete the spelling of these words with: a ae air are

__robics   rep__   softw__   __line   veget__rian
p__rent   prep__   ch__   __port   __roplane

b Which spellings are usually used:

a at the start of words?
b in the middle?
c at the end?

c There are a few exceptions. How many ways of spelling /eə/ can you find in these words?

millionaire   prayer   questionnaire   swear
their   there   underwear   where

d Spellcheck. In pairs, take turns to choose nine words and test your partner's spelling. Then check your spelling together.

NOTICE -ly adverbs

5 a Complete the sentences from this unit with the adverbs in the box.

constantly   independently   potentially   publicly
reasonably   seriously   strongly   thoroughly

1 Homeopathy has been tested _____.
2 I would like to see homeopaths debating _____ with their critics.
3 There have been a number of articles criticising homeopathic remedies as _____ lethal.
4 Our students take their responsibilities very _____.
5 They're expected to work _____.
6 Bright, modern, _____ priced events marquee.
7 I'd _____ recommend it.
8 The present machine breaks down _____.

b Test each other in pairs. A – say 1–8 without the adverbs. B – remember the adverbs. Then change roles.

Self-assessment

Can you do these things in English? Circle a number on each line. 1 = I can't do this, 5 = I can do this well.

talk about health treatments	1 2 3 4 5
express belief and scepticism	1 2 3 4 5
persuade someone of your point of view	1 2 3 4 5
tell people what to expect	1 2 3 4 5
support an argument	1 2 3 4 5
make and justify recommendations	1 2 3 4 5
write a proposal	1 2 3 4 5

• For Wordcards, reference and saving your work → e-Portfolio
• For more practice → Self-study Pack, Unit 12

13 Compromise

13.1 goals
◉ describe disagreements and compromises
◉ make your case in a disagreement

Living space

a car park

leaflets

bungalows

a cul-de-sac

a green

the local council

LISTENING

1 a You're going to listen to Liesbeth talking about a disagreement in her neighbourhood and how she dealt with it. The pictures show things from her story. Can you guess what the disagreement was about?

b 🔊 3.25 Listen to check.

2 🔊 3.25 Listen again. Which of these statements are true? Which are false?

1 It was the local council's idea to change the green into a car park.
2 Liesbeth lives next to the green.
3 She produced a leaflet to explain different opinions.
4 She organised a meeting of all the people in her street.
5 They persuaded the council not to make a car park.
6 The disagreement had a positive effect on the atmosphere in the street.

3 Talk together.

1 What do you think of the way Liesbeth dealt with the disagreement?
2 She says the compromise was 'a good deal all round'. Do you agree?
3 Could a story like this happen where you live?

VOCABULARY

Disagreement and compromise

4 a How are the expressions in each pair similar or different in meaning?

1	a get everyone's opinion	4	a thrash something out
	b organise a petition		b talk something over
2	a call a meeting	5	a propose an alternative
	b organise a demonstration		b propose a compromise
3	a have a word with someone	6	a take legal advice
	b make an official complaint		b take legal action

b Which of these things did Liesbeth or her neighbours do?

SPEAKING

5 What would you do, if anything, in these situations? Use the expressions in 4a and your own ideas.

- someone gets permission to build a nightclub opposite your home
- you get food poisoning after dining at a local restaurant
- a firm of decorators does a terrible job in your home
- your neighbour's car alarm keeps going off in the middle of the night

6 Have you (or has someone you know) ever been in a serious disagreement with a person or organisation? What was it about? What happened? How did it end?

Workspace

Yousef

LISTENING

1 Look at the picture. How do you think Yousef feels? Where you work or study, do you have enough space?

2 ◖3.26 Listen to the conversation between Yousef and his manager, Leo. What does Yousef want? Does he get what he wants?

3 a ◖3.26 Listen again and make notes on:

1 Yousef's ideas.　2 Leo's objections.　3 what they agree to do.

b Compare your notes, then read the script on pp156–7 to check.

VOCABULARY
Making your case

4 Complete the extracts with the expressions in the boxes.

> Y ¹_____, would it be possible for me to have my own office?
> L We just don't have the room. ²_____, it's not just you. Agustin and Rachel should really have their own offices too.
> Y Yes, ³_____. The company upstairs wants to rent out some rooms.

And besides
I've been thinking
I've thought about that

> Y Couldn't we at least ask about the price?
> L Come on, Yousef, ⁴_____ how things are with money at the moment. ⁵_____ there's no way Karin would agree.
> Y Well, ⁶_____, I've got another idea.

I'm afraid
in that case
you know

> Y I could move into the little photocopying room.
> L ⁷_____ the photocopier? We'd have to move it somewhere.
> Y ⁸_____. It could go in the corridor, next to the drinks machine.
> L Are you sure it would fit? ⁹_____, that room's too small.

But what about
In any case
That's no problem

5 In pairs, write another short conversation between an employee and manager, or a student and tutor. Begin with *I've been thinking*, ... Write about ten lines. Include expressions from 4.

PRONUNCIATION
Prominent words 3

6 a ◖3.27 Listen. Underline the prominent word (the word with extra-strong stress) in each group of words.

// I've been thinking // would it be possible // for me to have my own office? //
// We just don't have the room // And besides // it's not just you //

b With your partner from 5, read aloud the conversation you wrote and mark the groups of words. Then choose a key word to be prominent in each group.

c Listen to another pair's conversation. What's it about? Do they reach an agreement?

SPEAKING

7 a In A/B pairs, read the situations. Think of reasons to support your point of view.

❶ You run a small business together. A – you'd like to employ an assistant. B – you think this would be expensive and unnecessary.

❷ You're flatmates. A – you're a keen cyclist and you keep your bike just inside the front door. B – you hate having a dirty bike in your flat.

b Have a conversation for each situation. Try to come up with a compromise.

8 Compare your decisions as a class. Which were the most creative compromises?

In the middle

> **mediate** /ˈmiːdieɪt/ [I or T] *verb*
> to talk to two separate people or groups involved in a disagreement to try to help them to agree or find a solution to their problems:
> *Negotiators were called in to mediate **between** the two sides.*

READING

1 Read the definition and talk together.

1 Do you ever have to mediate between friends, family or people at work? Give examples.
2 What skills and qualities do you think a good mediator needs?

2 a You're going to read an interview with a professional mediator, Isobel Clark. Do you think these statements are true or false?

1 People often try mediation at the suggestion of lawyers and the police.
2 There are usually two mediators at a mediation meeting.
3 A mediator's job is to listen carefully and suggest compromises.
4 A mediation meeting can often take five or six hours.
5 Mediators need to have good communication skills.

b Read the interview to check.

Real professionals
The mediator

Conflicts at work, family feuds, neighbourly disagreements ... Isobel Clark has over 20 years' experience of workplace, relationship and community mediation

Can you give us an example of what you do?
[1]Recently I did a mediation between two families living in neighbouring houses. In one of the families, the father had a passion for restoring old cars. He'd work on these cars outside until quite late at night, and the front garden was full of bits of old car, oil cans and the like. The other family hated the noise and the mess but – as quite often happens, I'm afraid – they simply put up with the problem and hoped it would go away. This went on for some years until they finally complained to the police – and then of course the relationship between the neighbours broke down completely.

How do you, the mediator, get involved?
[2]Some people seek mediation independently, but many come to us on the recommendation of the police, doctors or lawyers. In this case, it was the police. Once we got into mediation,

the families came to an agreement very quickly. The car enthusiast agreed to tidy the garden and not to work on his cars so late, and both families agreed to be more open and honest with each other in future. Like most people we see in mediation, these were basically reasonable people who just needed to sit down together and talk things over in a structured way.

How many people are usually involved in a mediation?
[3]There are usually two mediators and ideally we should be visibly different – male and female, different ages, different ethnicities – as this often reflects the participants themselves. We invite each participant to bring along a supporter, who can be anyone who knows what's been happening. Sometimes they bring two supporters along but each side must have the same number so there's a perceived balance of power.

What does the mediator actually do?
[4]As a mediator, you're responsible for everything and nothing! On the one hand, you set up and guide the discussion at all times. On the other hand, mediators never suggest, advise or problem-solve. The purpose of mediation is to allow the participants to come up with solutions for themselves. If people feel you favour one side or the other, they'll lose confidence in you.

How long does it take?
[5]A session won't usually last longer than two hours. If people haven't sorted out their differences after that, then they're not going to, at least on that occasion! It also gets difficult for mediators to keep up their concentration.

What does it take to be a good mediator?
[6]You have to be able to listen and ask questions which show how people are feeling and what the real problems are. From time to time, you summarise what they say: 'So, you're upset because ...'. When they see things from a distance, objectively and without emotion, they can begin to move towards a solution. A mediator recognises moments of change, when people face up to reality and are ready to compromise – for instance, the moment when they stop looking at the mediator and start looking at each other. Whenever I see that, I think, 'That's it. Job done.'

3 **Read again. Find reasons why:**

1 the neighbours needed mediation.
2 the mediation was a success.
3 mediators should be different.
4 meetings are not longer than two hours.
5 mediators ask questions.
6 mediators summarise people's words.

SPEAKING

4 **Talk together.**

1 Is it common for people or organisations where you live to use mediation?
2 Would you ever consider using a mediator for problems in your family or at work? Why? / Why not?
3 Do you think you could be a professional mediator? Would you enjoy it?

Let's talk it over

GRAMMAR

Verbs with adverbs and prepositions 2

1 **Notice how the verbs in the interview have three patterns:**

1	They hoped the problem would **go away**.	*verb adverb*
2	We invite each participant to **bring along** a supporter.	*verb adverb object*
	or Sometimes they **bring** two supporters **along**.	*verb object adverb*
3	They simply **put up with** the problem.	*verb adverb preposition object*

Now find these verbs in the interview. Are they like 1, 2 or 3?

go on (paragraph 1)   break down (1)   sit down (2)   talk over (2)   set up (4)
come up with (4)   sort out (5)   keep up (5)   face up to (6)

2 **Which one of these sentences is wrong? Why?**

1 Let's **talk over** this problem.
2 Let's **talk** this problem **over**.
3 Let's **talk over** it.
4 Let's **talk** it **over**.

3 **Find a verb in 1 which has a similar meaning to:**

1 accept that something exists
2 continue
3 disappear
4 fail
5 organise
6 tolerate

4 **a** Add one word to complete each statement in the quiz. Sometimes it can go in two different places.

Dealing with conflict – what's your style?

Think about your relationships with friends and family. How true are these statements for you?
Rate them from 0 to 4. 0 = not true at all 4 = completely true

 1 ☐ I try to come up ⋀ agreements that satisfy everybody, no matter how long it takes.
               with
 2 ☐ In order to get the best result from the other side, I keep the pressure all the time.
 3 ☐ I prefer not to argue with people because many problems just go if you ignore them.
 4 ☐ I'll put up a compromise which isn't completely fair if it means we can move forward.
 5 ☐ I like to talk problems very carefully so I can understand everybody's point of view.
 6 ☐ I enjoy a good argument where people have strong opinions, even if it goes for hours.
 7 ☐ I'll tend not to face up a problem if it means damaging a relationship with a friend.
 8 ☐ I'd rather sort a problem by finding a compromise than spend a lot of time arguing with somebody.

Grammar reference and practice, p139

b Work alone and answer the quiz.

SPEAKING

5 **Tell each other about your answers to the quiz. Give reasons and examples.**

6 Look at the Analysis on p130 and follow the instructions. What's your main style of conflict management, according to the quiz? Do you agree? Why? / Why not?

Negotiate an agreement

13.3 goals
⊙ describe disagreements and compromises ♻
⊙ make your case in a disagreement ♻
⊙ negotiate a formal agreement

TASK LISTENING

1 Read the caption. What kind of mistake do you think the hotel might have made?

2 **3.28** Listen to Caitlin and Ethan's meeting.

1 What was the mistake?
2 How did the hotel deal with the problem?
3 Do Ethan and Caitlin seem satisfied with their agreement in the end?

3 a **3.28** Listen again. What's the significance of these figures?

a	75	d	$5,856
b	175	e	$2,500
c	$2,843	f	20%

b Read the script on p157 to check.

Caitlin is a director of a children's charity. She recently organised a fundraising event at a local hotel but, because the hotel made a mistake, the event was not a success and the charity lost money.

TASK VOCABULARY

Negotiating an agreement

4 a Complete the sentences with these words.

> accept   agree   be   compensated   depends
> entitled   gather   have   offer   prepared

Stating your position	1	We believe we should be _____ for our losses.
	2	I feel we're _____ to a 50% refund of the cost.
Finding out what the other side wants	3	I _____ you'd like to work out some compensation.
	4	What exactly did you _____ in mind?
Making a proposal	5	We're _____ to add an extra $250.
	6	We can _____ a refund on the room rental.
Rejecting a proposal	7	I'm afraid we can't _____ to cancel the entire cost.
	8	I don't think we can _____ that.
Setting a condition	9	That _____ on what we agree.
	10	We'd _____ willing to come here again provided we can sort out this problem.

b In pairs, write a few words to help you remember each sentence. Then cover 4a and try to remember them.

believe compensated losses – I believe we should be compensated for our losses.

TASK

5 Work in two groups.

Group A – look at the situation on p129.
Group B – look at the situation on p130.

6 a Get into A/B pairs. Have your meeting and try to negotiate the best possible agreement for your side.

b Go back to your group and tell each other what you agreed. Who do you think negotiated the best agreement for your side?

Keyword *put*

put = move or place something

1 a ●3.29 Listen to four people talking about the disastrous dinner organised by Caitlin's charity (see the previous page).

   1   Who works for the charity? Who works at the hotel?
   2   How do you think each person feels? Why?

b Compare your ideas, then read the script on p157 to check.

2 a The speakers use eight expressions with *put*, all with the same basic pattern. Find and write them in a table like this.

put	something/someone	preposition	something
put	half the guests	in	a little side room

b Which expressions are about moving or placing something physically? Which are more abstract?

3 a Work alone. Write four or five sentences expressing your opinions or experiences with *put*.

I think the government should put more money into primary education.
My husband's always putting me in really embarrassing situations.

b In groups, listen to each other's sentences and ask questions.

> Why primary education in particular?

> What kind of situations?

Multi-word verbs with *put*

4 a Can you guess the meanings of the multi-word verbs in these sentences?

```
1    He asked me to put on a suit jacket to ensure my job offer was for real. Unit 11
2    I'm not trying to put you off but travel writing has to be something you want to do passionately. Unit 9
3    Maybe we could put some notices up outside. Unit 8
4    Well, you're only a beginner. You just need to put in some practice. Unit 1
```

b Now do the same with these sentences. The verbs look the same as the ones in 4a but have different meanings.

   1   Do you mind if I **put** the television **on**?
   2   I know I should see a dentist but I keep **putting** it **off**.
   3   The hotel was full so I asked Abbas to **put** me **up** for a few days.
   4   It's a very old building but we've decided to **put in** central heating.

5 a Cover the sentences in 4a and 4b, then complete 1–8 below.

Find someone who:
   1   likes to put music _____ when they're working.
   2   once put _____ a notice in their neighbourhood.
   3   always puts a tie _____ when they go to work.
   4   keeps putting _____ something important.
   5   quite often puts friends _____ at the weekend.
   6   puts _____ a lot of practice for a sport every week.
   7   recently put _____ a new bathroom or kitchen at home.
   8   was put _____ a subject by a horrible teacher at school.

b Talk to different people in your class and try to find at least one person for each statement 1–8. Ask questions to find out more.

> Do you put music on when you're working?

> If I'm at home, yes.

> What kind of thing do you listen to?

13 EXPLORESpeaking

1 🔊 3.30 Listen to three conversations.

1 Why is Tomek unhappy?
2 Why is Barry disappointed?
3 Why is Sarah surprised?

2 a Read and complete 1–10 in the conversations with these expressions.

> definitely   terribly   absolutely   at all   complete
> single   very, very   far   total   on earth

b 🔊 3.30 Listen again to check.

c Practise in pairs. A – say sentences 1–10 from the conversations without the expressions in the gaps. B – close your book. Listen and make A's sentences more emphatic using the expressions from 2a. Then change roles.

3 a Which sentences, a or b, are used in the conversations? Why?

1	a It's a very big order.		b It is a very big order.
2	a We'd like a bigger discount.		b We would like a bigger discount.
3	a We've tried our best.		b We have tried our best.
4	a I see your point.		b I do see your point.
5	a I like it usually.		b I do like it usually.
6	a She worked really hard.		b She did work really hard.

b Answer the questions.

1 You can add emphasis by stressing **be**, **have** and modal verbs like **would**. What other modals can you think of?
2 What verb do you add for emphasis if the sentence doesn't have **be**, **have** or a modal verb?

c Practise in pairs. A – say the first sentence of each pair in 3a. B – close your book. Listen and make A's sentences more emphatic. Then change roles.

4 Use the language in 2 and 3 to make these sentences more emphatic. Then compare your ideas.

1 Although I don't usually like fiction, I enjoyed *All the Pretty Horses*.
Although I don't usually like fiction at all, I did enjoy **All the Pretty Horses**.
2 I hated my first job. However, I learned a lot.
3 I'm not very good at cooking but I make good lasagne.
4 I don't normally watch horror films but I'd go and see *The Descent*.
5 I think it's better to be happy than famous.
6 For me, voting in elections is a waste of time.
7 When I was at school, I found chemistry impossible.
8 I think I'm more sensible now than I was ten years ago.

5 a Work alone. Change your sentences from 4 so they're true for you.

Although I don't usually like biographies at all, I did enjoy Bruce Lee: Fighting Spirit.

b In groups, listen to each other's sentences. Ask questions to find out more.

❶

GREG	Hello?
TOMEK	Hi, Greg, it's Tomek. I'm calling about the email, er, you sent us. It's about the price you quoted ...
GREG	Oh, er yeah.
TOMEK	Well, erm, it is a very big order so, er, we would like a bigger discount than usual.
GREG	Yeah, we have tried our best. [1]That's _____ the best price we can manage.
TOMEK	[2]Sorry but we don't understand that _____. [3]It's a _____ bigger order than usual.
GREG	OK, erm, I do see your point. Look, I'd like to talk to someone and call you back, OK?
TOMEK	I'd appreciate that. Do you think you could call back today?

❷

LING	Hi, Barry. How was the film?
BARRY	Bad. [4]It was _____ bad.
LING	Really?
BARRY	Yep. [5]It was _____ rubbish.
LING	But I thought you were a big fan of sci-fi.
BARRY	I do like it, usually. [6]But this was a _____ waste of time. [7]The plot was _____ ridiculous.
LING	Wow! I'm glad I decided not to go.

❸

ESIN	... but anyways it all worked out fine in the end. By the way, Ashley got her exam results yesterday morning. Nine As.
SARAH	You're joking!
ESIN	No. [8]She got top marks in every _____ subject.
SARAH	[9]How _____ did she manage that?
ESIN	She did work really hard.
SARAH	Well, good for her. [10]She must be _____ happy about it.

13 Look again ♻

Review

VOCABULARY Disagreement and compromise

1 a Can you remember the missing verbs?

1   g_____ everyone's opinion
2   c_____ a meeting
3   h_____ a word with someone
4   th_____ o_____ an agreement
5   o_____ a demonstration or petition
6   m_____ an official complaint
7   p_____ a compromise
8   t_____ legal advice or legal action

b Talk together. Decide in what order you'd do the things 1–8 in this situation:

You live in a small block of flats. You hear that the management of the building are planning to paint the block a bright orange colour. You're horrified at this idea and determined to stop it.

First of all, I'd probably have a quiet word with the managers. If that didn't work, I'd …

○ ○ ○ ○

GRAMMAR Verbs with adverbs and prepositions 2

2 a 🔊 3.31 Listen to seven extracts and decide what the situation is in each case. Who's speaking? Who are they talking to? Where are they? Then compare your ideas.

b 🔊 3.31 Listen again. Note down the verbs with adverbs and prepositions in each sentence.

c In pairs, try to remember and write the seven extracts. Use the verbs to help you.

CAN YOU REMEMBER? Unit 12 – Belief and scepticism

3 a Put the expressions in order.

1   for it me works
2   and it's tested tried
3   it no proof that there's works
4   can effects its see you
5   a it's more nothing placebo than
6   basis has it no scientific

b In groups, say what you think about this advice.

Ten steps to a happier life

1   Get plenty of exercise.
2   Smile and laugh whenever possible.
3   Do nice things for other people.
4   Take vitamin B.
5   Keep busy with lots of activities.
6   Get a pet.
7   Think positive.
8   Dress in cheerful colours.
9   Eat a healthy diet and avoid caffeine.
10 Form good, lasting relationships.

Extension

SPELLING AND SOUNDS /əʊ/

4 a Underline the letters in these words which make an /əʊ/ sound.

placebo   negotiate   approach   ocean   download
arrow   hero   homework   bungalow   overseas

b Find words in 4a to match these spelling patterns.

1   /əʊ/ is usually spelled o.
2   But it's often spelled oa in the middle of words.
3   And it's often spelled ow at the end of words.

c There are a few exceptions in some common words. Which letters make an /əʊ/ sound in these words?

shoulder   soul   toe   though   mauve

d 🔊 3.32 Listen and write eleven words. Then check your spelling on p157.

NOTICE Expressions with keep

5 a Complete the extract from Liesbeth's story.

❝
So, I tried to think how we could solve this problem, not having it all turned into a car park but also ªkeep the _____ on the road and ᵇkeep everybody _____.
❞

Check the script on p156. Notice the patterns:

a   **keep** + something
b   **keep** + something/someone + description

b Which of these expressions are like A? B?

1   When I was younger I used to **keep a diary**.
2   I always **keep my appointments**.
3   It's never good to **keep someone waiting**.
4   I know how to **keep a secret**.
5   If I drink coffee after noon, it **keeps me up** at night.
6   I always **keep my fingers crossed** when my flight takes off.
7   When it comes to politics, I try to **keep an open mind**.

c Are the sentences 1–7 true for you? Talk together.

Self-assessment

Can you do these things in English? Circle a number on each line. 1 = I can't do this, 5 = I can do this well.

describe disagreements and compromises	1	2	3	4	5
make your case in a disagreement	1	2	3	4	5
talk about dealing with conflict	1	2	3	4	5
negotiate a formal agreement	1	2	3	4	5
use different ways of adding emphasis	1	2	3	4	5

• For Wordcards, reference and saving your work → e-Portfolio
• For more practice → Self-study Pack, Unit 13

14 Changes

14.1 goals
- talk about the future
- make predictions about the world

Reading the future

READING

1 Read about Ian Pearson, who has an unusual job. What does he do? What skills or attributes does he need in his work?

I work as a futurologist. I study the future. My day-to-day work involves tracking developments across the whole field of technology and society, figuring out where it is all going next, and how that will affect our everyday lives. My main tools are: a strong background in science and engineering, trends analysis, common sense, reasonable business insight, knowing when to listen to other people, and a whole lot of thinking. I usually get it right, but since the future is never totally predictable, I sometimes get it wrong too, about 15% of the time.

2 a Ian has made predictions about these things. In groups, imagine how each invention might work.

1 active contact lenses
2 active skin
3 digital jewellery
4 solar power stations
5 automatic transport systems
6 external brains

b Read the article to check your ideas.

Predictions for an inventive future

Active contact lenses In 1991, I predicted the invention of an active contact lens, which would use tiny lasers to project a picture onto your retina, allowing you to include any image in your normal vision. A company in the US has already made a prototype with four pixels, but in the future, we'll see high-definition lenses with full 3D virtual reality for games-playing and so on.

Active skin It will be possible to print electronic circuits straight onto the skin. They'll only last a few days, which could be perfect for security passes or ultra-secure fingerprint technology. I'd be surprised if a prototype isn't available in about five years. If we combine active skin and contact lens displays with the incredible miniaturisation of IT, you won't need a keyboard or a mobile phone because you could just touch your skin to access the Internet or call up a friend, and see everything in your active contact lens!

Digital jewellery I predict that mobile phones will become obsolete by 2020. Voice recognition will be so advanced that a simple piece of digital jewellery will be able to connect and dial as soon as you say the word. There's also the possibility that 'thought recognition' could allow you to just think the number. This is already in its early stages: the technology exists that allows you to move a screen cursor simply by having electrodes hooked up to your brain.

Solar power stations The amount of sunlight falling onto the Sahara is a couple of kilowatts per square metre. If you can make solar panels that are 30% or 40% efficient – something which will be available in the very near future – and you cover just 10% of the Sahara, you'd easily solve the world's energy needs. To make that possible, we'd need superconducting cables to get the electricity to the rest of Africa and the world, but once that technology's there, I can see the Sahara turning into a vast solar power station.

Automatic transport systems By 2020, self-driving vehicles could be quite common. Further into the future, we could very well have a country-wide transport system of small electric cars that would use electrified railways. You could tell a car where you want to go and lie back as it drives to the station, gets on the rails, drives quickly just inches from the cars in front, then gets off at the other end and drives you to your destination.

External brains By 2050, I can see us having probes that pick up signals from all over the brain. We'll then be able to use thought recognition and create computerised brain models in which you could run ultra-fast thought processes before feeding them back into the brain, massively increasing IQ. After the invention of a few key technologies, the next step could be uploading a brain onto a computer, then programming it into an android.

3 Read again. According to Ian, are these statements true or false?

1 A simple kind of active contact lens already exists.
2 We'll have permanent electronic 'tattoos' for identity purposes.
3 We might be able to phone someone just by thinking their number.
4 The Sahara could supply 30–40% of the world's energy needs.
5 Cars could be running on electric railways by 2020.
6 One day robots may be able to think in the same way as people.

SPEAKING

4 Talk together.

1 If these predictions came true, how would you feel about them?
2 Which do you think would have the most significant impact on the world? How?
3 Which predictions do you find the most and the least convincing? Why?

I'd be surprised if ...

VOCABULARY

Predicting the future

1 Which group of highlighted expressions A–C expresses the most certainty? Which expresses the least certainty?

A 1 In the future, **we'll see** high-definition lenses with full 3D virtual reality.
  2 **You won't need** a keyboard or a mobile phone.
  3 **I predict that** mobile phones will become obsolete by 2020.

B 4 **I'd be surprised if** an active skin prototype isn't available in about five years.
  5 **I can see** the Sahara turning into a vast solar power station.
  6 Further into the future, **we could very well** have a country-wide transport system of small electric cars.

C 7 There's also **the possibility that** 'thought recognition' could allow you to just think the number.
  8 **The next step could be** uploading a brain onto a computer, then programming it into an android.

VOCABULARY

Future time expressions

2 a Look at the sentences in 1 again and find four time expressions. Write them below.

1	in ____ ____	5	within a few years	9	in about ten years' time
2	by ____	6	within my lifetime	10	by the end of the century
3	in ____ ____ ____	7	in the short term	11	before long
4	____ into ____ ____	8	in the long term	12	Looking ahead, ...

b Compare ideas. Which expressions in 2a would you say are about:

a the near future?   b the distant future?   c the future in general?

c Look at these pairs of sentences. Which mean the same, and which are different?

1 a Mobile phones will become obsolete in 2020.
  b Mobile phones will become obsolete by 2020.
2 a It will become available in about five years.
  b It will become available in about five years' time.
3 a Oil will run out in a few years.
  b Oil will run out within a few years.

3 Use expressions from 1 and 2a to write six sentences predicting the future. Think about, for example:

your company or college   your country's economy   international relations
the mind and body   your city's population   transport and travel   sports
the media and information exchange

SPEAKING

4 In groups, compare your predictions and give reasons for them. Choose the two predictions you think are most likely to come true, and the two that are least likely.

5 Tell the other groups which predictions you chose and why. As a class, decide which are the two most and two least likely predictions.

Yes Man

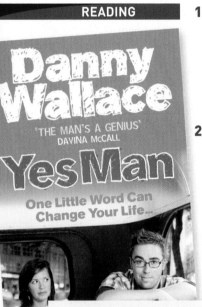

READING

1 a Look at the cover of *Yes Man*, by Danny Wallace. Do you know – or can you guess – what it's about?

b Read the blurb on the back of the book to check. How do you think Danny's decision could affect his life?

2 Read an extract from Danny's book.

1 How does Danny feel?
2 How long does he plan to say 'yes' to everything?
3 Why doesn't he want the double-glazed windows?

Danny Wallace

Yes Man

Danny Wallace had been staying in. Far too much. Having been dumped by his girlfriend, he was avoiding people. Texting them instead of calling them. Calling them instead of meeting them. That is until one day when a mystery man on a late-night bus told him to ... 'SAY YES MORE'. These three simple words changed Danny's life forever.

Yes Man is the story of what happened when Danny decided to say YES to everything.

I was angry at myself. I had wasted half a year after being dumped. Half a year gone. Thrown away. Swapped for toast, and evenings in front of the telly.

I had to get back out there. I had to start living life, rather than just living.

And it was obvious how.

Say Yes more.

I would say Yes more. Saying Yes more would get me out of this rut. It would rekindle my love for life. It would bring back the old me. I just needed a little kickstart. A little fun. A chance to live in a completely different way. I could treat it like an experiment. A study in my own behaviour. A study in positivity, and opportunity, and chance.

A day. Yes. A day of relentless positivity. What harm could that do? A day of saying Yes. Yes to anything. Anything and everything.

'Hello, can I speak to Mr Wallace, please?'
'Yes!'
'Hello, Mr Wallace, I'm phoning from Mark 1 Double Glazing in London. Would you have a moment to talk about double glazing, sir?'
'Yes!'
'Have you ever thought about having your house or apartment double-glazed at all?'

'Yes!'
'And have you been put off in the past by high prices at all?'
'Yes, I have, Yes.'
'Can I ask you, would you be interested in a free, no-obligation quote for double glazing on your property, Mr Wallace?'
'Yes!'
'Okay ... well, what we can do is, we can certainly send one of our representatives round to your residence. Is there a particular time or day that's good for you?'
'You suggest a time.'
'Right. How are you fixed for Tuesday, Mr Wallace?'
'Yes, Tuesday. Yes.'
'2 pm?'
'Yes. Um ... I should warn you, though ... I am already fully double-glazed.'
'You're what, sorry?'
'I already have double glazing throughout my flat.'
'Well, wait a second ... why would you want a quote?'
'Well, you asked, and –'
'I have to go now, Mr Wallace, okay?'
'Yes.'
And that is how my Yes experiment started.

---

3 Find these expressions in the first part of the extract. Discuss what they could mean, using the context to help you. Then check in a dictionary or ask your teacher.

1 dumped
2 get back out there
3 get out of this rut

4 rekindle my love for life
5 a little kickstart
6 relentless

SPEAKING

4 Talk together.

1 Would you ever be prepared to try an experiment like Danny's? Why? / Why not?
2 Do you know of anyone who got tired of their old life and made a big change? How? What was the result?

I'll have published ...

Eamonn from Ireland

1 🔊 3.33 Listen to Eamonn and Liliya talking about their lives.

1 Who likes planning things? Whose approach to life is more spontaneous?
2 Who mentions these topics – Eamonn, Liliya or both?
money work home children flying holidays writing

2 🔊 3.33 Eamonn and Liliya each mention three predictions or hopes. Listen again.

1 What are they?
2 What details do they give about each one?

Liliya from Russia

GRAMMAR

Future progressive and future perfect

3 a Which of these sentences from the listening describes:

a an action finished before a point in the future?
b an activity in progress at a point in the future?

> 1 In about ten years' time, my wife and I **will** probably **be living** in Portugal.
> 2 Hopefully, I'll **have published** another novel by the end of next year.

b How do you make the two forms?

1 future progressive: *will* + _____ + _____
2 future perfect: *will* + _____ + _____

4 You can use expressions other than will in progressive and perfect forms about the future. How do these highlighted expressions differ in meaning from will?

1 In a few years, I **may** be living abroad.
2 In ten years, I **hope** to have set up a business.
3 In five years' time, I **might** have bought a new flat.
4 By 2020, I **should** be nearing the end of my career.
5 In ten years' time, I **expect** to have done a doctorate.

Grammar reference and practice, p140

5 Look in Eamonn's and Liliya's scripts on pp157–8. Find more sentences where they use progressive and perfect forms to talk about the future.

PRONUNCIATION

Fluent speech 4 – double contractions

6 a 🔊 3.34 Listen to Eamonn's sentences. Notice that *have* is pronounced /əv/, making two contractions in a row: *'ll've*. Practise saying the sentences.

Hopefully, I'll have published another novel by the end of next year.
By that time, I'll have saved up enough money to buy a place with a sea view.

How would you say *will not have*?

b Practise saying these sentences with double contractions.

1 She will have got her exam results by then.
2 They will have completed it by the weekend.
3 They will not have decided before tomorrow.
4 It will have stopped raining soon.
5 I will not have started college until September.

You can *say* double contractions but it's not usual to *write* them.

SPEAKING

7 Tell a partner your predictions, hopes and expectations for your future, and give reasons. Talk about your:

ambitions interests relationships appearance possessions status ...

Use the future progressive and future perfect with suitable time expressions.

I think I'll be/have ...   I should be/have ...   I hope to be/have ...
Ideally, I'd like to be/have ...   I might be/have ...   I expect to be/have ...

8 Get into new pairs and tell each other what you learned about your first partner. Would you say their approach to life is more planned or more spontaneous?

14.3 Target activity

Choose the right candidate

14.3 goals
- talk about the future ♻
- describe personal hopes and expectations ♻
- take part in a job interview

TASK READING

1 a Look at the picture of a research station in the Antarctic. Can you guess:

1 how many people work there?
2 what jobs they do?
3 how they spend their free time?

b Read the job advertisement to check.

www.jobopportunities.com

Human Resources Assistant

Are you looking for a big change in your life? One that combines true adventure with employment? How would you like to be one of the few people that have the chance to live and work in Antarctica, a unique and unspoiled environment? We are looking for a Human Resources Assistant to fill a two-year position beginning from March 1. This position will draw on all your skills and add a valuable, attention-getting job experience to your CV.

Responsibilities Provides support to the Human Resources Manager. Handles all issues with total confidentiality. Helps to create and maintain employee files. Assists the Manager in matters related to salaries, employee evaluation and training. Up to 70 employees, many of them scientists, work in the research station.

Requirements A degree is preferred, but professional experience can be accepted instead of a degree. Should be computer literate with a good knowledge of Excel and Word. Must be attentive to detail, able to work independently and have strong organisational and people skills. Must be in good health. Preference will be given to candidates who can contribute significantly to the social life of the station.

Living and working in the Antarctic In summer, temperatures average –10°C on sunny days. In winter, temperatures often drop below –20°C, sometimes down to –50°C. Mechanics, engineers, a chef and a doctor are in the station at all times. Popular free-time activities include skiing, snowboarding, dog sledding, bird and animal watching, photography and films.

2 Read the advert again. Find the following key information:

1 job title
2 duration of job
3 start date
4 duties
5 required attributes
6 preferred attributes

TASK VOCABULARY

Interview questions

3 Replace the <u>underlined</u> parts of the questions with a–h to make new questions.

1 What are your reasons for <u>applying for this position</u>?
2 What would you say are <u>your greatest strengths</u>?
3 Are you confident that <u>you'll complete the full two years</u>?
4 What contributions will you make to <u>good staff relations</u>?
5 How will you handle <u>living in a closed community</u>?
6 What do you hope to have achieved <u>after six months in the job</u>?
7 What do you intend to do <u>after this job</u>?
8 What do you think you'll be doing in <u>five years' time</u>?

a by the time you go home
b you have the right people skills
c spending so much time indoors
d wanting a change in your life
e with the skills you gain
f the social life of the station
g ten years
h your weaker points

TASK

4 In pairs, prepare for a job interview for the position of HR Assistant.

1 Make a list of questions you'd ask an applicant. Use 3 and your own ideas.
2 Now imagine you're the applicant. Say how you'd answer your own questions.

5 Change pairs. Have job interviews. Take turns to be interviewer and candidate.

6 a Go back to your first partner. Discuss the people you interviewed and decide who you'd offer the job to.

b Who were offered jobs? Why? Would anyone *really* like to work in the Antarctic?

Across cultures Recruitment

READING

1 Read the advice for people who are preparing for a job interview abroad. What information would you give these people about customs in your country?

Preparing for a job interview abroad

- Access the official tourism site for the country or city where you are being interviewed. Most large cities and almost all countries have a national ministry or board of tourism that publishes information regarding local customs.
- Know what topics of conversation are considered appropriate in business situations or job interviews. Some cultures consider too much personal information to be rude, while in other cultures, it is offensive if you do not enquire about someone's family before conducting business.
- Have business cards printed in English on one side and the language of the country of your interview on the reverse side. Many countries exchange business cards in any professional meeting.
- Know local customs regarding non-verbal communication. Research whether a handshake is appropriate or if bowing is expected. Some cultures consider prolonged eye contact aggressive.
- Learn the customs regarding names. In many countries, using a first name is reserved for good friends or is used only after meeting many times.

LISTENING

2 🎧 **3.35** Listen to the two pairs of speakers discussing recruitment and interviews in their countries. Which pair talks about these topics – Iain and Barbara, Lixing and Cian, or both?

covering letters   CVs   internships   interviews   job advertisements
personalities   salaries

Lixing from China

Iain from England

3 a 🎧 **3.35** Listen again. Which countries do these sentences refer to?

1 CVs usually include a main objective, details of experience and references.
2 You should submit a covering letter along with your CV.
3 Interviews can be quite conversational, to show how you'd deal with clients.
4 Salaries aren't usually discussed until you're offered the job.
5 Interviews for new graduates tend to focus on personality and psychology.
6 New graduates should usually have some internship experience.
7 To get to the interview stage, you really need to sell yourself in your CV and covering letter.
8 Interviewers sometimes observe candidates having group discussions, to see how they interact.

Barbara from Venezuela

Cian from Ireland

b Read the scripts on p158 to check.

VOCABULARY
Recruitment

4 a In pairs, look at the sentences in 3a again. Note down one or two expressions from each sentence which could be useful for talking about recruitment.

1 CV   a main objective

b Compare your choices with another pair or as a class.

SPEAKING

5 Read a final piece of advice from the website. Why should you research an organisation before you go for an interview there?

- Remember that differences in the recruitment process are not just a matter of national borders. Each profession and organisation has its own 'culture'. Finding out about an organisation can be just as important as knowing the local customs. Check their website and even contact employees to find out if there are any guidelines you should follow.

6 a Prepare to talk about how recruitment is done in a field of work you know about.

1 Choose topics from 2 and any other topics you think are important.
2 Choose expressions you noted in 4a to help you talk about your topics.

b Tell each other about recruitment in your field. What are the main differences?

1 When do people have to write formal letters or emails saying 'no'? For example:

refusing a job application   turning down a dinner invitation   ...

2 Read the letter and email. What do the writers say 'no' to? What reasons do they give?

Dear Mr Brackley,

[1]We'd like to thank you for coming to the interview for the position of Financial Services Advisor on 14 August. [2]We were pleased to have the opportunity to discuss your qualifications and expectations.

We have given your application a great deal of consideration but [3]we regret to inform you that [4]we are unable to offer you a position at this time. There was considerable competition for the position and many of the applicants had many years of experience in banking. We feel that you have a great deal of potential but do not yet have the necessary experience for this position.

[5]Would you mind if we keep your records on file? [6]We will certainly contact you if any suitable vacancies arise in future.

Yours sincerely,

Chris Pattinson

Christopher Pattinson
Human Resources Manager

Delete   Reply   Reply All   Forward   Print

Dear Estelle,

[7]Many thanks for helping us with the preparations for the Avondale Community Summer Party last month. [8]We very much appreciated the efforts you made to decorate the community centre and grounds. Your contribution played a significant role in the success of the event.

You asked if you could help out again with the Autumn Festival. [9]I am sorry to say that we already have enough volunteers for that event and that, as far as we know at this point, [10]we will not be needing any more.

[11]We have your contact details, of course, and [12]we will be sure to get in touch if we require your assistance for any future event. Thank you very much again.

Best wishes,
Gudrun Olsen

---

3 a Look at the expressions 1–12 in the letters. Which do the writers use to:

a thank people or express appreciation?   b say 'no'?   c refer to possible future contact?

b Now add these expressions to the right groups a–c.

We will let you know if ...	We'd like to take this opportunity to thank you ...
Unfortunately, it is not possible to ...	I have made a note of your telephone number ...
We're sorry to have to tell you that ...	We'd like to express our gratitude for ...

4 a Read the two situations. In pairs, choose one of them.

1   Marina Vargas has been invited by Liang Shen to present a paper at an economics conference in Taiwan. She can't attend but wants to participate in future events held by his organisation. She might be able to go in the first half of next year. Marina writes to Liang Shen.
2   Kevin Hall was assistant coach for the Children's Basketball Club last season, which was very successful. He wants to do it again. However, the coach has resigned, the future of the Club is in doubt, and they don't need him at present. Casey Mann, the Club director, writes to Kevin.

b Plan a formal letter or email of refusal together. Decide:

1   how many paragraphs you need, and what each will be about.
2   what details you should include in each paragraph.
3   which expressions to use from 3a and 3b.

5 Work on your own. Write your letter or email.

6 Read your partner's letter or email. Do you think it's clear enough? Is it polite?

Review

VOCABULARY Predicting the future

1 a Complete Kimi's predictions about her son with these expressions.

> I'd be surprised if   the next step could be
> I predict that   could very well   I can see
> there's the possibility that

My son is training to be a vet. He's a hard worker so ¹_____ he'll do very well in his final exams and ²_____ he didn't find a position right away at an animal hospital, though ³_____ he might work at a zoo or maybe an animal park. In several years' time, he ⁴_____ have his own clinic and – who knows? – ⁵_____ opening his own animal hospital. He has always loved animals so ⁶_____ him being a success in this field. He'll enjoy every minute of it!

b Write a paragraph about the future of someone you know well. Use expressions from 1a.

c Exchange paragraphs with a partner. Ask questions to find out more details.

GRAMMAR Future progressive and future perfect

2 a Complete 1–4 using the future progressive or future perfect. Then write two more questions.

1 What / you / achieve / in a year's time?
2 What / you / do / at 1.30 pm tomorrow?
3 How many people / you / speak to / by the end of today?
4 What / you / do / at midnight on New Year's Eve?

b Ask and answer the questions.

CAN YOU REMEMBER? Unit 13 – Making your case

3 a Put the lines of the conversation in order.

How about going to the cinema tonight? _1_

So I can do the shopping. In any case, you need an evening off. ___

That's no problem. We can do it tomorrow. ___

Good idea, but what about the shopping? ___

You know I'm working all day tomorrow! ___

b Which highlighted expressions in 3a could you replace with these expressions?

> In that case,   And besides,
> I've thought about that.   I'm afraid

c Work in pairs. You're friends with different ideas about how to spend the weekend. Make conversations like the one in 3a. Take turns to start.

Extension

SPELLING AND SOUNDS /ɪə/

4 a Complete the spelling of these words with: e ear eer ere

__phones   __rings   car__   cl__   disapp__
engin__   p__riod   s__rious   sinc__   sph__

b Which spelling is usually used:

a at the start of words?
b in the middle?

Which three spellings can be used at the end of words?

c ● 3.36 Spellcheck. Listen and write ten words. Then check your spelling on p158.

NOTICE Planning and spontaneity

5 a Look at Eamonn's and Liliya's scripts on pp157–8 and complete these expressions.

I tend to …	react to ¹c_____.
	react to the way things are ²g_____.
	act on the ³s_____ of the moment.
	plan ⁴a_____.
	make sure everything's in ⁵p_____.
	respond to things ⁶s_____.
	respond to things on a ⁷d_____ basis.

b Who do you know, or know of, that behaves in the ways described above? Give examples.

Self-assessment

Can you do these things in English? Circle a number on each line. 1 = I can't do this, 5 = I can do this well.

⊙ talk about the future	1 2 3 4 5
⊙ make predictions about the world	1 2 3 4 5
⊙ describe personal hopes and expectations	1 2 3 4 5
⊙ take part in a job interview	1 2 3 4 5
⊙ write a formal letter or email of refusal	1 2 3 4 5

• For Wordcards, reference and saving your work → e-Portfolio
• For more practice → Self-study Pack, Unit 14

Activities

Unit 1, p7, I'm not really convinced 5

1

Team Sports Participation Reduces Likelihood Of Youths Becoming Smokers

Participating in team sports will reduce the chance of a young person becoming a smoker, according to a new report.

2

Fathers Spend More Time With Children Who Look Like Them

Darwin's theory of evolution predicts that men will take more care of children that look like them. Now a study has been published suggesting that this is true.

3

Foods Bad For The Teeth Are Also Bad For The Body

Dental problems may be a warning of future, more serious health problems resulting from poor diet.

4

Does Size Matter? Study Shows Taller People Earn More Money

Taller men are able to earn more money than shorter men simply because taller people are perceived to be more intelligent and powerful, according to a new study.

5

Doctor's Compassion May Help Cure Colds Faster

Some cold medicines often produce unpleasant side effects. A new study shows, for the first time, that a doctor's sympathy may be a better way to speed recovery.

Unit 2, p18, Target activity 6a (Student A)

Situation 1

You're a **customer** of EPC, a company which provides your home internet and cable TV connection. You're not satisfied with EPC's service because you work from home and you need the internet for your work, but last month the internet wasn't working properly. You've registered a complaint on the EPC website and now you're expecting a call from one of their customer service managers.

Before you talk, **decide on the answers to these questions**:
1 What exactly were the problems with the internet? How long did they last?
2 How many times did you contact EPC about the problems? What did they say or do?
3 How did the problems affect you? How much did they cost you in time or money?
4 Was the cable TV service OK, or were there problems with that too?
Choose language from **Vocabulary** *Explaining a complaint* to use in your answers.

Situation 2

You work as a **customer service manager** for ThomAir, an international airline. One of your customers has registered a complaint on your website and asked for someone to phone him/her. You know that this is a very regular customer and that he/she is very unhappy about something that happened recently, but you don't have any details. Your job is to find out exactly what the problem is and to offer appropriate compensation.

Before you make the call, **think about**:
1 how to open the call.
2 what questions you could ask.
3 what kinds of action or compensation you could offer.

Unit 2, p15, Not my day 7a (Student A)

Situation 1

It's evening. You arranged to meet Student B at the cinema today but when you arrived an hour ago, he/she wasn't there. You haven't received any messages from Student B. You're a bit worried. Maybe he/she just missed the bus, or maybe there's been an accident. Phone and find out what happened.

Situation 2

Recently it was your birthday and you got lots of gifts and cards by post from friends and family. You thanked everyone but there were two gifts – a book and a watch – that had no sender's name or address on them. This evening, you're at a party and you see Student B, an old friend. You think maybe he/she sent you the gifts, but you're not sure so you don't want to ask.

Situation 3

Student B invited a group of friends you have in common to a party at his/her house. You didn't get an invitation and didn't even know about the party until someone told you about it the next day. You think Student B left you out on purpose, but you don't understand why. You feel upset. A few days later, you're out shopping when you suddenly see Student B coming towards you.

Unit 4, p 32, Two voices 1b (Group B)

Article | Discussion

🔍 Log in/create account

Bohumil Hrabal – the close watcher of trains

by Mats Larsson

"BOHUMIL HRABAL TRAGICALLY DEAD" said the headline on the front page of *Mladá fronta*, the Czech Republic's most popular daily newspaper. The 82-year-old Hrabal died instantly when, on 3 February 1997, he fell from a fifth-floor window of a hospital in Prague. According to witnesses, he was trying to feed the pigeons at his window when the table he was standing on fell over. But the particular significance of the fifth floor in Hrabal's life and work has led some to wonder whether his death was an accident or suicide. His Prague apartment was located on the fifth floor and his fear of falling from this floor was well known. Suicides by jumping from a fifth-floor window occur several times in his writings.

During Hrabal's lifetime, nearly three million copies of his books were printed in his native Czechoslovakia and he has been translated into twenty-seven languages. One of his most famous works, *Dancing Lessons for the Advanced in Age*, is a story written in a single sentence, which came out in more editions than any other of his works. *Closely Watched Trains*, his book about a little train station under German occupation, is one of many of his novels adapted for film. Directed by Jirí Menzel, the movie won an Oscar for Best Foreign Film in 1967.

Although he started out as a poet, Hrabal had his first breakthrough with a collection of short stories at the age of 49. From 1963 to 1968, he published eight works but was then banned from publishing. Only in 1975 did he regain the right to publish, but still several of his most important works could only be published abroad. After the Velvet Revolution in 1989, a number of Hrabal's previously banned books were published, and the first of his collected writings – in nineteen volumes – came out in 1991.

Everything Hrabal wrote was based on real events; nothing was invented. As one of his admirers put it, instead of a brain, Hrabal had a hard disk which stored everything. While sitting among his admirers at the Golden Tiger, a favourite pub in Prague, Hrabal could effortlessly recite long passages from books he had read during his youth.

Unit 2, p15, Not my day 7a (Student B)

Situation 1
You and Student A have arranged to meet at a cinema tomorrow evening. You've written the date in your diary and you're looking forward to it. At the moment you're in a café, chatting with another friend who you haven't seen for a long time. Suddenly, you get a phone call from Student A.

Situation 2
Recently you bought a birthday gift for Student A – a watch – and sent it to him/her by post. A week has passed but you haven't heard anything from Student A. You think maybe he/she didn't like the watch but you feel too embarrassed to phone and ask. This evening, however, you're at a party and you see Student A. You decide to ask about the watch.

Situation 3
You recently invited a group of friends to a party, which everyone enjoyed. Strangely, one of your closest friends, Student A, didn't come – even though you'd sent him/her an invitation. You think maybe Student A was away somewhere or got confused about the date. A few days later, you happen to meet Student A in a local shop. Find out what happened.

Unit 2, p18, Target activity 6a (Student B)

Situation 1
You work as a **customer service manager** for EPC, a company which provides internet, telephone and cable TV services to people's homes. One of your customers has registered a complaint on your website and asked for someone to phone him/her. You know that the customer pays for an internet connection and cable TV and that he/she is very unhappy, but you don't have any details. Your job is to find out exactly what the problem is and to offer appropriate compensation.

Before you make the call, **think about**:
1 how to open the call.
2 what questions you could ask.
3 what kinds of action or compensation you could offer.

Situation 2
You're a regular **customer** of ThomAir, an international airline. You're unhappy with ThomAir because last Tuesday your evening flight to an important meeting was cancelled and you were moved to a flight on Wednesday morning. You paid a lot for the ticket because you wanted to fly on that particular day. You've registered a complaint on the ThomAir website and asked for a representative of the company to call you.

Before you talk, **decide on the answers to these questions**:
1 Why was it so important for you to fly on Tuesday?
2 When did you hear about the cancellation? Where did you spend Tuesday evening?
3 How did the cancellation affect you? How much did it cost you in time or money?
4 Have you already spoken to anyone at ThomAir about this? What did they say or do?
Choose language from **Vocabulary Explaining a complaint** to use in your answers.

Unit 5, p43, Keyword 4 (Group A)

Hi Keith,
As you know, I'm putting together the agenda for Monday's meeting. I was wondering if you had any last-minute points to add?
Leona

1

Sorry Keith: I did ask about changing the date as promised, but half the sales team are on a training course from Tuesday! So it looks like we'll have to go ahead on Monday as planned. Hope you can still make it (even if only the morning part?) L.

3

Thanks for your understanding about the date, and yes, the time/venue are unchanged. Here's the agenda. Could you have a quick look through before I send it round? As you'll see, it's pretty full. L.

5

Unit 5, p44, Explore speaking 5a (Group B)

Situation 1
You're colleagues deciding where to have the company party. You think it should be in a café with a garden.

Situation 3
You're guests on a radio show discussing what kind of books teach you more about life. You believe non-fiction books do this.

Situation 2
You're friends at university considering if you should have a cleaning rota in your flat. You think it's a bad idea.

Situation 4
You're a married couple deciding what kind of animal to get as a pet. You'd prefer to have a tortoise.

Unit 7, p57, I saw atoms dancing … 3a (Student A)

Unit 8, p67, Across cultures 1b

alphabet – Greek
boss – Dutch
cotton – Arabic
hamburger – German
ketchup – Cantonese

marriage – French
opera – Italian
plaza – Spanish
robot – Czech
sauna – Finnish

shampoo – Hindi
ski – Norwegian
tsunami – Japanese
yoghurt – Turkish

Unit 9, p77, Look again 2b

1 an exam
2 an application form
3 a newspaper
4 the workplace
5 a recipe
6 a family kitchen

Unit 10, p84, Explore writing 6

A possible summary of *Forget space travel. The ocean is our final frontier.*

Even though we spend a fortune on space exploration, we still know very little about the deep sea on our own planet. Water pressure makes deep-sea exploration very difficult but we know there are many unknown life forms there and instruments suggest the presence of huge creatures. Space exploration is best done by machines but deep-sea exploration needs to be done by people, using both ships and submersibles. Marine exploration can help us to understand the origins of life as well as helping us to develop new medicines and sources of food and energy.

Activities

Unit 5, p39

Digha II by Ananta Mandal

Nighthawks by Edward Hopper

One of the Family by Frederick Cotman

Returning Home by Hilda Vogl

Unit 7, p60, Explore speaking 4a (Student A)

Situation 1
You notice your friend is limping. You want to know what happened.

Situation 2
You recently had some bad news and find it hard to concentrate at work. What was the news? Do you want to talk about it with your boss?

Situation 3
You've just started a new job, which is the same as your neighbour's. You'd like to know what salary and benefits your neighbour gets so you can check that you're being treated fairly.

Situation 4
You split up with your girlfriend/boyfriend a few days ago. What happened? Are you ready to talk about it with a friend?

Situation 5
Recently your colleague has completely changed their hairstyle and the kind of clothes they wear. You're curious to know why.

Situation 6
You recently received a lot of money. How much? Where did you get it from? Are you willing to talk about it with a cousin?

Unit 5, p43, Keyword 4 (Group B)

Not to worry. I'll be there, though I might have to miss the afternoon as you suggested. Are the time and venue still as agreed last time (9.30 in Media Room B)? K.	Nothing to add thanks, but as I mentioned last week, Monday's pretty busy for me. I can do some rescheduling but would rather not. Any chance of a different day (Tue or Thu)? K.	This all looks fine to me Leona, but I'd put the time and room number at the top. As you probably remember, someone usually goes to the wrong room or turns up late! K.
2	4	6

Unit 6, p47, Consequences 3

1   A woman takes paper from the office for her kids to use at home.
2   A man withdraws $100 from a cash machine but $200 comes out. He keeps all the money.
3   A woman applies for a job she knows she can do but lies about her qualifications in order to get it.
4   A man buys lots of tickets for a major football match so he can sell them online to the highest bidder.
5   A woman sees her friend steal an expensive watch from a shop. She's shocked but does nothing.
6   A man says his daughter is younger than she really is to get a cheaper cinema seat.
7   A woman uses her brother's address to get her child into a better school than the one in her district.
8   A man says he's never had a serious illness to get a lower insurance rate. He's had two serious illnesses.

Unit 7, p58, Target activity 6a and 6b

CASE STUDY 2: KOFI

* Kofi is a university student with a part-time job in a coffee shop.
* He works with Rob, the manager, and Rob's sister, Freda.
* He's noticed Freda giving free coffee to her friends a few times – it could be more often.
* When £20 went missing, he overheard Freda telling Rob it was probably "Kofi's mistake" – it wasn't.
* He also saw Freda cleaning tables that weren't hers and keeping the tips.
* He feels Freda's acting coldly towards him and treating him as a rival.
* He doesn't want to lose his job – student jobs are hard to get.
* Rob seems to value Freda (his sister, full-time employee, 3 years' experience) more than Kofi (part-time employee, 4 months' experience).

CASE STUDY 3: ROSARIO

* Rosario lives and works in one of two ground-floor flats.
* A family with two small children lives next door.
* She often hears the children playing in the back garden, screaming loudly. She can't concentrate on her work.
* She often sees the children eating in the garden and throwing leftover food on the ground.
* She noticed a rat coming into her garden from next door a month ago – and sees more rats running around now.
* She's spoken to the neighbours. They were friendly, but nothing's changed.
* The police won't be interested unless a crime is being committed.
* The owner of the building lives in another city and is very difficult to contact.

Unit 7, p57, I saw atoms dancing … 3a (Student B)

Unit 8, p66, Target activity 5a (Student A)

Situation 1

You and Student B share a second-floor flat. It's April, and you've just received an enormous water bill for the first three months of the year – more than double the normal amount! You're going to talk with your flatmate to try and work out what happened and what to do next.

Before you talk, think about these facts. What do they suggest could (or can't) have happened? Get ready to explain your ideas.

- *The water meters are in the corridor outside your flat.*
- *Last month the building administrators installed new water meters.*
- *You saw a young man reading the water meter last week.*
- *You had guests for a week in February.*
- *You bought a dishwasher in the January sales.*
- *A cleaner comes to your flat once a week.*
- *You both went away on holiday for two weeks in March.*
- *Living in the flat underneath you, there's an old man who loves complaining.*

Situation 2

You and Student B live together in a house. You went together to a party last night and when you got home, you found that your new flat-screen TV had been stolen. You've called the police and are waiting for them to arrive. You're going to talk with your flatmate to try and work out what happened and what to tell the police.

Before you talk, think about these facts. What do they suggest could (or can't) have happened? Get ready to explain your ideas.

- *Nothing seems to be missing from your room.*
- *The upstairs bathroom window's open.*
- *As you walked into your street, you noticed a van driving away in the distance.*
- *You don't think you've seen it before.*
- *When you got home, the front door was unlocked.*
- *The front door is undamaged.*
- *You can open the front door from the inside without a key.*
- *You had your outside windows cleaned recently by a friend and his partner.*
- *The TV is a big one: sixty inches.*

Unit 9, p71, First of all, ... 3a (Group B)

Imagine you're going to give a tour of a factory where **glass bottles** are made.

1 Read the information below. Check any words you don't know in a dictionary.
2 Make brief notes to help you give your tour:
   powder (sand, soda ash, limestone) – furnace (up to 1675ºC) – ...
3 Choose expressions from **Vocabulary** *Organising a description* to help you organise what you say.
4 Practise giving your tour with someone else from your group.

Glass is made out of various ingredients such as sand, soda ash and limestone.

1 *Melting the ingredients*
   – The bottle-makers crush the ingredients for glass to a powder and mix them up.
   – They melt the powder in large furnaces at high temperatures (up to 1675°C).
   – The melted glass emerges from the furnace, moving along a special channel.
   – As it moves along, it cools slightly and becomes a bit thicker.
2 *Forming the bottle*
   – A knife cuts the soft glass into simple cylinders.
   – The cylinder moves along and is pushed into a mould to half shape it.
   – Then it goes into another mould, where it's formed into its final shape.
3 *Cooling and finishing*
   – The glass shrinks and hardens as it cools.
   – To make it strong, the bottle goes into a special oven.
   – It's re-heated, then slowly cooled for 20–60 minutes.
   – It's examined to make sure it's perfect.
   – After that, it's ready for packaging and shipment.

Unit 10, p82, Target activity 5a (Student A)

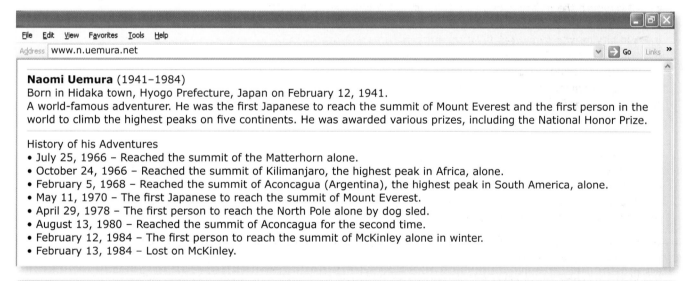

Naomi Uemura (1941–1984)
Born in Hidaka town, Hyogo Prefecture, Japan on February 12, 1941.
A world-famous adventurer. He was the first Japanese to reach the summit of Mount Everest and the first person in the world to climb the highest peaks on five continents. He was awarded various prizes, including the National Honor Prize.

History of his Adventures
• July 25, 1966 – Reached the summit of the Matterhorn alone.
• October 24, 1966 – Reached the summit of Kilimanjaro, the highest peak in Africa, alone.
• February 5, 1968 – Reached the summit of Aconcagua (Argentina), the highest peak in South America, alone.
• May 11, 1970 – The first Japanese to reach the summit of Mount Everest.
• April 29, 1978 – The first person to reach the North Pole alone by dog sled.
• August 13, 1980 – Reached the summit of Aconcagua for the second time.
• February 12, 1984 – The first person to reach the summit of McKinley alone in winter.
• February 13, 1984 – Lost on McKinley.

www.climbhistorystory.org

Naomi Uemura

Born in Hidaka, Hyogo Prefecture in 1941, Naomi Uemura was the second Japanese to reach the summit of Mt. Everest (May 11th 1970) or perhaps the first. As the story goes, Teruo Matsuura (who was one of the 39 climbers, 77 Sherpas and one woman on the expedition) reached the top first. Although Naomi Uemura led almost all the route from the last camp to the top, at the final moment, he gave way to the elder Matsuura. Uemura would go on to solo climb Kilimanjaro in Africa, Aconcagua in South America, Mt. Blanc in Europe, and McKinley in North America.

His other adventurous exploits are impressive as well, including rafting solo 6,500 kilometers down the Amazon River and trekking 12,000 kilometers solo across the Arctic from Greenland to Alaska. On May 1st 1978, he was the first person to reach the North Pole alone. The trip took Uemura 57 gruelling days by dogsled.

On his 43rd birthday (February 12, 1984), he became the first solo climber to reach the summit of 6,194-meter Mt. McKinley (Denali) in winter. He lost radio contact the following day and is presumed dead.

Unit 7, p60, Explore speaking 4a (Student B)

Situation 1
You recently hurt your leg. How? Do you want to talk about it with a friend?

Situation 2
You've noticed that one of your employees looks distracted and their work is not of its usual high quality. You decide to talk to the employee privately and ask what's wrong.

Situation 3
You receive a good salary and benefits from your company. What are they? Are you willing to give details about them to your neighbour?

Situation 4
Your friend split up with their girlfriend/boyfriend a few days ago. You're extremely curious to know the details.

Situation 5
Recently you completely changed your hairstyle and the kind of clothes you wear. What were your reasons? Are you willing to discuss them with a colleague?

Situation 6
You've noticed your cousin has suddenly become a lot wealthier for no obvious reason. You want to know how.

Unit 8, p66, Target activity 5a (Student B)

Situation 1
You and Student A share a second-floor flat. It's April, and you've just received an enormous water bill for the first three months of the year – more than double the normal amount! You're going to talk with your flatmate to try and work out what happened and what to do next.

Before you talk, think about these facts. What do they suggest could (or can't) have happened? Get ready to explain your ideas.

- *The water meters are in the corridor outside your flat.*
- *Last month the building administrators installed new water meters.*
- *You saw a middle-aged woman reading the water meter last week.*
- *Your flatmate had guests for a week in February.*
- *You've employed a cleaner since this time last year.*
- *You both went away on holiday for two weeks in March.*
- *You've got a very old washing machine.*
- *A nice family of five lives opposite you.*

Situation 2
You and Student A live together in a house. You went together to a party last night and when you got home, you found that your new flat-screen TV had been stolen. You've called the police and are waiting for them to arrive. You're going to talk with your flatmate to try and work out what happened and what to tell the police.

Before you talk, think about these facts. What do they suggest could (or can't) have happened? Get ready to explain your ideas.

- *A pair of trainers is missing from your room.*
- *The upstairs bathroom window's open.*
- *As you walked into your street, you passed a man walking in the opposite direction. You think you've seen him before.*
- *When you got home, the front door was unlocked.*
- *The front door is undamaged.*
- *You can open the front door from the inside without a key.*
- *Two friends of your flatmate recently came to clean the windows outside.*
- *The TV is a big one: sixty inches.*

Unit 9, p71, First of all, ... 3a (Group A)

Imagine you're going to give a tour of the factory where they make **Maldon salt**.

1 Read the information below. Check any words you don't know in a dictionary.
2 Make brief notes to help you give your tour:
   Blackwater River (middle, saltiest) – tanks – ...
3 Choose expressions from **Vocabulary** *Organising a description* to help you organise what you say.
4 Practise giving your tour with someone else from your group.

The Maldon Crystal Salt Company has been producing table salt for over 200 years. It exports salt around the world, where its texture and taste have made it popular with gourmets and chefs.

1 *Getting and cleaning the water*
   – The company uses water from the Blackwater River.
   – The water comes from the middle of the river, where it's saltiest.
   – The water is put in large storage tanks and left to settle.
   – They filter out tiny pieces of sand and mud.

2 *Making the crystals*
   – They pour the water into large stainless steel pans and heat it to boiling point.
   – Any impurities that come to the surface are removed.
   – The temperature is carefully controlled for 15 to 16 hours.
   – As the water evaporates, salt crystals form on the surface.
   – The crystals slowly grow until they sink to the bottom because of their weight.
   – Eventually the water reduces to the same level as the crystals.

3 *Drying the crystals*
   – The salt-makers carefully pick up the crystals, put them in bins and leave them to drain.
   – They put them in the drying boxes.
   – When totally dry, the salt is ready for packing and distribution.

Unit 10, p82, Target activity 5a (Student B)

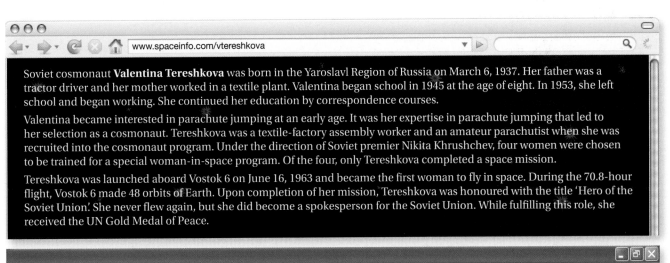

www.spaceinfo.com/vtereshkova

Soviet cosmonaut **Valentina Tereshkova** was born in the Yaroslavl Region of Russia on March 6, 1937. Her father was a tractor driver and her mother worked in a textile plant. Valentina began school in 1945 at the age of eight. In 1953, she left school and began working. She continued her education by correspondence courses.

Valentina became interested in parachute jumping at an early age. It was her expertise in parachute jumping that led to her selection as a cosmonaut. Tereshkova was a textile-factory assembly worker and an amateur parachutist when she was recruited into the cosmonaut program. Under the direction of Soviet premier Nikita Khrushchev, four women were chosen to be trained for a special woman-in-space program. Of the four, only Tereshkova completed a space mission.

Tereshkova was launched aboard Vostok 6 on June 16, 1963 and became the first woman to fly in space. During the 70.8-hour flight, Vostok 6 made 48 orbits of Earth. Upon completion of her mission, Tereshkova was honoured with the title 'Hero of the Soviet Union'. She never flew again, but she did become a spokesperson for the Soviet Union. While fulfilling this role, she received the UN Gold Medal of Peace.

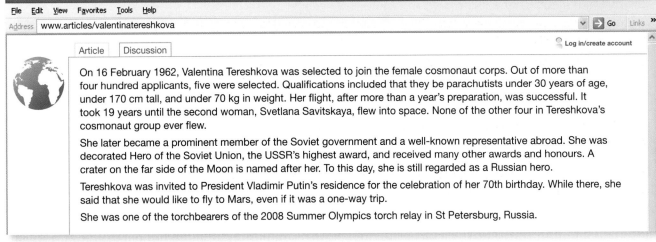

File   Edit   View   Favorites   Tools   Help

Address   www.articles/valentinatereshkova   Go   Links »

Log in/create account

Article   Discussion

On 16 February 1962, Valentina Tereshkova was selected to join the female cosmonaut corps. Out of more than four hundred applicants, five were selected. Qualifications included that they be parachutists under 30 years of age, under 170 cm tall, and under 70 kg in weight. Her flight, after more than a year's preparation, was successful. It took 19 years until the second woman, Svetlana Savitskaya, flew into space. None of the other four in Tereshkova's cosmonaut group ever flew.

She later became a prominent member of the Soviet government and a well-known representative abroad. She was decorated Hero of the Soviet Union, the USSR's highest award, and received many other awards and honours. A crater on the far side of the Moon is named after her. To this day, she is still regarded as a Russian hero.

Tereshkova was invited to President Vladimir Putin's residence for the celebration of her 70th birthday. While there, she said that she would like to fly to Mars, even if it was a one-way trip.

She was one of the torchbearers of the 2008 Summer Olympics torch relay in St Petersburg, Russia.

Unit 8, p66, Target activity 7

Possible explanations

Situation 1

It's unlikely that the guests or the cleaner can be the reason for the big water bill: the guests were only with you for a week, and the cleaner's been working for you for a year, so why would she suddenly start using lots of water? The old washing machine is also unlikely: if it had leaked, the water would surely have gone into the flat below, where your bad-tempered neighbour would have no hesitation in complaining. It's hard to see how the holiday could be significant: again, if there'd been a flood while you were away – or if someone had been using your flat! – you would surely have heard about it. The most likely explanation seems to be that the water company has made a mistake: there's a problem with the new meters, they've been connected up wrongly, or an employee has made a mistake. The fact that two different people came to look at the meters in such a short space of time is suspicious. Perhaps the water company has received complaints from other users?

Situation 2

It's impossible to be sure exactly what happened, but here's a scenario which fits the facts. First, the fact that two such specific items were taken – and one of them so big – suggests that the burglary was planned and that there was more than one burglar. At least one burglar must have come in through the open bathroom window and opened the front door from the inside, possibly to allow an accomplice inside. The burglars would then have been able to carry the TV outside. They must have worked quickly and quietly, probably after dark, and they must have had a vehicle to put the TV in and drive away. How did the first burglar get up to the window? Surely a ladder, which the burglars would then have taken away as they left the scene. Obviously, suspicion must fall on the partner of Student A's friend who came to clean the windows. The significance of the man and the van you saw when coming home is not clear.

Unit 10, p82, Target activity 5a (Student C)

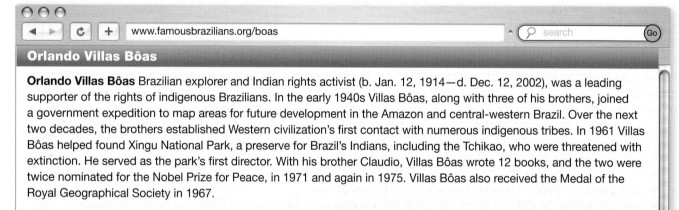

www.famousbrazilians.org/boas

Orlando Villas Bôas

Orlando Villas Bôas Brazilian explorer and Indian rights activist (b. Jan. 12, 1914—d. Dec. 12, 2002), was a leading supporter of the rights of indigenous Brazilians. In the early 1940s Villas Bôas, along with three of his brothers, joined a government expedition to map areas for future development in the Amazon and central-western Brazil. Over the next two decades, the brothers established Western civilization's first contact with numerous indigenous tribes. In 1961 Villas Bôas helped found Xingu National Park, a preserve for Brazil's Indians, including the Tchikao, who were threatened with extinction. He served as the park's first director. With his brother Claudio, Villas Bôas wrote 12 books, and the two were twice nominated for the Nobel Prize for Peace, in 1971 and again in 1975. Villas Bôas also received the Medal of the Royal Geographical Society in 1967.

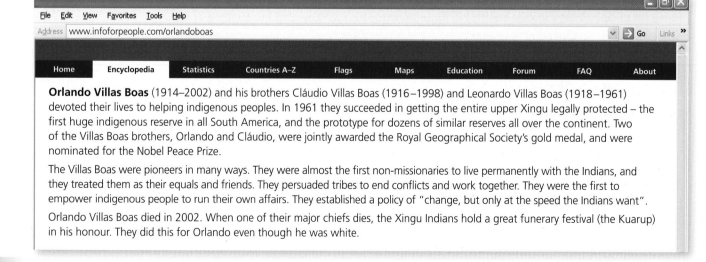

File   Edit   View   Favorites   Tools   Help

Address www.infoforpeople.com/orlandoboas

Home   Encyclopedia   Statistics   Countries A–Z   Flags   Maps   Education   Forum   FAQ   About

Orlando Villas Boas (1914–2002) and his brothers Cláudio Villas Boas (1916–1998) and Leonardo Villas Boas (1918–1961) devoted their lives to helping indigenous peoples. In 1961 they succeeded in getting the entire upper Xingu legally protected – the first huge indigenous reserve in all South America, and the prototype for dozens of similar reserves all over the continent. Two of the Villas Boas brothers, Orlando and Cláudio, were jointly awarded the Royal Geographical Society's gold medal, and were nominated for the Nobel Peace Prize.

The Villas Boas were pioneers in many ways. They were almost the first non-missionaries to live permanently with the Indians, and they treated them as their equals and friends. They persuaded tribes to end conflicts and work together. They were the first to empower indigenous people to run their own affairs. They established a policy of "change, but only at the speed the Indians want".

Orlando Villas Boas died in 2002. When one of their major chiefs dies, the Xingu Indians hold a great funerary festival (the Kuarup) in his honour. They did this for Orlando even though he was white.

Unit 12, p94, Placebo? 4 (Group B)

THE BELIEVER: JEANETTE WINTERSON
Picture this. I am staying in a remote cottage without a car. I have a temperature of 39°C, spots on my throat, delirium, and a book to finish writing. My desperate publisher suggests I call Hilary Fairclough, a homeopath, who sends round a remedy called Lachesis, made from snake venom. Four hours later, I have no symptoms whatsoever.

Right now, there is a fierce debate between those, like me, who trust homeopathy because it works for them, and those who call it nonsense, without clinical proof or any scientific basis. There have been a number of articles in the press criticising homeopathic remedies as worthless at best, and potentially lethal at worst, if they are being taken instead of tried and tested conventional medicines.

Good homeopaths know the value of conventional medicine and do not seek to weaken that value. Yet the long-term critics of homeopathy want it dead. Two weeks ago, an article in a leading medical journal called on doctors to tell their patients that homeopathic medicines offer no benefit. But where is the scientific sense in saying that because we don't understand something, even though we can see its effects, we have to show no respect for it or suppress it?

The placebo effect is common to all kinds of treatment, and it is valuable. But it is also true that many who visit a homeopath do so as a last resort, when nothing else is working. That such people often see an improvement suggests that the remedies themselves are contributing to the wellness of the individual.

Objections to homeopathy begin with what are viewed as the impossible dilutions of the remedies. Yet recent discoveries point to a whole new set of rules for the behaviour of substances in tiny quantities. We do not know whether this concerns homeopathic dilutions, but it may offer a clue.

I would like to see homeopathy better regulated. I would like to see homeopaths debating publicly with their critics, as well as initiating more research. There will always be dishonest homeopaths and bad homeopaths, but that is true of any profession.

Above all, we should be careful of dismissing the testimony of millions who say the remedies have worked for them.

Jeanette Winterson is a novelist and journalist.

5 Group B – read again. What examples does Jeanette give of:

1 homeopathic treatment that worked for her?
2 how some people criticise homeopathy?
3 improvements she thinks should be made to the field of homeopathy?

Unit 13, p106, Target activity 5 (Group A)

Read the situation.
You represent the **Hailey Arts Club**. You're going to have a party at the Torrington Hotel to launch your summer exhibition. Two months ago, you asked the Hotel to arrange a party for 100 people. You agreed a price and signed an agreement. There are only four days to go until the party but unfortunately, you've sold just 50 tickets. You now want a smaller party – and a lower price! You're going to meet the manager of the Hotel to try and renegotiate your agreement. Key facts:

o the price you originally agreed with the Hotel was $6000
o you've sold 50 tickets for $70 each (= $3500)
o you asked the Hotel to provide food and drink for 100 people
o you also asked the Hotel to hire a band and provide souvenirs with the Arts Club logo for all the guests
o the Hotel has already made some arrangements and spent some money – but you don't know how much
o legally, the Hotel can insist that you pay the full price …
o … but you're a regular customer of the Hotel and have always had good relations in the past

Prepare for the negotiation. Think about these questions.
1 What's the highest price you can accept? How much money are you prepared to lose?
2 What price will you ask for? What arguments will you use?
3 Can you offer the Hotel something instead of money?

Decide which expressions from 4a you could use.

Unit 13, p105, Let's talk it over 6

> ### Dealing with conflict – analysis
>
> Add up your score for each pair of statements as shown in the table. The highest score indicates your main style of conflict management.
>
> | Statements | Total | Style |
> |---|---|---|
> | 1, 5 | | **Collaboration:** Both sides get what they want.
Pros: Creates trust and positive relationships.
Cons: Time consuming, energy consuming, not always possible. |
> | 2, 6 | | **Competition:** Your aim is to win.
Pros: Goal-oriented, can be quick.
Cons: May create anger, destroy relationships. |
> | 3, 7 | | **Avoidance:** You avoid confrontation.
Pros: Does not increase conflict; delays difficulties.
Cons: Unresolved problems. |
> | 4, 8 | | **Compromise:** Both sides get something of what they want.
Pros: Useful in complex issues without simple solutions.
Cons: No one is ever completely satisfied. |

Unit 13, p106, Target activity 5 (Group B)

Read the situation.

You represent **the Torrington Hotel**. Two months ago, the Hailey Arts Club asked you to arrange a party for 100 people. You agreed a price and signed an agreement. There are only four days to go until the party but unfortunately, the Club has sold just 50 tickets. They now want a smaller party – and a lower price! You're going to meet the secretary of the Club to discuss the situation. Key facts:

- the price you originally agreed with the Club was $6000
- you've already bought food ($1000) and drink ($1000) for 100 people
- you've ordered souvenirs with the Arts Club logo for all the guests ($500)
- you've bought room and table decorations ($500)
- you've hired a band ($500 deposit, non-refundable)
- you've promised overtime payments to staff ($1000)
- legally, you can insist that the Club pay the full price …
- … but they are regular customers and you've always had good relations in the past

Prepare for the negotiation. Think about these questions.

1 What's the lowest price you can accept? Could you use any of the things you've bought for other events?
2 What price will you offer? What arguments will you use?
3 Can you offer the Club something instead of a lower price?

Decide which expressions from 4a you could use.

Grammar reference and practice

1 PRESENT PERFECT SIMPLE AND PROGRESSIVE

MEANING

The basic purpose of the **present perfect simple** is to say something about *the present* by describing something which happened or started in the past. It can be useful to think about the present perfect simple as having three main uses:

1 describing a period from some time in the past until now.
I've been to Malaysia three times (in my life).
I've only seen Julia twice since January.
You can use the present perfect simple in this way to summarise experiences and achievements.

2 describing an activity, state or habit which started in the past and is still going on.
I've lived in the same place since 1960.
They've used the same doctor for twenty years.
You often use the present perfect simple in this way to answer the question 'How long ...?'

3 emphasising the present result of past events.
I think my battery has run out. (= now my mobile isn't working)
Darya's talent for numbers has made her a lot of money.
(= now she's quite rich)

Because the present perfect simple is about the present, you can't use it with finished past time expressions.
I've been to Malaysia in 2007.

The **present perfect progressive** has two main uses:

1 describing an activity, state or habit which started in the past and is still happening. This is similar to the second use of the present perfect simple above, so you can say:
I've lived in the same place since 1960.
OR *I've been living in the same place since 1960.*
They've used the same doctor for twenty years.
OR *They've been using the same doctor for twenty years.*
In situations like these, native speakers most often choose the progressive.

2 describing a past activity which has a direct result now. The result comes from the activity, and it doesn't matter if the activity is finished or not. Compare:
I've painted my room. (simple) *It looks great!* (result of completed activity)
I've been painting my room. (progressive) *I feel exhausted.*
(result of activity – maybe finished, maybe not)

Remember that some verbs are not usually used in progressive forms. Many of these are verbs for talking about:
1 thoughts (*believe, know, remember, understand,* etc.)
I'm believing you. I believe you.
2 emotions (*love, like, hate, prefer,* etc.)
I've always been loving you. I've always loved you.
3 senses (*see, hear, smell, taste,* etc.)
I'm seeing you! I see you! I can see you!

4 ownership (*have, own, possess,* etc.)
Are we having any milk? Do we have any milk?

Because these verbs often describe states rather than actions, they are sometimes called **state verbs**.

FORM

Present perfect simple
have / has + past participle
❓ *How long have you lived here?*
➕ *I've lived here since nineteen-sixty.*
➖ *I haven't lived here long.*
✔/✘ *Yes, I have. No, I haven't.*

Present perfect progressive
have / has + *been* + *-ing* form
❓ *What have you been doing?*
➕ *I've been painting my room.*
➖ *I haven't been sleeping.*
✔/✘ *Yes, I have. No, I haven't.*

PRONUNCIATION

Look at the FORM section above. The • shows which syllables are usually stressed.

Notice how you usually stress past participles and *-ing* forms like *lived* and *painting*.
In questions and positive sentences, you don't usually stress *have* or *been*.
In negative sentences and short answers, you usually stress *have*.
been is pronounced /bɪn/.

PRACTICE

Make questions and sentences. Use the present perfect simple or present perfect progressive. Sometimes both are possible.

1 Adam / cycle competitively since he was a teenager.
2 Guess what! I / finally / join the sports club.
3 I have an awful feeling that I / break my toe!
4 Mia / prepare for her final exams for months.
5 I'm not really crying. I / cut onions!
6 Sonia / be married since she was eighteen.
7 you ever / think about becoming a vegetarian?
8 You look exhausted! What / you / do?
9 Not again! You / already / watch this film twice.
10 Sorry I didn't hear the phone. I / work in the garden.
11 you / finish your coffee? Would you like another?
12 I / only / see Ben a couple of times since we left school.

2 PAST SIMPLE AND PAST PERFECT SIMPLE

MEANING

The **past simple** is by far the most commonly used form in descriptions of the past. You can use it to talk about several different kinds of past situation, for example:

- a momentary action. *The teacher sat down.*
- a number of actions. *Gomez scored five goals in two matches.*
- a habitual action. *We visited my aunt every summer.*
- an activity or state which lasted for a period of time. *I lived in Paris for five years.*

You can use the **past perfect simple** to show that something happened earlier than another event in the past. For example, the past perfect is common in clauses after past simple verbs which describe speech, thoughts and sensations.

PAST	EARLIER PAST
She told me	*that she'd cheated in the exam.*
They noticed	*that he hadn't touched his dinner.*
I heard	*that Amelia's cat had died.*

Often the use of the past perfect is optional and only for emphasis.
After I arrived, the party started. (I arrived – party started)
After I'd arrived, the party started. (I arrived – party started)
These sentences have the same meaning. Because of the word *after*, the order of events is clear.

But sometimes the past perfect is necessary to make the order of events clear.
When I arrived at the station, the train left. (I arrived – train left)
When I arrived at the station, the train had left. (train left – I arrived)
You often need the past perfect in sentences with *when*.

FORM

Past simple
❷ *How many goals did Gomez score?*
❶ *He scored five goals.*
❸ *He didn't score any.*
✓/✗ *Yes, he did. No, he didn't.*

Past perfect simple *had* + past participle
❷ *Had you met each other before the party?*
❶ *We'd met a few times.*
❸ *We hadn't met for years.*
✓/✗ *Yes, we had. No, we hadn't.*

PRONUNCIATION

Look at the FORM section above. The • shows which syllables are usually stressed.

Notice how you usually stress main verbs like *score(d)* and *met*.
In questions, you don't usually stress *did* or *had*.
In negative sentences and short answers, you usually stress *did* or *had*.

PRACTICE

Complete each sentence with the past simple and past perfect simple in the correct place.

1 When I got home last night, I _____ (realise) I _____ (lose) my keys.
2 I _____ (decide) not to go to university by the time I _____ (be) eighteen.
3 Last night, I _____ (text) all my friends to say I _____ (get) a job in another city.
4 My son _____ (love) our skiing holiday – he _____ (never see) real snow before!
5 My boss _____ (promise) me a day off so I _____ (be) upset when I had to work yesterday.
6 My brother _____ (tell) me this morning that he _____ (find) a good flat near his college.

2 PAST PROGRESSIVE AND PAST PERFECT PROGRESSIVE

MEANING

You can use the **past progressive** when you want to focus on a moment in the past when an activity was in progress.
This time yesterday, we were walking along the beach. (focus: this time yesterday)
When I met Sally, I was working in a café. (focus: the time I met Sally)

You can also use the past progressive to emphasise that an activity was in progress at every moment over a period of time.
I'm not surprised you're tired. You were working all weekend.

You use the **past perfect progressive** to describe an activity over a period that started before another past event and continued up to it, or until a short time before it.

When I arrived, everyone had been waiting for hours.
I guessed that Maria had been crying.

FORM

Past progressive *was / were* + *-ing* form
❷ *What were you doing when you heard the news?*
❶ *I was listening to the radio.*
❸ *I wasn't watching TV.*
✓/✗ *Yes, I was. No, I wasn't.*

Past perfect progressive *had been* + *-ing* form
❷ *What had he been doing before he joined the army?*
❶ *He'd been studying at university.*
❸ *He hadn't been working.*
✓/✗ *Yes, he had. No, he hadn't.*

PRONUNCIATION

Look at the FORM section above. The • shows which syllables are usually stressed.

Notice how you usually stress main verbs like *doing* and *studying*.
In questions and positive sentences, you don't usually stress *was / were*, *had* or *been*.
In negative sentences and short answers, you usually stress *was / were* or *had*.

PRACTICE

Choose the best option.

1 When I arrived at the shop, the owner was just closing up / had just been closing up.

2 They only reached an agreement after they were negotiating / 'd been negotiating for two days.

3 Everyone was still working / had still been working even though it was ten at night. They were exhausted.

4 I met my future husband when I was living / 'd been living in Dubai.

5 I didn't meet my neighbours until I was living / 'd been living here for three or four months.

6 By the time the train arrived, we were waiting / 'd been waiting for over an hour.

3 HABITS AND TENDENCIES – PAST AND PRESENT

MEANING

You can use a number of different forms to talk about habits and tendencies.

1 The most common forms are the **present simple** and the **past simple**.
We buy a TV guide every Friday.
When I was a boy, we always spent our holidays abroad.
All the examples in 2–4 below could also be in the present simple or past simple.

2 You can use *will* (present) and *would* (past) to describe people's regular habits, or how they usually behave in particular situations.
When you ask Dad for money, he'll always say 'no' at first.
My grandmother would help anyone who asked her.

3 You can use *used to* to describe past states and habits.
When I was younger, we used to live about a hundred metres from a pool.
We used to go swimming every weekend.

Used to is only for talking about the past. There is no present form.
~~I use to go swimming every weekend at the moment.~~

There is an important difference between *used to* and *would*. You can only use *used to*, not *would*, for past states.
When I was younger, we used to / ~~would~~ live about a hundred metres from a pool.
We used to / would go swimming every weekend.

In a longer speech about past habits and routines, you normally start with *used to*, then continue with *would*.
When I was younger, we used to go swimming every weekend. Every Saturday we'd get up at about eight, then our mum would help us pack our swimming things and our dad would ...

4 You can use the **present progressive** and the **past progressive** with expressions like *always*, *constantly*, etc. These forms are used to emphasise that something happens / happened all the time, or very often. They can suggest that the speaker finds / found the situation surprising, unusual or annoying.
We're always looking for ways to improve our services for customers.
Be quiet, will you? You're always interrupting me.
Wayne's constantly giving his girlfriend expensive presents.

FORM

will / would + infinitive
❓ What would she do?
➕ Mum would help us pack.
➖ She wouldn't go with us.
✔/✘ Yes, she would. No, she wouldn't.

used to + infinitive
❓ What did you use to do?
➕ We used to go swimming.
➖ We didn't use to stay at home.
✔/✘ Yes, we did. No, we didn't.

You may sometimes see *used* in written questions and negatives, but many people consider this to be incorrect. In speech there is no difference, as the usual pronunciation of both 'used to' and 'use to' is the same: /'juːstə/.

PRONUNCIATION

Look at the FORM section above. The • shows which syllables are usually stressed.
In positive sentences and questions, you usually stress *used* and the main verb, but not *will / would* or *did*.
In negative sentences and short answers, *will / won't*, *would / wouldn't* and *did / didn't* are also stressed.

PRACTICE

Read Paula's description of a job she had. Change the <u>underlined</u> expressions using *used to*, *would* or *was / were always -ing*.

I [1]<u>was</u> a freelance writer in Argentina. I mostly wrote book reviews but I [2]<u>also did</u> restaurant reviews quite often, so it was a really varied job. The restaurant reviews were a great way to get free meals, though sometimes I [3]<u>did</u> more than one review in a day so I [4]<u>ate out</u> two or even three times. I [5]<u>worried</u> about my weight! The newspaper [6]<u>told</u> the restaurants that I was going to visit, so they [7]<u>made</u> special dishes, which was great in one way, though it made it difficult to write an accurate review. Of course, my boyfriend [8]<u>asked</u> if he could come with me because the meals were free, though it happened once that they didn't charge me but they charged him. It was an expensive place, so we ended up paying quite a lot!

Compare and explain your answers in groups.

4 USING THE PASSIVE

MEANING

In English, you usually put the person or thing you want to talk about (the **topic**) at the beginning of a sentence. New information (the **comment**) comes after the topic.

Topic	Comment
Umm Kulthum	*was probably the most famous singer of the Arab world in the 20th century.*

The **passive** gives you a way of keeping the topic, or things closely related to the topic, in the usual position at the beginning of a sentence.

Topic	Comment
She	*is known as 'the Voice of Egypt' and 'the Star of the East'.*
Her music	*can often be heard on radio and television.*

Notice how, in this extract, the writer chooses **active** or **passive** forms to keep the focus on <u>Bohumil Hrabal and his work</u>.

*Although <u>he</u> **started out** as a poet, <u>Hrabal</u> had his first breakthrough with a collection of short stories at the age of 49. From 1963 to 1968, <u>he</u> **published** eight works but **was** then **banned** from publishing. Only in 1975 **did** <u>he</u> **regain** the right to publish, but still <u>several of his most important works</u> **could** only **be published** abroad. After the Velvet Revolution in 1989, <u>a number of Hrabal's previously banned books</u> **were published**, and <u>the first of his collected writings</u> – in nineteen volumes – **came out** in 1991.*

You can use **by** after the passive to say who does or did an action.
She was noticed by Zakariyya Ahmad, a famous musician.
However, this is often not necessary.
She is known ~~by people~~ as 'the Voice of Egypt'.

A number of common expressions include the passive.
she was born in … it's estimated that … she's known as … it's said that …

FORM

You make all passive forms using *be* + past participle.

Present simple *am / is / are* + past participle *She is known as 'the Voice of Egypt'.*
Past simple *was / were* + past participle *She was noticed by Zakariyya Ahmad, a famous musician.*
Present perfect *have been / has been* + past participle *About a million copies of her records have been sold every year.*
Modal verb + *be* + past participle *Her music can often be heard on the radio.*

PRONUNCIATION

You usually stress the past participle but not auxiliary verbs (*be*, *have*, modals).
Her music can often be heard on the radio.

But in negative sentences, you also stress the negative word.
Her music isn't often heard these days.

PRACTICE

Complete the sentences with the correct form of the passive. Use the verbs in brackets.

1 Budget airlines nowadays _____ often _____ by passengers. (criticise)
2 A few weeks ago, I _____ to join a Citizens' Action Group. (invite)
3 Sorry, but your car _____ until next Monday. (can't, repair)
4 Since the 1990s, many of our toys and games _____ from China. (import)
5 She _____ just _____ for an Oscar. (nominate)
6 As far as I'm concerned, he _____ to prison. (should, send)
7 _____ the results of the survey _____ yet? (announce)
8 Are you sure the staff _____ about the new regulations last week? (inform)

5 DESCRIBING OBJECTS – PAST PARTICIPLE CLAUSES

MEANING

You can use a **past participle clause** to describe a noun or a noun phrase.
More than 5 million lighters made by Bic are sold every day.

Here the past participle clause *made by Bic* describes the noun phrase *5 million lighters*.

Notice how:

1 past participle clauses have a similar meaning to **relative clauses** with a passive verb form.
More than 5 million lighters which are made by Bic are sold every day.

2 past participle clauses have nothing to do with past time. The expression 'past participle clause' is used because this kind of clause starts with a past participle (*made*).

There are two kinds of past participle clause.

1 You use **a defining clause** to show exactly which things or people you're talking about.
I read an interesting survey conducted by the New York Times.

2 You use **a non-defining clause** to add extra details about things or people.
A recent survey on reading habits, conducted by the New York Times, attracted a lot of attention.

Sometimes, the choice of defining or non-defining clause depends on the feelings of the speaker.
It's a famous picture painted by Yeames. (= *painted by Yeames* identifies the picture)
It's a famous picture, painted by Yeames. (= *painted by Yeames* is an extra detail)

FORM

A defining clause goes directly after the noun phrase, without a comma.

A non-defining clause can go in different places:
1 directly after the noun phrase, but with commas.
This picture, painted by Yeames in 1878, shows a dramatic scene of a family in danger.
2 before the noun phrase, if the noun phrase is the subject of the sentence.
Painted by Yeames in 1878, this picture shows a dramatic scene of a family in danger.

PRONUNCIATION

Speakers make it easier for people to understand them by dividing their speech into logical groups of words.

If a past participle clause is defining, it makes a single group of words with the thing it describes.
// It's a famous picture painted by Yeames //

If a past participle clause is non-defining, you put it in a separate group of words.
// It's a famous picture // painted by Yeames //

PRACTICE

Choose the right expressions to complete the defining past participle clauses.

called	built	grown	imported
taken	made	located	directed

1 The most expensive thing I ever lost was a bracelet _____ of silver and pearls.
2 I really enjoy horror films _____ by Guillermo Del Toro.
3 Whenever I can, I buy fruit and vegetables _____ locally.
4 Guests stay in beautiful chalets _____ in a forest near the mountains.
5 I tend to buy a lot of cotton clothes _____ from Turkey.
6 They live in a delightful old house _____ in the 1920s.
7 One of my favourite possessions is a family photo _____ at my wedding.
8 Recently I tried out a new exercise machine at my gym _____ 'the Power Plate'.

6 CONDITIONAL CLAUSES – PRESENT AND FUTURE

MEANING

Conditional sentences have two parts.

CONDITIONAL CLAUSE	MAIN CLAUSE
If the weather's bad tomorrow,	*they'll have to cancel the match.*

You can start a conditional clause with different **linking expressions.**
I'll lend you the car as long as / provided you promise to be careful. (= 'you *must* promise to be careful' (emphatic))
Even if he wins this match, he can't win the tournament. (= 'he might win but it won't make any difference')
Unless the taxi gets here soon, we're going to be late. (= 'if the taxi doesn't get here soon, …')

Notice that you only usually use **as long as** and **provided** to describe conditions for situations which you feel are positive or desirable.
As long as / Provided we leave now, we'll catch the train.
~~As long as / Provided we don't leave now, we'll miss the train.~~

You can use different **tenses** in conditional clauses:
1 You use the **present tense** when you feel that a situation is **real** (a fact or a possibility).
If I eat mushrooms, they make me sick. (= a fact)
If he's late, I'm afraid we'll have to cancel the meeting. (= a possibility)

2 You use the **past tense** when you feel that a situation is **unreal** (unlikely or impossible).
If we had a bit more money, we could think about moving to a new flat. (= unlikely)
If my uncle were alive now, he'd be 102. (= impossible because he's dead)
Notice that, although these sentences use the past tense, they're not about past time. They describe hypothetical situations in the present or future.

FORM

Real conditionals:

PRESENT TENSE	PRESENT TENSE OR MODAL
If I eat mushrooms,	*they make me sick.*
If he's late,	*we'll have to cancel the meeting.*

You can use a main clause with or without a modal verb, depending on whether you want to talk about facts, possibilities (*will*, *might*), habits (*will*), abilities (*can*), etc.

Unreal conditionals:

PAST TENSE	WOULD / COULD + INFINITIVE
If we had a bit more money,	*we could think about moving to a new flat.*
If my uncle were alive now,	*he'd be 102.*

In the main clause you use the past form of a modal verb, usually *would* or *could*.

Notice how:
1 You can use a conditional clause before or after a main clause.
If we had a bit more money, we could think about moving to a new flat. (with comma ,)
We could think about moving to a new flat if we had a bit more money. (without comma)

2 In unreal conditional clauses, you can use *were* instead of *was*.
If my uncle was / were … If I was / were …

PRONUNCIATION

You usually say a conditional sentence with at least two groups of words //…//.
// If we had a bit more money // we could think about moving to a new flat //
// We could think about moving to a new flat // if we had a bit more money //

PRACTICE

Put the underlined verbs in 1–6 in the correct form and add modal verbs. Use the information about the speakers in brackets ( ) to help you decide whether to make real or unreal conditionals.

1 If the business <u>be</u> successful, we <u>think</u> about opening a second branch. (a confident businessman)
2 If you <u>order</u> slightly more units, we <u>consider</u> reducing our price further. (a cautious negotiator)
3 I probably <u>think</u> about applying to university if I <u>pass</u> all my exams. (a pessimistic student)
4 Friends, if we <u>win</u> tonight's vote, it <u>be</u> a great victory for our country. (an optimistic political leader)
5 To be honest, if they <u>give</u> me the job, I <u>be</u> amazed. (a poorly qualified job applicant)
6 I <u>turn</u> off that television if you two <u>not stop</u> arguing about what to watch! (an impatient parent)

Compare your sentences. If there are any differences, explain the choices you made.

7 DESCRIBING SCENES – PRESENT AND PAST PARTICIPLE CLAUSES

MEANING AND FORM

You can use **present and past participle clauses** to give information about a noun or a noun phrase.

He was interrupted by someone visiting on urgent business.
(= present participle clause)

'Kubla Khan' is an unfinished poem inspired by a dream. (= past participle clause)

Present participle clauses have an **active** meaning.
He was interrupted by someone visiting [= who visited] on urgent business.

Past participle clauses have a **passive** meaning.
'Kubla Khan' is an unfinished poem inspired [= which was inspired] by a dream.

Notice how:

1 present and past participle clauses have nothing to do with present and past time. You can use them to talk about things in the past, present or future.

2 participle clauses can be used to describe scenes in sentences with verbs like *see, hear, feel* and *remember* and sentences with *There is / was ...* .
I heard Henry telling Jacques that he was going out for lunch.
There's someone waiting for you at reception.

PRONUNCIATION

See Grammar reference for Unit 5, Past participle clauses.

PRACTICE

Complete the sentences with the present or past participle form of the verb in brackets.

1 A few weeks ago, I saw him _____ dinner in a restaurant with a blonde woman. (have)

2 Have you seen that great website _____ to classic science fiction? (dedicate)

3 It's one of those things _____ by plumbers to join pipes. (use)

4 I found them all _____ basketball in the school gym. (practise)

5 Look. There's still an old price tag _____ to this coat. (attach)

6 I heard my professor _____ my last essay with one of his colleagues. (discuss)

7 All the politicians _____ with the scandal have resigned. (connect)

8 I stared out of the window at the rain _____ down. (pour)

8 MAKING DEDUCTIONS ABOUT THE PAST

MEANING

You can use these **expressions with modal verbs** to give your opinions about the likelihood of events in the past.
The fire must have started by mistake. (= I'm sure it started by mistake)
It may well have started by mistake. (= I think there's a good chance)
It may have / might have / could have started by mistake. (= it's possible, but I'm not sure)
It can't have started by mistake. (= I think it's impossible)

Notice that we don't use the following **expressions** for making deductions about the past.
It ~~can have~~ started by mistake. (use *may have, might have* or *could have*)
It ~~mustn't have~~ started by mistake. (use *can't have*)

FORM

modal verb (**not**) + **have** + past participle
The fire can't have started by mistake.

PRONUNCIATION

You usually say modal verbs and *have* without stress.
/mʌstəv/
The fire must have started by mistake.

PRACTICE

Choose the correct option.

1 The streets are all wet. It may have / must have rained.

2 He's late. Considering the poor state of his car, it can't have / may well have broken down.

3 I might have / must have left a light on in the flat. I mean, I probably didn't but I'm a bit worried.

4 "What's that noise?" "It could have / couldn't have been the postman. He gets here much later."

5 Lightning could have / can't have started the forest fire. It's been very stormy recently.

6 That's a huge painting. It must have / could have taken a long time to complete.

7 We felt a bit ill after dinner. It might have / can't have been the fish because it was fresh.

8 "Where did this cake come from?" "Tanya may have / must have brought it but I'm not sure."

8 CONDITIONALS – PAST AND PRESENT

MEANING

1

Fact about the past:	*I didn't marry Juli.*
Fact about the past:	*We didn't have kids.*
Imaginary action and result:	*If I'd married Juli, we could have had kids.*

This sentence links an imaginary action in the past with an imaginary result, also in the past. This kind of sentence is sometimes called a **third conditional**.

2

Fact about the past:	*He went to China.*
Fact about the present:	*He's married.*
Imaginary action and result:	*If he hadn't gone to China, he might not be married.*

This sentence links an imaginary action in the past with an imaginary result in the present. This kind of sentence is sometimes called a **mixed conditional**.

FORM

1

If + past perfect , modal verb + *have* + past participle
If I'd married Juli, we could have had kids.
(**'d** = had)

2

If + past perfect , modal verb + infinitive
If he hadn't gone to China, he might not be married.

If + past perfect , modal verb + infinitive + *-ing*
If my company hadn't decided to move, I'd probably still be doing the same job.

In modern English, many people say *if* with *would(n't) have* instead of the past perfect.
If I'd have married Juli, we could have had kids.
(**'d** = would)

PRONUNCIATION

You usually say a conditional sentence with at least two speech units //...//.
// *If he hadn't gone to China // he might not be married //*

PRACTICE

Find and correct one error in each sentence.

1 If she'd arrived a little earlier, she could got the express train.
2 I might still working in an office if I hadn't won the lottery.
3 He might had become a landscape gardener if he hadn't been allergic to flowers.
4 If he'd locked the window, the cat couldn't have get out.
5 The party would been successful if there hadn't been a power failure.
6 If that taxi hadn't stopped for us, we'd still stand at the bus stop in the rain.
7 This soup would have been perfect you hadn't added that last teaspoon of salt!
8 If she'd come back for a second interview, we have offered her the job.
9 She have seen everything much better if she'd had her glasses with her.
10 If everyone comes by public transport, we wouldn't have this parking problem now.

9 VERBS WITH ADVERBS AND PREPOSITIONS 1

MEANING

Verbs with **prepositions** or **adverbs** are sometimes referred to as multi-word verbs.
We put the pages into this machine. (verb + preposition)
It sticks all the pages together. (verb + adverb)
In multi-word verbs, both prepositions and adverbs are sometimes called **particles**.

You can often work out the meaning of a multi-word verb from the meaning of the separate verb and preposition or adverb. In the examples above, the meanings of *put into* and *stick together* are obvious from the meanings of *put*, *stick*, *into* and *together*.

FORM

The patterns which go with a multi-word verb depend on:
* whether there's an object after the verb.
* whether the particle is a preposition or an adverb. A preposition has an object, but an adverb doesn't.

In this unit there are three common kinds of multi-word verb:
1 *Pour the milk into the mixing bowl.*
   (verb with object + preposition with object)
2 *We passed through Dresden hours ago.*
   (verb + preposition with object)
3 *She picked her bag up.* (verb with object + adverb)

In multi-word verbs with an object and an adverb, you can put the adverb before or after the object.
She picked up her bag.   *She picked her bag up.*
But if the object is a pronoun (*me, it, they*, etc.), the adverb must go after it.
~~She picked up it.~~   *She picked it up.*

PRONUNCIATION

In multi-word verbs:
* prepositions are not usually stressed.
* verbs and adverbs are usually stressed.
* adverbs are usually stressed more strongly than verbs.

You can use these rules to help you say multi-word verbs of all kinds.
Pour the milk into the mixing bowl.
We passed through Dresden hours ago.
She picked her bag up.
She picked up her bag.

PRACTICE

Put the underlined expressions in the correct order. In some cases, two answers are possible.

1 Add the flour and salt, then slowly the bowl / pour / into / the milk, stirring all the time.
2 Can you help me with this printer? I want to print / this envelope / an address / onto.
3 Please over / turn / the worksheet and look at question 2.
4 Could you from school / pick / the kids / up? I'm stuck at work.
5 I forgot to the agenda / attach / email / this morning's / to.
6 The company are taking a big risk. They've a lot of / this project / put / money / into.
7 If we put / single beds / these two / together, we can make a big double bed.
8 Do watch out with that knife. You'll off / cut / your finger if you're not careful.

10 USING THE -ING FORM

MEANING AND FORM

You can use the -ing forms of verbs in several different ways.

1 You can use -ing forms in the same way as **nouns**, for example as the **subject** or **object** in a sentence.
*Chocolate / Smoking **is** bad for you.*

2 You can use -ing forms **after a preposition**, again in the same way as **nouns**.
You shouldn't have taken the car without permission / asking.

3 You can use -ing forms **after certain verbs**, for example:
admit, avoid, consider, deny, dislike, enjoy, fancy, feel like, finish, give up, imagine, involve, keep, mind, miss, practise, risk, can't stand, suggest, understand.
Notice how all of these verbs can also be followed by a normal noun.
I need to finish painting this room.
I need to finish this job.

4 You use -ing forms in **progressive verb forms**.
We were staying with my aunt when we heard the good news.

5 You can use -ing forms as **adjectives**.
The first thing I saw when I woke up was her smiling face.

6 You can use -ing forms **after linking words**, especially those to do with time.
Make sure you add the sugar after / before / while heating up the milk.
Linking words followed by -ing forms include:
before, after, since, until, when, while, whenever, if, even if, unless.

PRONUNCIATION

Because they function as verbs, nouns or adjectives, -ing forms are usually stressed in a sentence.

You shouldn't have taken the car without asking.

I found the film really disturbing.

Make sure you add the sugar before heating up the milk.

PRACTICE

Choose the correct word for each sentence and write it in the proper place.

completing giving pressing raining fascinating
relaxing playing riding learning disturbing

1 It's been heavily like this all week, so everything's wet.
2 I don't usually find horror films. They're just funny.
3 I sometimes feel ill when in the back of a car.
4 Excuse me. Would you be interested in a questionnaire on your local government?
5 After work, I enjoy in front of the TV with a cold drink.
6 Because my mother's French, the language has been fairly easy for me.
7 You can do it by the 'Control' and the 'S' key at the same time.
8 This is an absolutely book. You must read it!
9 Computer games won't help you pass your exams!
10 His job involves presentations around the world.

Then match each -ing word in the sentences with a use 1–6 in MEANING AND FORM above.

11 PATTERNS AFTER VERBS

MEANING AND FORM

A number of different **patterns** can be used after <u>verbs</u>.

Objects
• *The government has <u>announced</u> a new policy.* (noun)
• *I was wrong – I <u>admit</u> it.* (pronoun)
• *You <u>promised</u> me a pay rise.* (indirect + direct object)

Clauses
• *We <u>agreed</u> (that) there'd been a mistake.* (*that* clause)
• *She <u>asked</u> if she could leave early.* (*if* clause)
• *I don't <u>understand</u> what you're saying.* (*wh-* clause)

Other verbs
• *They're <u>refusing</u> to sign the contract.* (infinitive with *to*)
• *How can we <u>avoid</u> paying?* (-*ing* form)

Prepositional phrases
• *We <u>apologise</u> for the delay.*
• *They don't <u>agree</u> about anything.*
• *Dalton <u>confessed</u> to the murder.*
• *We need to <u>decide</u> on a time.*

Sometimes you can combine an object and another pattern.
• *They <u>promised</u> me (that) I'd get a pay rise.* (object + *that* clause)
• *My doctor <u>advised</u> me to quit smoking.* (object + infinitive with *to*)
• *He <u>challenged</u> me to a game of squash.* (object + prepositional phrase)

There are no simple rules for working out which patterns can go with a verb. Many verbs can have a number of different patterns and verbs with a similar meaning sometimes have different patterns, for example:
I <u>advise</u> you to get legal advice.
~~I advise that you get legal advice.~~
~~I recommend you to get legal advice.~~
I recommend that you get legal advice.

You can find information about verb patterns in good learner dictionaries.

PRACTICE

Complete the sentences with the verbs in the correct form.

1 The employees have threatened _____ (go) on strike unless they're paid more.
2 She looked embarrassed and admitted _____ (she / not / check) her email for a week or so.
3 I think I'd better apologise _____ (Frank / be) so late.
4 More and more people complain _____ (TV / be / not) as good as it used to be.
5 We've challenged _____ (Brandon College / a football match) next weekend.
6 I'd like to thank _____ (everybody / come) to this seminar today.
7 Unfortunately, the clients refused _____ (wait) any longer and left before Bob arrived.
8 I'd advise _____ (you / get rid of) that car as soon as possible.
9 Have you heard? James and Aga have announced _____ (they / get married).
10 You promised _____ (write) to me at least once a week.

12 WILL BE -ING

MEANING

You can use will be -ing to let people know about future events.
I'll be finishing college next year.
We'll be meeting again next Thursday.
It can often be used instead of other future forms like *will*, the present progressive and the present simple.

will be -ing gives the impression that a future event is a matter of simple fact. It does *not* refer to the speaker's personal wishes or intentions.
I'll phone you on Monday. (sounds like it could be the speaker's decision)
I'll be phoning you on Monday. (doesn't refer to the speaker's wishes but rather a simple fact)

Because will be -ing avoids the idea of intentions or decisions, it can be useful when you want to:

1 suggest that you have no control over a future event.
   Unfortunately, over the next six months we'll be reducing our workforce by 15%.
2 reassure people that an event is normal and 'natural'.
   We'll be flying today at around 40,000 feet.
3 sound friendlier and less distant.
   In my presentation I'll be talking to you about some new concepts in marketing.
4 make a question sound less direct.
   Will you be visiting us again soon?

FORM

❓ *Will you be visiting us again soon?*
➕ *Yes, I'll be visiting again in April.*
➖ *I'm afraid I won't be visiting again until July.*
✔/✗ *Yes, I will. No, I won't.*

PRONUNCIATION

Look at the FORM section above. The • shows the syllables which are usually stressed.

Notice how you usually stress *won't* and *–ing* forms. You don't usually stress *will* (*'ll*) unless it's at the end of a sentence.
be is usually unstressed and can be said as /bɪ/.

PRACTICE

Use the verbs in the box and *will be –ing* to complete the paragraph.

bring get have join meet present start try out watch

Just to confirm, we ¹_____ in Events Room 2 tomorrow at 9.00. Jessica ²_____ the meeting with a report on the latest trends in computer gaming. She ³_____ also _____ the latest sales statistics for the top twenty most popular games. After that, we ⁴_____ into groups to brainstorm ideas for our new project, SunBlast. Around 12.30, the caterers ⁵_____ in some lunch for us. Oh, and we ⁶_____ a coffee break at 10.30, before the brainstorming. In the afternoon, we ⁷_____ a video on the latest developments in virtual reality games. Blake Simms from Cobalt ⁸_____ us for that and afterwards we
⁹_____ some new games he's been developing.

13 VERBS WITH ADVERBS AND PREPOSITIONS 2

MEANING

You can often work out the meaning of these verbs, also referred to as multi-word verbs, from the meanings of the separate words which make them up.
Please sit down.
In this example, the meaning of *sit down* is obvious from the meanings of *sit* and *down*.

However, multi-word verbs can also have idiomatic meanings which you simply have to learn.
I'd like to set up a meeting for Friday. (= organise, arrange)
In this example, it's not possible to work out the meaning of *set up* from *set* and *up*.

Some multi-word verbs have a number of different meanings.
Can you go away, please? I'm trying to work. (= leave this place)
It's no good ignoring the problem. It won't just go away. (= stop, disappear)
We usually try to go away at least once a year. (= go somewhere on holiday)

FORM

The patterns which go with a multi-word verb depend on:
* whether there's an object after the verb.
* whether the particles are prepositions or adverbs. A preposition has an object, but an adverb doesn't.

In this unit there are three common kinds of multi-word verb:
1 *The meeting seemed to go on for hours.* (verb + adverb)
2 *We managed to sort a lot of things out.* (verb with object + adverb)
3 *Alain came up with loads of good ideas.* (verb + adverb + preposition with object)

In multi-word verbs with an object and an adverb, you can put the adverb before or after the object.
We sorted out a lot of things.   *We sorted a lot of things out.*
But:
1 if the object is a pronoun (*me, it, they*, etc.), the adverb must go after it.
   ~~We sorted out them.~~   *We sorted them out.*
2 if the object is a long phrase, the adverb usually goes before it.
   We sorted out a problem with my car.
   ~~We sorted a problem with my car out.~~

PRONUNCIATION

See Unit 9 Grammar reference, Verbs with adverbs and prepositions 1.

PRACTICE

Rewrite the sentences using the multi-word verbs in the correct form.

a	sit down	e	break down	i	face up to
b	go away	f	come up with	j	bring along
c	sort out	g	talk over	k	keep up
d	set up	h	go on	l	put up with

1 She finally <u>accepted</u> the fact that she wasn't going to get the job.
2 There's going to be a new department at work. They've asked me to help <u>organise</u> it.
3 How can people <u>tolerate</u> noisy neighbours?
4 If you ignore a problem, it won't just <u>disappear</u>.
5 I've got some questions. Do you have a few minutes to <u>discuss</u> them?
6 No one imagined the meeting would <u>continue</u> for so long.
7 Anna's nice. Next time you come to my place, why don't you <u>come with</u> her?
8 I think we should <u>meet</u> soon and discuss the issue.
9 Negotiations between the two companies have <u>failed</u> completely.
10 We've finally <u>thought of</u> a deal which satisfies everybody.
11 We've got a problem with our email. I'll let you know as soon as we've <u>solved</u> it.
12 I couldn't <u>maintain</u> the energy and discipline needed to train for the marathon.

14 FUTURE PROGRESSIVE AND FUTURE PERFECT

MEANING

You can use both future progressive and future perfect forms to focus on a specific point in the future.

You use the **future progressive** to describe an activity in progress at <u>a point in the future</u>.
Just think. <u>This time tomorrow</u> we'll be flying over the Indian Ocean.
I'll probably be staying at my parents' <u>at New Year</u>.

You use the **future perfect** to say an action will be finished some time before <u>a point in the future</u>.
We'll have finished all the painting by <u>the end of the week</u>, no problem.
<u>This time next year</u>, Jerome will have graduated.

FORM

Future progressive *will* + *be* + *-ing* form
❓ *What do you think you'll be doing in ten years?*
➕ *I'll probably be running my own business.*
➖ *I'm pretty sure I won't be living in this city.*
✅/❌ *Yes, I will. / No, I won't.*

Future perfect *will* + *have* + past participle
❓ *What do you think you'll have achieved by 2020?*
➕ *I'll definitely have changed companies by then.*
➖ *I probably won't have started a family.*
✅/❌ *Yes, I will. / No, I won't.*

In place of *will*, you can use other modal verbs like *may*, *might* and *should*.
I may / might / should be running my own business.
You can also use verbs like *hope to*, *expect to* and *would like to*.
I hope to / expect to / would like to have started a family.

PRONUNCIATION

Look at the FORM section above. The • shows the syllables which are usually stressed.

Notice how you usually stress main verbs like *doing*, *achieved* and *hope*.
You don't usually stress the auxiliaries *be* or *have*.
You don't usually stress modal verbs except when they're negative (*won't*) or at the end of a sentence (*I will. I won't.*).

PRACTICE

Complete the sentences with the future perfect or future progressive, using the verbs in brackets.

1 In fifty years' time, the world _____ of oil completely. (may, run out)
2 I'm not sure if I can meet you at eight. I _____ late. (might, work)
3 He _____ her the good news by the end of the day. (will definitely, tell)
4 When you read this, I _____ on a beach in Thailand. (will probably, lie)
5 They _____ lunch by the time they get here. (should, have)
6 She _____ for us at the station at 10.00. (will, wait)
7 I _____ somewhere else in five years' time. (expect, live)
8 By the end of today's workshop, we _____ to every one of you. (hope, speak)

Unit 1

🔊 **1.1**

JENNIFER Hi Derek.

DEREK Hi.

J Good weekend?

D Yeah. Went to see a film, played a bit of golf, you know.

J How's the golf?

D Oh, don't ask.

J Well, you're only a beginner. You just need to put in some practice.

D Hmm, maybe.

J Yeah, I read an interesting article about that a couple of weeks ago.

D Yeah?

J Yeah, it said if you want to be really good at something, it's all a question of practice, deliberate practice.

D Well, that's not saying anything new, is it? 'Practice makes perfect', and all that.

J But the point is, a lot of people don't really *believe* that practice makes perfect. They think it's all down to natural talent, whatever that means.

D But surely that's not the whole picture. You need *some* talent, too.

J Yeah, but I think the article was trying to say that nowadays talent's overrated.

D But I don't get the bit about 'deliberate' practice. Is that different from normal practice?

J Er, I'm not a hundred per cent sure, to be honest. It's something to do with focusing on your technique, and focusing on your results at the same time.

D Hm. I'm not really convinced.

J Well, I'll have to find the article for you. Another thing it said – again, maybe it's not a new idea – is that people should do things they enjoy.

D Because we enjoy things we're good at?

J No, more the other way round ... if you like something, then you do it a lot, you get a lot of practice, and then you get good at it.

D Hm. I hadn't really thought about it in quite that way before but it makes a lot of sense.

J So what about you and your golf? Do you enjoy it?

D To be honest, no, not really. I like the walking and the scenery and the company. I just don't like the bits in between when you have to hit the ball.

J 'Golf is a good walk, ruined,' as someone said.

D Who said that?

J I don't remember.

D Hm.

J Now, have you ever played tennis?

🔊 **1.2**

DARYA I've always been good with numbers. Erm, for example, when I was a child, I realised I could add up numbers very quickly, just by looking at them really. At the time it just seemed like a good trick but looking back I have to say it's been useful in lots of different ways. For instance, when I'm shopping, you know, putting things in my basket, I always know exactly how much I should pay at the check-out. So you could say my talent has saved me a lot of money! Numbers are also essential to my work. I've recently passed my final engineering exams and I'm starting a new job next month. The mathematics can be quite complex and you need to be able to think logically. Of course, there's much more to being an engineer than maths – it takes imagination too, and the ability to compromise – but, yes, it's definitely a great help.

CIAN I suppose one of the big, er, passions of my life is water sports, in particular sailing. I started sailing when I was nine in my local sailing club that's in my home village in Ireland. Erm, I've been sailing pretty consistently ever since. Erm, I sailed all the way through my teens. I managed to be lucky enough to sail in countries all around Europe. Erm, I've done it, er, for my university, I did it for, erm, my country a few times. The main skills you need for sailing, I suppose, [are] erm, two part. It's a, there has to be a mixture of, er, the physicality and the mental approach. I mean you have to be physically fit and strong and, erm, have plenty of endurance because the races can be very long, a couple of hours at some stages, in some places, but at the same time you have to be mentally very aware. You have to be very much focused not only on yourself but on everyone else and all the conditions around you.

HYUN-AE Well, when I was young, my family moved around a lot – my father was a diplomat – so I went to lots of different schools and met people from lots of different places and backgrounds. I think that experience gave me a lot of my people skills ... by which I mean, erm, I like meeting new people, I'm a good listener, I'm good at helping people get on with each other, that kind of thing. It comes in really useful at work, of course. For the last eight years, I've been running a social club in the area. Erm, it's a club for elderly people, paid for by the local government. Obviously I use my people skills there ... being an effective communicator is an important part of management, maybe the most important. I've done a couple of degrees, in psychology and social work, and more recently I've been studying in the evenings so I'm quite tired. But qualifications aren't everything. I think the most important thing is that you should be genuinely interested in other people, open to them. You can't fake that. People will sense that you're faking it sooner or later.

🔊 **1.3**

1 be **physically fit**, be **strong**, have plenty of **endurance**, have **good eyesight**, have **a good sense of balance**, have **quick reflexes**

2 be **good with numbers**, be able to **think logically**, be **focused**, have a lot of **self-discipline**, have plenty of **imagination**, be **well organised**

3 be **a good listener**, be **an effective communicator**, have **the ability to compromise**, be able to **delegate**, be able to **manage groups**, be **sensitive to** people's feelings

🔊 **1.4**

INTERVIEWER Does a game designer need qualifications?

HARRY Ah, that's a, that's a tough question because, er, people want to become game designers and so we're getting universities who are offering courses in, er, in game design but, if I were speaking personally, I think actually a broad, a broad qualification can help you. So I did, er, physics and maths and chemistry, and then I did, er, English literature and art history, and then I carried all of that pretty much through to university level so I ended up doing a couple of degrees, erm, a science degree and an arts degree. Er, but I think, erm, the gist of it is, a good technical base is great. But obviously it's a creative pursuit as well, so, learn to write well, erm, and, you know, there's, er, good things to be learnt from art history and English literature, and er, history.

I How do I get my foot in the door at a games company?

H Ah, there are a number of ways you can kind of get your foot in the door and just get known by the, er, by a studio. Erm, so, you can apply for jobs just like, erm, you would with any industry. However, er, it's it's a bit tough to do with no experience. So, a good way of getting that experience is to apply for work experience positions, you know, sort of, er, unpaid sort of, er, work for a month on, er, in a studio, or work on a title with a studio. Erm, you can also come in, er, there are entry-level positions, like, er, the quality assurance testers. Er, often that's sort of, er, a nice feeder into becoming a game designer. You come on as a tester, test the game, become known, er, you often have the opportunity to provide feedback to the designers and you can prove er, you know, that you're, that you're a good candidate for moving into a design role.

I   Does a games designer need to know how to code?

H   A game designer doesn't need to know how to code, but it, er, helps. Erm, he will, er, be well served if he understands, he or she, understands the technical limitations of, er, what can be achieved with the code. Er, but, that said, you don't absolutely have to know it. It's something you can learn on the job.

I   Does a games designer need to be a good artist?

H   Hm, er it helps to be able to draw a little bit, er, but I don't think you need to be precious about it. Er, so, yeah, game designers, erm, are often required to sort of visualise ideas, erm, and if you can sketch even feebly, I think it helps. But no, you don't have to be a great artist.

I   I have an idea for a game. Erm, what should I do with it?

H   Keep it to yourself. If you really want that game made, try and get a job in the industry and then present it formally, internally. Erm, or if you don't want to do that and it's a, it's an idea that might be achieved with a couple of mates, hook up with a couple of mates and, er, see if you can make it together. There are lots of places that, er, are now springing up online for you, that give you the tools to make, erm, games, and people are making quite adventurous, creative games, er, with very little background in, er, in the industry.

1.6

Egypt   engine   gadget   genuine ginger   hijack   jacket   jewel justice   majority   object   passenger

Unit 2

1.7

PAULINE   Hello?

RAINER   Er, hi, Pauline. It's Rainer. Erm, are you on your way?

P   On my way? No, I'm in the Burlington office.

R   Burlington? But the meeting starts in five minutes!

P   Five minutes? What meeting?

R   The one with the Layton Group.

P   Hang on, I thought you'd cancelled that meeting.

R   No, we didn't cancel it.

P   But on Monday, Chris told me he'd cancelled all meetings because of the flu. He sent me a text.

R   Er, Chris is off sick, but I think he meant all *his* meetings ...

P   But that's not what he said. He said *all* meetings ... and mentioned 'widespread flu' so I assumed it had spread through your whole office.

R   No ...

P   Oh, I'm awfully sorry.

R   No, it isn't *your* fault. It's *Chris's* fault. But we were counting on you to sort things out with Layton.

P   I know, but, er, after Chris had texted me, I made other appointments for today. I don't know ...

R   OK, well, don't worry about it, Pauline. We'll manage.

P   Look, what if I call for a taxi? I can be there in twenty minutes – though I won't be as well prepared as I'd like.

R   What about your other appointments?

P   We'll just have to get everything done super fast.

R   That would be fantastic, Pauline. Thanks.

P   That's OK. I'm on my way.

RAINER   ... so she arrived fifteen minutes later, got the Layton people to sign the contract, and then rushed off again.

LIANA   Well, good for her. But speaking of mix-ups, *we've* got one to discuss, too.

R   Oh really? What about?

L   Your mother's birthday present. Erm, you said you'd ordered that plant we talked about ...

R   Yeah, I did.

L   Well, I phoned your mum to wish her 'Happy Birthday' and to see if she likes the plant –

R   And it hadn't arrived?

L   Oh no, she said she'd received it – she even thanked us – but the problem is, it isn't a *plant*. It's a *tree* – some monster potted thing that takes up half her living room. She says it's beautiful but it's like living in a jungle.

R   Oh.

L   Now, I was sure I'd circled the plant in the garden centre catalogue so you'd know which one to buy.

R   Yeah, but by the time I got to the office, the catalogue had disappeared. Maybe it fell out of my bag, I don't know. But I was pretty sure I could remember the name of it.

L   I see. Well, that explains it.

R   So I ordered it by phone, erm, but it wasn't the *normal* price. It was a *special* price. They were having a sale, they said. How was I supposed to know it was that big?

L   I knew something had gone wrong but I couldn't imagine what. Well, we'll have to rescue your mum. I suppose the logical thing is to return the tree to the garden centre.

R   We can't. Like I said, it was in some kind of sale.

L   Oh dear. Well, then, the other option is to take it to your office.

R   Yeah, by truck. This is absolutely *not* my day.

1.9

RAINER   It isn't your fault. It's Chris's fault.

LIANA   The problem is, it isn't a plant. It's a tree.

R   It wasn't the normal price. It was a special price.

1.10

Er, my worst ever journey – though it was kind of funny, too – erm, happened in India a few years ago. I wanted to get a train from Delhi to a town called Dehra Dun near the Himalayas. But, erm, half an hour before my train was due to leave, I realised I had come to the wrong station. I was sure my friend had told me to go to the station in New Delhi but in fact my train went from the Old Delhi station. I jumped in a taxi but when I got to Old Delhi, my train had already left. So, erm, I bought a new ticket, waited a few hours and got on the next train. Everything was fine until I noticed one of my bags had disappeared. I remembered that a strange man had walked through the carriage some time before, so maybe he'd taken it. Unfortunately, there was an old camera in it with some pictures that I'd taken of my grandmother just before she died, and also a hat some close friends had given me. The other passengers were very kind and tried to help, but it was too late. Later, we stopped at a little station in the countryside. Suddenly, a wave of water came through the open window and soaked me to the skin! I'd forgotten it was the Hindu festival of Holi, when people throw paints and water at each other. It's all meant to be fun, of course, but by that time I'd lost my sense of humour!

1.11

JESSICA   Who are the guys in these paintings, Shiori?

SHIORI   Well, that one's Sen no Rikyū, who was a famous tea master. You've probably heard of the Japanese tea ceremony.

J   Sure.

S   And the other one is Toyotomi Hideyoshi, a warlord, very important in Japanese history.

J   And were they both around at the same time?

S   Oh yes, in the ... sixteenth century, I think. Actually, there's quite an interesting story about them.

J   Yeah?

S   Yeah. Erm, well, the first thing you have to understand is that Rikyū was a very, er, spiritual man who believed in simple, natural things. So when he did the tea ceremony, for instance, he would carefully choose tea bowls and pots and so on which were still beautiful, of course, but also very simple.

J Right.

S So anyway, one day, Hideyoshi was riding past Rikyū's house –

J Hideyoshi's the soldier, right?

S The warlord, yes. So he was riding past Rikyū's house when suddenly, he noticed that the garden was full of these fantastic flowers, er, morning glory flowers.

J OK.

S And it was such a beautiful sight that he stopped and he asked Rikyū to hold a tea ceremony for him there the next day – and, of course, Rikyū agreed reluctantly.

J Why do you say he was reluctant?

S Well, they were totally different people – one was a thoughtful, quiet man and the other was a rich, powerful soldier who'd been fighting all his life. But Rikyū didn't have a lot of choice.

J So what happened?

S Well, when Hideyoshi arrived at the tea house the next day as they'd agreed, he saw that Rikyū had deliberately cut down all the flowers! Not one flower was left in the garden.

J Really? That's awful.

S Well, yes, Hideyoshi was furious. He'd been expecting to see this amazing garden again but instead he found all the flowers completely destroyed.

J Strange.

S So he rushed into the tea house ... but when he got inside, Rikyū was just sitting there calmly, waiting to make tea for him.

J OK.

S But behind Rikyū, he saw a simple brown pot ... and in the pot was one absolutely perfect morning glory flower.

J Only one?

S Only one. And when Hideyoshi saw it, he immediately understood why Rikyū had cut down the flowers.

J So what was the reason? I'm not sure I understand it.

S Well, people have different ideas, ...

🔊 1.12

JESSICA So what was the reason? I'm not sure I understand.

SHIORI Well, people have different ideas, but to me, he was saying that a simple thing has the greatest beauty ... that one perfect thing is enough and all the rest is just detail. What do you think?

J I'd need some time to think about that! But it is a fascinating story.

S Yes, I don't know why but I love it. You know, er, some years back, the Japanese director Teshigahara made a film about Rikyū and he included the story of the morning glory flowers, so

it's quite famous. It always seems to make an impression on people.

J Yeah.

🔊 1.13

In the south of Poland, in a town called Wieliczka, there's a famous salt mine. According to a traditional story, mining started in Wieliczka because of a Hungarian princess called Kinga. Kinga was preparing to marry Bolesław, the Duke of Kraków, so she asked her father, King Bela, for a present which she could give to her husband. Salt was very valuable at the time, so Bela gave her one of his salt mines in Hungary. As she was leaving for Poland, Kinga took a gold ring from her finger and threw it into the deepest part of the mine. After Kinga had been living in Kraków for some months, she suggested to Bolesław that they should find a place to establish a salt mine. They started their search the next day. They'd been travelling for only a few hours when they reached the village of Wieliczka, and Kinga felt sure that this was the right place. The Duke's servants started digging. Almost at once they hit a hard stone and, on lifting it from the earth, saw that it was a block of pure salt and that inside the block, something was shining. Kinga looked into the block and recognised the ring which she had thrown into the mine in Hungary, hundreds of miles away. Nowadays the mine at Wieliczka is like a huge underground city, with more than 2000 rooms and 300 kilometres of passages. Not much actual mining happens there, but it's a huge tourist attraction.

🔊 1.14

MAUREEN Hello?

IAN Er, hello, my name's Ian Wells, I'm the manager of your local branch of Ian's Pizzas.

M Ah.

I I wonder, do you have a moment to talk?

M Er, yes, I think so.

I Good. Er, I understand that you placed an order with us yesterday evening ...

M Yes, that's right.

I ... and the bill came to eighteen pounds and forty-five pence.

M Well probably, but the food took ages to arrive. Erm, that's why I only paid ten pounds.

I Ah, I see.

M I suppose that's why you're calling?

I Yes. Erm, obviously, if we got something wrong, then I'm very sorry.

M Well, it was quite a few things actually.

I Right ... you put in your order at about eight, is that right?

M No, that's the thing. I'd already ordered before that, at seven o'clock,

and they said they'd deliver in about forty minutes.

I The normal time.

M The normal time, yes. But at eight o'clock the pizzas still hadn't arrived, so I phoned again and they said they'd lost the order!

I Oh, well I'm very sorry about that.

M So anyway, I gave them the order again and we waited. Again, I was told it would take forty minutes.

I And when did the order arrive?

M It was just after nine. So by that time, erm, we'd been waiting more than two hours. The delivery boy said he'd got lost on his bike.

I Right.

M And then, after I'd taken the pizzas inside, we found that they were all cold and one of the boxes was wet. They looked like they'd been sitting outside for ages, so we couldn't eat them.

I Hm. That's really not good enough, is it?

M Well, no. In fact, I ended up ordering some Chinese food instead. Er, it cost me another ... twenty pounds?

I Right.

M And of course they weren't delivering by that time, so I had to go to the trouble of collecting it myself. So ... yeah, the whole thing caused a lot of inconvenience.

I Yep, I completely understand. Look, we are sorry about all this. I'm going to look into things in a bit more detail at this end and try to make sure this doesn't happen again.

M Well, yes, it was a pity.

I Meanwhile, if I may, I'd like to return your ten pounds and give you some vouchers which you can spend on future orders.

M Oh.

I Someone'll put them through your door this evening.

M Well, yes, that would be great.

I OK, well, thank you very much for your time and, er, sorry again.

M That's all right, thank you for calling. Bye now.

I Bye bye.

🔊 1.15

If you're visiting Portugal, one thing to keep in mind is there's a big difference between big cities and the countryside. Er, people have a tendency to learn languages in the big cities. English is basic but also, because of immigration or family that's spent time abroad or something, some people know French, or Spanish, or maybe Italian or German. And people everywhere will try to help in whatever way they can. Erm, in big cities, it's usually quite easy for foreigners to get by. But in the countryside ... if I think about my own town, apart from some of the young people, most people won't speak English so knowing some sentences, some expressions in Portuguese might help if you go to the countryside. When it comes to relations between Portuguese people, er, generally speaking, I think people used to be more open and friendly. For example, some years ago, you could often see people smiling on the street and being quite friendly, even to people they didn't know. Erm, and on the bus you'd say good morning or good evening and even start conversations with strangers. Not any more, not even in small cities. People tend to keep to themselves now, especially in big places like Lisbon and Porto. With family and friends, though, we like conversations, discussions. It's quite interesting to observe a group of people in a coffee shop. They're all talking at the same time, possibly in a way that looks like arguing. But it's just sharing opinions in a loud voice, that's all. This is typical, especially in the north of the country. Erm, people in the south, er, they're often a bit quieter, calmer, maybe because of the climate. It's so hot in the south sometimes, you have no energy to do anything. In the north, people can be very opinionated. Er, traditions vary from city to city, from area to area. Erm, for example, weddings are quite big in the countryside, all the family gathered together. In the cities, things are more expensive, the groups are smaller and they do things in a slightly different way. Some cities, you might not even have a choir, while in the countryside, a wedding without singing is not a wedding. Portuguese cuisine is good and food is a very, very important part of daily life. Er, people will usually have, er, between three and six meals a day. Er, lunch and dinner are taken quite seriously and even work schedules are organised around eating times. So everyone gets a lunch break from thirty minutes up to two hours where we either go home to cook or go to local restaurants. Erm, coffee is a big part of the culture too, and by coffee I mean like espresso. Because you have a big meal at lunchtime, it's obvious that half an hour later you feel tired, you want to sit down, you want to go to sleep. So when you go back to work in the afternoon, it's kind of compulsory to have a coffee and you will typically have at least three, four coffees a day. It's just a normal thing.

Unit 3

🔊 **1.16**

DON Hmm ...

CARRIE Oh, you're finally looking at that brochure.

D Yeah. There are some interesting things, aren't there?

C Yes, but the trick is finding something we both want to do. Are you *sure* we should do the same course, Don?

D Yeah, so we can talk things over afterwards and stuff. I haven't taken a course for years so it would be nice to have some support.

C That makes sense.

D And anyway, we've both been a bit lonely ever since Sonia and Adam went off to university so ...

C ... so we should do something together, right?

D Right.

C OK, then. Erm, any thoughts on which course to take?

D Well, I think ... for me, it's a choice between, er, two or three?

C OK. Which ones?

D I like the sound of this one, er, Bollywood Workout. It could be ...

C No, there's no way I'm doing that!

D Oh, come on. It could be fun.

C For you maybe but, as I'm sure you remember, I can't dance. I'll look like an idiot.

D Well, this is your chance to learn.

C No thanks. What else did you like?

D OK. Erm ... yes, what about Creative Writing?

C Yes, it's a thought ... but I can't make up my mind about it. I'm not sure I'd have time to do the homework.

D Good point, actually.

C Hm.

D OK. Which ones did *you* like?

C Well, actually, I wouldn't mind doing a course in First Aid. It's certainly a useful thing to know.

D Hm. That doesn't really appeal to me very much.

C No?

D No. Boring. What else?

C OK. I'd be happy with either Malaysian Cookery or the psychology course. It's up to you.

D Hm.

C Psychology?

D Yeah, I've got mixed feelings about that one. It looks interesting but it could be a lot of work. Two lessons a week ...

C ... for twelve weeks. Yes, it *is* quite a big commitment. Let's do the cookery course then, OK?

D Yeah ... yeah, all right.

C Great, I'll give them a call when we get back. I just hope there are some places left. We've left it a bit late.

D Ah, I'm sure it'll be fine. Hm ...

C What?

D I wonder who has to do the washing up?

🔊 **1.18**

Write down:
a course you'd like to sign up for if you had more time.
a goal you're working towards at the moment.

a big responsibility you've taken on in the last five years.
a course or competition you dropped out of.
a skill you had to work on really hard when you were younger.
a subject you wish you'd carried on studying for longer.
an activity you feel you should do regularly, but find difficult to keep up.
something you wish you hadn't given up.

🔊 **1.19**

ALEX ... so when I saw the notice in the paper, I immediately thought of Bill.

LIZ Bill?

A Yeah, my old driving instructor. I still see him around sometimes.

L Your driving instructor?

A Yeah. I had driving lessons about ... oh, fifteen years ago?

L And you still remember him?

A Well, he made a big impression on me. Er, I'd just turned seventeen and, erm, my parents said that, as a birthday present, they'd pay for me to have driving lessons.

L That's a nice idea.

A Well, it certainly *was* – because they said they'd pay until I passed and normally people will have maybe fifteen or twenty lessons ...

L Right.

A ... er, but I was such a terrible driver that I didn't pass until I was eighteen. I probably had about ... oh, sixty lessons in all.

L Sixty!

A Yeah, it was an expensive present. Erm, anyway, my driving instructor – Bill – was an ex-policeman, and he had a little company called Sure-Pass Driving ...

L OK.

A ... and I have to say, I've never met anybody so patient.

L Really?

A Yes. He was the calmest person I've ever met. I mean, I was a really terrible driver. I was always getting things wrong, er, and on a few occasions we got into some dangerous situations.

L Right.

A But, erm, Bill always kept calm. Er, he would never shout, never lose his temper. He was quite a quiet guy but, er, one of those people who have a lot of, erm, inner strength, you know? Nothing seemed to bother him.

L Did you ever consider giving up?

A Yeah, I did. I mentioned it to him a few times but he'd always encourage me to carry on in that quiet way of his. He seemed to have confidence in me and of course that was really motivating.

L So, he was a good teacher.

A Yeah, absolutely. I didn't really appreciate it at the time but looking back, I think he was quite a positive influence on me.

L You mean in general? Not just on your driving?

A Exactly. He taught me a lot about, well, determination. And, er, I suppose he was a kind of role model for me.

L Being calm and patient ...

A Yeah, I think they're really important things in life, so ... well, I owe him a lot.

L Well, maybe you *should* nominate him. When's the deadline?

🔊 1.20

KAREN Well, what do you think?

NIKLAS Well, obviously, you can use it to play different ball games, not just tennis.

K Yes. Er, or you could ... cut it in half, use it as a cup?

N OK, yes.

K Or put it in the garden to catch rainwater, you know, for the birds to drink.

N Sure. And using it as a stress ball would be good. You know, you squeeze it to get rid of stress –

K – or to exercise, to build up hand strength.

N Yep.

K Erm, what else?

N Erm, you could put a string through it and hang it up. My cat would play with it for hours.

K Yes. Er, or put it behind a door, so the door doesn't hit the wall.

N I suppose you could use them for packing things, fragile things.

K How do you mean?

N Well, if you wanted to send something fragile in the post, you'd pack lots of tennis balls all around it, so it wouldn't break.

K Yes, though it would be a bit expensive, wouldn't it? Erm, maybe you could –

BEN OK, thanks everyone, time's up. Let's see how you did. Who'd like to go first?

🔊 1.21

ALAN Have you read about this young headteacher in India? Babur Ali?

MIKI Babur Ali? No.

A Well, he's only sixteen but he's set up a school, with a proper curriculum and teachers and ...

M But isn't he still a student himself at that age?

A Yes. Apparently, he goes to quite a good school but it's too expensive for a lot of kids in his area. So basically, after he gets home from school, he teaches them what he's learned.

M But who funds his school and pays for the teachers?

A Surprisingly, he managed on his own at first but nowadays he gets funding from the regional government and from donations. Personally, I think it's amazing.

M Hmm, then perhaps we should send a donation, too.

A Us?

M Yeah. Seriously, I think we should consider it.

MATHIAS Well, yesterday evening, one of the branches of that big tree outside my flat broke off and crashed straight through my neighbours' living room window.

CORRIE Wow! Was anyone hurt?

M No. Thankfully, the whole family was out. Funnily enough, they were on their way home at the time of the accident but got stuck in a traffic jam. If they'd arrived back a few minutes earlier...

C Obviously, they had a lucky escape. But what's going to happen to the tree now?

M Frankly, I think it should be cut down. I don't think it's safe.

🔊 1.22

ERYN Is Dominic coming tonight?

OMAR No. Unfortunately, he can't make it. He's still at the office.

E Again? He's always working late these days.

O Well, between you and me, I think his company's in trouble. He may even go out of business.

E I didn't know that. That's terrible!

O Yes, but hopefully it won't come to that. To tell you the truth, I think owning your own business is quite stressful.

E Yeah. Personally, I'd rather be an employee than an employer. What about you?

O Oh, I'd agree with that. But basically, I'd like to be so rich that I didn't have to work at all.

🔊 1.23

ashamed   chef   distinguish
machine   moustache   parachute
share   shoulder   squash   sugar

Unit 4

🔊 1.24

CIAN One of the most, er, obvious and in some ways controversial pieces of public art in Ireland is what's known as the Millennium Spike or Spire. It's situated in the very middle of Dublin on the main ... the main street called O'Connell Street. You can see it from anywhere in the city essentially and you'll ... you'll always know where you're going if you aim for the Spike.

It was erected to celebrate the Millennium so it was unveiled, er, at the very end of 1999. It's, er, a very controversial piece because it, its design, while simple, is almost, erm, it's almost over-simplified. It ... It's very ... it is abstract. Erm, at the time it was heavily criticised but I think people are beginning to warm to it now they see it as part of the landscape and because it's taller ... because it's taller than pretty much the rest of Dublin, it does dominate the skyline ... so, I mean, we've kind of gotten used to it. Er, personally, I wasn't very pleased about it at the time. I'm, I suppose I'm more used to it now.

BERYL If you drive north on the A1, which is the road that goes from the south right ... of England right up to Scotland, as you pass the town called Gateshead, on a hill by the side of the road, you'll probably spot the Angel of the North. The Angel of the North was put up during the 1990s. It's a huge sculpture, as the name suggests, in the shape of an angel. It's constructed in steel, erm, steel, the steel industry was very important in ... in that part of the world, so that's quite significant. I like it. I don't think it's a wonderful scul ... sculpture but I like it because it's a landmark and I think everybody who goes past, of any age, probably says, 'Oh, look. There's the Angel of the North.' So it signifies an arrival somewhere.

DOMINIKA A few years ago a palm tree appeared on one of the main, erm, streets in the capital city of Poland, Warsaw, and, erm, it was in the middle of winter. It was a little bit like, erm, like a palm tree in the middle of a ... of a concrete desert, which was actually at the time also covered in snow. Erm, and a lot of people, erm, didn't know what to make of it and then it turned out that it was, erm, an art project by by a female Polish artist, who thought it would be first of all a good way of, er, brightening up, erm, the bleak, erm, winter landscape but also, I suppose ... I don't know, a way of, erm, maybe surprising people and showing them something that they didn't expect. It did cause quite a lot of controversy but then people actually also grew to love it and ... and it became, almost, er, a landmark and people would look forward to seeing it, er, on their way to work. I always, I quite like, erm, the idea of of using the city space in in an imaginative way and so I thought it was a very good example of, erm, of just brightening up a bleak part of Warsaw.

🔊 1.26

1 It was erected to celebrate the Millennium.
   It was put up during the 1990s.
2 It was unveiled at the very end of 1999.
   It was opened to the public in 2006.
3 It was heavily criticised at first.
   It was badly received.
4 It caused a lot of controversy.
   It made a big impression on people.
5 People didn't know what to make of it.
   People were baffled by it.
6 People grew to love it.
   People warmed to it after a while.
7 It became a landmark.
   It became a tourist attraction.
8 People see it as part of the landscape.
   People regard it as an eyesore.

🔊 1.27

Jang Nara was born in Seoul in March 1981. She is considered one of the best entertainers in South Korea.
She started out as an actress in her primary school days, when she was invited to appear in the play Les Misérables. Later, in high school, she modelled in a number of television ads. Jang had her first real success as a singer in 2001, when her debut album was released. 300,000 copies of the album were sold, and she was awarded Best New Singer of that year.
At the same time, her acting career continued to develop. She was hired to star in popular sitcoms and dramas, and she was also invited by a Chinese television station to star in the successful drama My Bratty Princess. She is very popular in China, where she is known as 'Zhang Na La'.
In addition, she has been recognised for her charity work in different countries. She was appointed a goodwill ambassador by one Chinese charity, the first foreigner to receive this honour.

🔊 1.28

CONOR   OK, so, there's lots to see. Er, where should we start?
MEI   Well, you should see the Forbidden City, of course.
c   Yeah, definitely. Er, the Forbidden City's basically a palace, isn't it?
M   It was, yes. It was built by the Emperor Yongle, who was one of our most famous emperors.
c   Right. When was that?

M   Erm, as far as I can remember, it was in the, erm, fifteenth century. Actually I'm not really sure.
c   Right. So would that take all day or … ?
M   Oh, yes. There's, like, a thousand buildings! They say that it took a million workers fourteen years to complete.
c   Oh, right. I'll need a guide book, then.
M   Yes, though I think I'm right in saying that you can rent an audio tour. There's an office just inside the main entrance.
c   Sounds good.
M   Hmm … Let's see. Hmm … Another big landmark is the Temple of Heaven. That was also put up by the Emperor Yongle, by the way.
c   Busy man.
M   Yeah. I read somewhere that it's made completely of wood. There are no nails at all.
c   Oh, wow!
M   Anyway, it's in excellent condition now because they did a lot of restoration work before the 2008 Olympics.
c   Ah, of course, the Olympics. Now, is that place still open, you know, the Bird's Nest?
M   Oh, you mean the National Stadium? Yeah, it's quite a big tourist attraction these days.
c   Ah, good. I'd love to see it. It's an amazing building!
M   OK, well, I've heard that they have English-speaking guides there so they'll be able to give you lots of details – facts and figures – about the stadium.
c   Ah, great. And what about the Great Wall? That's pretty close to here, isn't it?
M   It's quite close, yes. Erm, the Badaling section, that's the most popular part, it's been restored with a lot of watchtowers and so on …
c   Uh-huh.
M   … erm, if I remember rightly, it's a two- or three-hour trip by bus.
c   Oh, OK.
M   Maybe we can go tomorrow? It's my day off.
c   Fine by me.
M   Great and then maybe the day after tomorrow you might consider …

🔊 1.29

BERYL   If anyone arrived in England on November the fifth, I think they'd get quite a shock in the evening, erm, because they'd hear a lot of bangs and a lot of lights in the sky. Erm, what they wouldn't know is that November the fifth is Bonfire Night in England. Erm, nowadays, erm, people celebrate it together. Mostly their local council will organise a bonfire and fireworks, whereas in the old days, people used to celebrate it in their … their back gardens but now

almost the whole town or village will turn out for the … this event where there will be a huge bonfire, with a guy sitting on the top, and a display of fireworks and all ages of people go, erm, people …
INTERVIEWER   Beryl, what is a guy, can you tell me?
B   Yes, the reason we have Bonfire Night is because about four hundred years ago, a group of conspirators tried to blow up the Houses of Parliament, hoping at the same time to kill the king.
I   Oh, right.
B   And the unlucky one who got caught was Guy Fawkes so the guy is actually Guy Fawkes but now the word 'guy' has got a more general meaning.
I   So it's not a real person. It's a kind of doll or something.
B   It's a kind of doll made out of wood, erm, straw, old clothes just to … to look like a … a figure on the top of the bonfire.
I   And what kind of atmosphere is there?
B   Erm, usually quite excited and people always think that the children will love it and most children do but a lot of young children are of course quite frightened by it because the bangs are very loud. So there's a lot of laughing, a lot of shouting and screaming – and crying as well – and an awful lot of 'Wows' …
I   I bet!
B   … as the fireworks go up.

DOMINIKA   Erm, I suppose, erm, the … one of the nicest things about being Polish is that you get, erm, to attend plenty of, erm, extravagant weddings and, erm, they may not be extravagant in terms of the kind of food they serve or the kind of, erm, drink but they are quite extravagant in terms of the effort made by the entire community and in terms of, also, the amount of time you'd spend … you'd spend celebrating. Er, Polish weddings traditionally, erm, go on for days on end.
INTERVIEWER   Days!
D   And, er … Oh, yes, and, erm, er, you tend to have, erm, well it's at least … traditionally it's at least two days, so first you celebrate the whole day and the whole night and then it's also, er, it's also quite, erm, it's quite normal to then have another celebration the day after, er, to help you recover.
I   Really.
D   So, erm, there is plenty of food served throughout the ceremony and, erm, you also, erm, … there are also quite a few, erm, peculiar things, for example, erm, the fact that the bride should wear something that she borrowed from somebody else, erm, to bring her good luck and … and also

the fact that she has to dance with, erm, every one of her guests.

I Every guest? Well, how many guests are there, then?

D Well, again, traditionally it's, erm, a wedding is a celebration for an entire community, er, and a big extended family so it can be anywhere between two hundred and four hundred people.

I So she must be exhausted.

D Oh, yes. It's quite a job being a bride.

🔊 1.30

autumn   community   impression
estimated   immigration   summary
summit   thumb   demonstration
remember   enormous   calm

Unit 5

🔊 2.1

During the English Civil War from 1642 to 1649, Parliamentarians and Royalists fought each other for control of the country. The Parliamentarians were unhappy with the way King Charles I ruled the country, while the Royalists were loyal to the King. The war ended in 1649 when Oliver Cromwell, a leading Parliamentarian, had the King executed and became leader of the country. This painting, by William Frederick Yeames, shows an imaginary scene from a Royalist household during the English Civil War. Parliamentarian soldiers have taken over the house and are questioning the little boy about the location of his Royalist father.

🔊 2.2

The young boy in the painting was based on Yeames' five-year-old nephew, James. Yeames was inspired to paint the picture after recognising that childhood honesty and innocence could have disastrous consequences. The boy will have been told that honesty is a virtue and that he should never lie. But will he realise that his father is in danger? We can only guess how he will answer. The small size of the boy, his blond hair and blue suit highlight his innocence. In order to save his father, he may have to lose some of his innocence and lie to the men who are questioning him.

Behind the boy, his sister stands crying, probably at the thought of what her brother may say, or of being questioned herself. The young girl was modelled on the artist's niece, Mary.

On the far left of the painting two other women, probably the boy's elder sister and mother, can be seen. The anxiety about his possible answer can clearly be seen on his mother's face. Through a doorway, more soldiers are visible and this further emphasises the family's helplessness.

This man is asking the boy where his Royalist father is. The soldier and the boy's father support different sides in the English Civil War. His expression seems calm and friendly. However, he may be behaving in this way to try and trick the boy into giving up his father.

Yeames portrays the Parliamentarian soldiers with some sensitivity. The guard with the sobbing young girl seems to be comforting her. This implies that he has some sympathy for their situation. Perhaps the guard has children of his own and would not like to see them questioned in this way.

The gentleman standing at the table appears to be opening the family jewel-box. This and the opened chest in the foreground of the painting suggest that the soldiers may be searching the house and helping themselves to the family's possessions.

🔊 2.3

JAMES Hey, what do you think about this one, Paloma?

PALOMA Mm ... It's interesting. I can't see it in the living room, though.

J No?

P No. It's too dark and gloomy.

J I suppose so.

P And it's the wrong ... shape.

J Too wide, you mean?

P Yeah. If it's going to go above the leather chair, it needs to be a bit more square.

J Well, how about this one? It's a good size.

P Are you joking? Ugh ...

J What? It's nice and cheerful.

P Yeah. We could put it in the toilet, perhaps.

J Oh, come on. The horse is nice.

P No, it isn't.

J OK. Have you got any suggestions?

P Yes, how about this? I love the strong colours.

J Yeah, they're very striking, aren't they?

P But?

J I'm not so sure about the style. For the room, I mean.

P Hmm, I see what you mean. No, it wouldn't suit the living room, would it?

J I can imagine it in the kitchen, though. It could go in that corner by the window.

P Yeah.

J OK, well, maybe we can do that. But we still need something for the living room.

P Well, I think *this* one would look nice in the living room.

J Yeah.

P Do you like it?

J Yes, I do actually. I like the way the sunlight comes down through the clouds.

P Me too. And it's nice and bright, so it'd make the room feel a lot bigger.

J Is the shape OK?

P Yes, I think so.

J OK, shall we get that one then? And the one with the tree for the kitchen?

P All right. Then we need to get some frames.

J All right. Er, what are the numbers of the posters?

🔊 2.5

CALLIE Right, well, as you know, we originally had a choice of six designs created for us by LogoForum. We've asked different people for their opinions and, er, we've narrowed it down to these three.

KIM Right.

BRETT Yes.

C Now, I think we're almost there but we really need to make a decision this afternoon. So ... Kim?

K Alright, well, I think all three designs have their strengths, but I think this one's the weakest.

B Really? I liked that one.

K Well, it's true that it emphasises the idea of 'forever' quite well – you know, the idea that you can give flowers any time – but the colours are a bit weak.

B Well, I wouldn't exactly say they're weak. I'd say the colours are low-key and, well, quite elegant.

K But even if that's the case, I don't think they look dynamic enough for our business. I mean, we're all about colour.

B But too much colour can look flashy if you're not careful.

K Yeah but look at this one – which is my favourite, by the way. It's pretty colourful but I wouldn't say it was flashy.

B Well, I think it's a bit strong myself, though I have to admit that the flower image is nice.

C OK, let's put these two aside for a moment and have a look at the third design. Brett, what are your thoughts?

B No, it wouldn't suit our business at all. It's too abstract, too cold, too much lettering. I'm surprised it got into the final three, to be honest.

C Yeah, I don't think it's very good either. Are we all agreed on that? Kim?

K Mm, I didn't think it was too bad actually. It's nice and modern. But I'll go along with the majority.

C OK, so let's eliminate this one. Now, back to the first two.

B Well, what do *you* think about them?

C Personally, I think we need a strong image that people won't forget, and for that reason, I agree with Kim on this one.

B OK ...

C Having said that, I take your point that the colours may be a bit too flashy. How about if we ask LogoForum to tone down the colours a little – the same colours but a shade or two lighter? Would that work for you?

B Well ... yeah, I guess it would help.

C Kim?

K Yeah, a shade or two's fine but no more than that. It has to be bright and easy to see.

C OK, then. These two are out and we're going with this one but we'll ask for a slight adjustment to the colours, right?

K Sounds good.

C Brett? It's not too late to change your mind.

B No. I'm fine with that.

C So, we're all in favour of it. Great! Well, thanks, both of you.

K That's all right.

C I'll go and call LogoForum now.

2.6

a What are your thoughts?
Are we all agreed on that?
Would that work for you?
Brett? It's not too late to change your mind.

b We're going with this one.
So, we're all in favour of it.

c Let's eliminate this one.
These two are out.

2.8

1 Are you joking?
I wouldn't exactly say
I'm not so sure about
Oh, come on.
Are you serious?
How can you say that?
I have to disagree with you there.
I wonder about that.

2 I have to admit that
I see what you mean.
I'd go along with you there.
Maybe you're right about that.

3 It's true that ... but
But even if that's the case,
That may be so, but
I take your point, but

Unit 6

2.9

ANGELA The government yesterday proposed tough new measures to deal with illegal file sharing. It wants the companies which bring the internet to people's homes – Internet service providers, or ISPs – to cut off people who download films and music illegally. But ISPs say it's not their job to police the web. Music journalist Robin Bland joins us now. Robin, thanks for joining us.

ROBIN Thank you.

A Why do you think the government's taking this action now?

R Well, for a long time, they've been under a lot of pressure from the music industry, the entertainment industry – who've always been very clear that, as far as they're concerned, file sharing is just another word for stealing. You wouldn't go into your local shop and steal a CD or a DVD, so why's it OK to do it online?

A That makes it sound very simple.

R Yes it does, but on the other hand, you have people who say that a lot of the files people download are things you couldn't buy even if you wanted to – videos of concerts, TV programmes which aren't out on DVD, things like that.

A Hm.

R There's also the argument that people use file-sharing sites to decide whether they like, say, a particular album and if they do, then they'll go out and buy it legally.

A So file sharing is a form of advertising.

R That's the theory, yes.

A But how much money does the music industry actually lose through file sharing? Have they said?

R Well, the music companies will tell you that their sales have gone down a lot in recent years, and that's true. But a lot of people think that, even if you stopped file sharing completely, it wouldn't lead to a big increase in sales.

A Why is that?

R Well, what they say is that, historically, music prices have simply been too high and that most people would be happy to buy the real thing provided the prices were lower.

A But the music companies say – don't they? – that they need to make a healthy profit so they can invest in new, young musicians ...

R That's exactly right. And of course, many musicians will say that if you like their music, well, you really should be prepared to pay for it!

A So, er, why are the Internet companies, the ISPs, so reluctant to take action against file sharing?

R An ISP is a business like any other. Why would they want to cut off their own customers? And finding out who's sharing files illegally – because there's lots of *legal* file sharing too – takes up a lot of time and money.

A So, where do you think this is headed?

R Well, I think there's a chance the ISPs will take action as long as they can all agree to act together. Obviously, unless that happens, ISPs will just be afraid of losing customers to their rivals.

A Interesting stuff. Robin Bland, thanks for being with us.

R Cheers.

2.11

BEN OK, erm ... what else?

RAMDAS Erm ...

B We've got a meeting with the web designers tomorrow, right?

R Yeah, first thing, at nine o'clock.

B OK, so let's have a look at the site map.

R Yeah, it's er right here. There were a couple of things I wasn't sure about.

B Me, too. I have some ideas, though.

R Great. What are they?

B No, go ahead.

R OK. Well, first thing, the 'Portrait advice' is in the wrong place.

B Uh huh.

R I think we should link that page to 'Portraits'.

B Yep, I agree. Hang on while I make the new link. ... What else?

R I think we should cut the 'About Us' page.

B Cut it? But we need it.

R Yeah, but if we leave it where it is, no one'll see it. It's better to move all that information to the homepage.

B So the homepage would have our pictures and all the info about us, right?

R Right. Otherwise, it'll be a bit empty. I mean, there's nothing much on the homepage right now.

B Except the links.

R Exactly. So it makes sense to use that space. That way, everyone'll read the information about us ... I hope!

B All right. ... So that's one less page.

R Right. Now what about you?

B My idea is to stick another page here and link it to the 'Contact us' page. It would tell people where the studio is.

R Like a map?

B Yeah, a map – and directions if you're coming by car, bus or on foot. We're not so easy to find.

R OK. So we'd call the page 'How to find us' or something.

B 'How to find us', yeah, that's good.

R Anything else?

B Yeah, it's a small thing but I think we should swap 'Landscapes' and 'Weddings'. Then all the people stuff will be grouped together.

R Ah, OK. So 'Landscapes' would be the last link on the list.

B Yep.

R OK, that's it, then. So the next thing is what pictures to include ...

2.12

LIESBETH I think it's really important, if you send out or receive a job offer, that you get it in writing in a letter, on a piece of paper, even though someone might have already told you by whatever – text or phone – that you got the job.

HUGO Yeah, I ... I think I would agree, though it is really increasingly common for people to call you first. Erm, like certainly that's ... that's happened to me quite a few times that the company will call me but then I'll receive a letter and especially if you're discussing things like contracts and ... then you need official documents ...

L Mm, absolutely.

H ... otherwise, you know, it starts getting problematic. But, for example, sending out applications, er, I ... I've done loads of applications on – online and it's much easier, much quicker, you know, to send an email with a ... a more or less similar message to five hundred companies instead of posting them all over the place.

L Mm, true, yeah. What do you think about thanking someone for a gift, though? I mean, would you still do that by email or whatever?

H For me, it's it's a generational thing. It depends who I'm thanking. So, erm, like, if I'm ... if it's a mate who's got me something for a birthday, then I'll probably just call him, erm, or text him.

L No. Yeah, it's definitely a generational thing. I mean, I've got this really old, erm, lovely uncle. He's really quite old, in his nineties, and I wouldn't dream of phoning him. If he sends me a gift, I will make a lovely handwritten ... clearly written letter, twice over, erm, with some news about myself and thanking him for the gift and what I like about it and there's no other way I'll possibly thank him.

H Yeah, I've got the same thing. I mean, if it's my ... my grandparents or someone like that, then I'll definitely send a letter because there ... there's that expectation. But with people my age, I I think that's more or less disappeared.

L Yeah.

🔊 2.13

For a long time, the government's been under a lot of pressure from the music industry, the entertainment industry – who've always been very clear that, as far as they're concerned, file sharing is just another word for stealing ...

But on the other hand, you have people who say that even if it's illegal, most file sharing doesn't in fact hurt the music industry ...

There's also the argument that people use file-sharing sites to decide whether they like, say, a particular album and if they do, then they'll go out and buy it legally.

The music companies will tell you that their sales have gone down a lot in recent years ...

But a lot of people think that, even if you stopped file sharing completely, it wouldn't lead to a big increase in sales ...

What they say is that, historically, music prices have simply been too high and that most people would be happy to pay for the real thing in a shop – rather than download it – provided the prices were lower ...

And of course, many musicians will say that if you like their music, well, you should really be prepared to pay for it!

Unit 7

🔊 2.14

INTERVIEWER ... that you founded a magazine called *Polyglossia* a little while ago. Erm, did you encounter any particular problems in founding it?

HUGO Well, first off, in terms of founding it, to begin with, er, the biggest problem was that it was just an idea and really I ... I was trying to find people, er, I found it really difficult to select different people and I had to have almost a type of interview my, er, with ... with prospective candidates and then once we'd set it up, there ... there were a lot of executive decisions that needed to be taken. So the magazine was called *Polyglossia* and specifically this magazine contained articles, or, contains articles in lots of different languages. This was really interesting but it presented us with a problem because what do you do with a casual reader who picks up the magazine and, say, has a knowledge of French but can't read Spanish, Swahili, German, Russian? ... And so what we decided to do, erm, or my way of solving this problem was to include English summaries of all of the foreign languages ... of all of the foreign-language articles and this meant that at least the reader would feel that they had an idea of what was going on in in each article and and all through the magazine.

I So this was fundamentally to increase your readership.

H Yeah, because, er, obviously if you have a magazine with eight or nine different languages and you don't make any accommodation for ... for someone who only reads two or three, then your readership is going to be null.

I And, erm, what did you learn from that kind of puzzle-solving experience?

H What did I learn from it? Well, I suppose really what I ... what I really learned was to put myself in ... in other people's shoes ...

I OK.

H ... and to ... to sort of, also sort of thinking outside of ... of the box ...

I Yes, definitely.

H ... outside of very concrete ideas that I had and also flexibility. You know, noticing that maybe ... learning to admit that original ideas may not be that good or that things need to be revised and ... yeah.

🔊 2.15

PRESENTER ... next week. In the next part of today's programme, we investigate the power of dreams. We all know the benefits of a good night's rest, but our sleeping minds are by no means inactive. Kathryn Harrison explains.

KATHRYN Published in 1818, Mary Shelley's *Frankenstein* is regarded by many as the world's first science-fiction novel. But did you know that the image of the famous monster came to the author in her sleep? In the summer of 1816, at the age of just nineteen, Mary visited the home of the poet Byron in Switzerland. Forced to stay indoors by stormy weather, Mary and Byron's other guests amused themselves by reading from a book of German ghost stories, and Byron suggested that they each write their own supernatural tale. A short time later, Mary got the idea for *Frankenstein* from a dream:

MARY When I placed my head upon my pillow, I saw a pale student kneeling beside the monster he had put together and then, on the working of some powerful engine, it came to life. I opened my eyes in terror, but then the idea broke upon me: 'I have found my story! What terrified me will terrify others, and I need only describe the monster which haunted my sleep.'

K The next day, Mary began writing. But it's not only in the arts that dreams have been important. One of India's greatest mathematical geniuses, Srinivasa Ramanujan, was inspired by dreams in which a Hindu goddess called Namagiri would appear and present him with mathematical formulae. As Ramanujan describes it:

SRINIVASA There was a red screen formed by flowing blood. I was observing it. Suddenly, a hand began to write on the screen. I was fascinated. The hand wrote a number of mathematical equations. They stuck in my mind. As soon as I woke up, I copied them down.

K Many of our most important scientists and engineers get a lot of inspiration from dreams as well. Perhaps the most famous scientific dream story of all involves the German chemist August Kekulé, who was trying to work out the chemical structure of benzene. One day in 1865, Kekulé had a strange experience:

AUGUST I was sitting and writing, but the work did not progress. My thoughts were elsewhere. I turned my chair to the fire and slept. I saw atoms dancing before my eyes. I had had visions of this kind before, but could now see larger structures, long rows of atoms connected together and twisting like a snake. But look! What was that? One of the snakes was eating its own tail, and the form, like a circle, spun before my eyes.

K Kekulé realised that benzene molecules, like the snake made of atoms in his dream, have the shape of a circle or ring. Thus he made one of the most important discoveries of nineteenth-century chemistry. So, the next time you have an unusual dream, why not think about what your mind is trying to tell you? It could give you the answer to a puzzle that's been bothering you, or the idea for a great work of art.

P That was Kathryn Harrison on the power of dreams. Now, as you may remember, in last week's competition we asked you to think of ...

2.17

TYLER So, this guy Chen ... what are his options?

FAISAL Well, it might be worth speaking to the two workers privately. You know, just ask them.

HAN Hmm ... There's something in that, I suppose.

T No. I think that would be tricky. He doesn't have any clear evidence, really, so they'd have every right to feel upset or insulted. They could even accuse Chen of trying to get them fired.

F Well, obviously he'd have to word it carefully.

T Even if he did that, they'd still see it as an accusation.

F Hm.

T I'd install a camera in the lab, get film evidence and prove who's doing it that way.

H Filming secretly? That's probably illegal, isn't it?

T Really? Well, erm, alternatively, he could hide somewhere and wait until the thief tries to take something.

H That's not really practical, though. He's got a job to do. He can't spend hours hiding and waiting.

F No ... Another option would be to lock the lab door when he goes out. Then, no problem!

H Yes. That's quite feasible.

T Er, I don't think so. Other people will need to use the lab even when he's not there.

H You know, what he really needs is an assistant.

F Hm, that's worth considering. He could get someone to supervise the lab, just while he's out.

T But *he's* an assistant him*self*. That's like having an assistant to an assistant!

H I guess you're right. Look, a different approach would be to inform the head of the lab about the losses.

T OK, but remember, the problem's been going on for weeks. The head will wonder why Chen didn't say anything about it before.

F Yeah, that's true.

H Then maybe he could just mention the microscope but nothing else. That's the most important thing.

F I wouldn't recommend that. It would be best just to tell the truth about all the missing things.

T OK, agreed. But should he name names?

H No, because he's not sure who did it. The two workers *could* be innocent.

F Well, that looks like the best solution then.

H Yes, all right.

T Fine by me. OK, er, what's the next one?

2.19

1

A I don't want to be nosy but I heard your brother's company just closed down.

B Yes, but I can't really talk about it.

2

A Well, happy birthday! I don't mean to pry but how old are you?

B I'd prefer not to answer that. It's a secret!

3

A Alistair told me you're not speaking. I know it's none of my business but what's the problem?

B Well, it's a difficult situation. It's just that he's sometimes so opinionated.

4

A Do you know why Jerry was fired?

B I do, but I'd rather not say. I promised not to gossip about it.

2.20

concentrate cottage equality
obvious opposition qualified
sausage swan warrior wallet

Unit 8

2.21

VIC My wife and I were in Toronto last summer and our Canadian friend, Neil, took us here and there sightseeing. He was a wonderful host, so on our last evening, we took him to dinner at a Moroccan restaurant. The food was so good that we kept ordering different dishes, trying out this and that. It was a perfect end to our trip. But for some reason, the mood changed when I paid the bill. Neil suddenly looked embarrassed and I don't know why. It can't have been because I paid. He knew I was going to. Oh, and the waiter – he might have been a bit angry. It's hard to say. Anyway, Neil was fine when he took us to the airport the next morning. But I still don't know what happened in the restaurant.

MADISON There was a really nice girl from Colombia in my first-year design class at college. Her name was Daniela. We got along quite well and often had lunch together, so when a friend decided to have a party one Saturday and asked me to bring some friends with me, one of the people I invited was Daniela. There was a barbecue of course and people were wandering in and out, talking and eating. Then suddenly I caught sight of Daniela. She was in a group but looking really bored ... anyway, not involved. I went over and talked to her but after a while she looked at her watch and said she had to go. Poor Daniela! I think she must have felt homesick.

VIRGINIA A strange thing happened the first time I went to Korea to see my friend, Haneul. I was paying her a return visit because she'd come to Italy two years before. When I saw her at the airport, I rushed over and greeted her but she looked – how can I put it? – a bit uncomfortable. She tried to smile but I had the feeling I'd done something wrong. Then after a moment, she said, 'I'm very happy to see you, Virginia. Let's go back to my apartment now.' Once we got home, everything was fine. Thinking back on it, we hadn't seen each other for two years, so she may well have forgotten what I looked like. But still, it was a strange reaction.

2.22

JEANETTE I was twenty-three years old, working for a firm of architects on the admin side. I was pretty happy – the work was interesting, and not bad money. Then one day the company announced it was moving to another state, and I thought, I have two options: I can either go with the company or stay where I am and get a new job. And then that evening I saw a college ad in one of the newspapers and I thought, well, maybe that's option three! I'd always wanted to study law, but it just never happened for one reason or another. So that's what I did, I went to college and got a law degree. And it was hard – a lot of work, money was tight and I had to take out loans. But I don't regret a thing. I'm fully qualified now and I work for a law firm in Boston.
But you know, if my company hadn't decided to move, I'd probably still be doing the same job. It's funny how things work out.

FERNANDO Well, when I was at college, I met this fantastic girl called Juli and we started going out together. Then when we graduated, we both got decent jobs and I thought, 'OK, I should ask Juli to marry me.' But I made a mistake – well, maybe it was a mistake – and I told my father first. He was totally against it. He said it was just a college romance, I needed more experience, and all that. I argued with him of course, and in the end I just thought, 'I've had enough of this, I'm going to ask her,' so I invited her to a restaurant and there we were, talking, having a nice meal – I could see our whole future together – and what happened? I didn't ask her. I still don't know why. Maybe deep down I knew my father was right. Anyway, after a few months, me and Juli split up and that was that. I'm in my early forties now, happy enough, but still single! I guess if I'd married Juli, we could've been happy, could've had kids, I really don't know. I wish I'd thought about it more carefully, that's all.

TRISTAN   For me, it was a normal school day when I was fifteen. Our head teacher told us that, if we were interested, he had the address of a guy in China who was looking for some English-speaking pen friends. Now, at the end of the day, on the way out of school, I saw the head teacher coming the other way. I wouldn't have spoken to him normally – he could be quite frightening – but he said 'Hello', so I asked him for the Chinese boy's address and he gave it to me. I wrote to the Chinese boy and eventually I visited him in Shanghai – we had a great time together, we're still friends, in fact – but the thing is, on the flight home, I ended up sitting next to someone really special who later – quite a few years later, in fact! – became my wife. We've got two children now. It's strange to think that if I hadn't seen the head teacher that day, my life would be completely different. I wouldn't have gone to China or been on that plane or met my wife or had kids! I'm glad things turned out the way they did, obviously.

🔊 2.24

JO   This is just ridiculous.
ANGELA   Yes, it is.
J   So ... what are we going to do?
A   I don't know. What are we going to *say*?
J   But it can't just have disappeared.
A   Look, we've looked everywhere. If it was here, we'd've found it.
J   So when was the last time you saw it?
A   I've told you, I don't remember. It's just ... not here now.
J   So you think it's outside?
A   Well, it might have jumped out the window, yes. Or fallen.
J   No, we'd have seen it outside, wouldn't we?

A   Not necessarily.
J   Angie, we're on the fourth floor.
A   OK, so what do you think happened?
J   Well, if it's not here and it didn't go out of the window, it must have gone out the front door.
A   How?
J   Well, last night, when we came back from shopping.
A   But I saw it when we came in, definitely.
J   Me too, but the door was open for quite a while. I had to go back down and get those bottles of water, remember?
A   Yeah, but somebody would've seen it on the stairs, one of the neighbours.
J   Hm.
A   They're nice. If they'd seen it, they would've said something.
J   Hmm ... You're wrong about last night, though.
A   What do you mean?
J   This bowl is *empty*.
A   So?
J   *So*, I distinctly remember putting out some food before we went to bed.
A   OK ...
J   So it must have been here overnight.
A   OK, well, that's good news, I guess. Has the front door been open since then?
J   No.
A   Yes, it has ... I went out to get some sugar, first thing.
J   Well, that's it then.
A   What?
J   Oh, come on. You know what you're like in the mornings. Half asleep until you've had, like, eight cups of coffee.
A   Well, I didn't see anything.
J   Oh, dear. We really need to find it before she gets back.
A   Dead or alive.
J   That's not funny.
A   Sorry.

🔊 2.25

JO   Oh, dear. We really need to find it before she gets back.
ANGELA   Dead or alive.
J   That's not funny.
A   Sorry.
J   Maybe we could put some notices up outside.
A   Yeah, or ask the neighbours.
J   When's she coming back, again?
A   She said Friday, in the evening, probably.
J   Well, that gives us two days. I ... What's that?
A   I don't believe this. Where's it coming from?
J   Seems to be coming from the bathroom ...

🔊 2.26

SAHANA   There are many different, er, languages in, in India but even more, er, dialects and even the, even the

one same language will be spoken very differently in different parts of the country. Erm, yes, there's a huge linguistic variety in India. And in fact, it's quite common to find in India now that, erm, especially with urban people of my generation, young people, in urban India, the, the only language they have in common is actually English, because the, their mother tongues, regional languages, are absolutely different and they don't understand or speak the regional languages. But also a lot of people will in school learn Hindi, which is which is the language spoken by the majority, erm, of the population in India.

LIESBETH   Erm, we have three official languages, sort of general, [uh-hum], Dutch and then there's one, there's Frisian, spoken in Friesland, which is actually older than Dutch. It's related to, it's clo – it's more closely related to English, [uh-hum,] than it is to Dutch. And one in the south, erm, and then lots of dialects as well. Everybody speaks at least two, they speak Dutch and English, and if they're in Friesland, they may speak Dutch, Frisian and English, [uh-hum,] and lots of people speak, learn other languages in school as well. It's just part of our tradition. We've always learned, you know, sort of sea-faring, trading nation and a very small nation, [Yes] so we've always gone and learned other people's languages to trade with them, so, a very linguistic country. [Yes]

🔊 2.27

SAHANA   I think it's become a lot less rigid, I mean, just as English, for instance, the English we speak now is quite different from, [uh-huh, yes] say, Victorian English. Similarly, erm, say Hindi or Bengali that we speak colloquially now is, erm, has definitely changed. Er, both Hindi and Bengali, I think, have absorbed a lot of words. For instance, there is no, there's no word in Bengali or Hindi for 'computer'. So if you're speaking a whole sentence in Bengali and you have to refer to a computer, you would say 'computer'. Older people are actually not very happy about the fact that, er, younger people who are equally proficient, erm, in say two languages tend to use words from both, in, in one single conversation or in one sentence, so, older people in general, I think, are a little more conservative, [Right, yes.] and puritanical about, erm, speaking one language.

LIESBETH Erm, it's, it's a very direct language and that's just a reflection of the character of the people, really. [uh-hum] Dutch are very direct people. People say what they mean. There's no sort of mincing of words, and it's not with any idea of being rude but it's sometimes perceived as rude by English people or people from other countries because it's very direct and, er, that's sort of reflected in, in the language.

2.28

1 A couple of years ago, I missed a flight from Paris to Buenos Aires because my alarm clock didn't go off. Later, I heard many passengers on that flight had got food poisoning. A few of them even ended up in hospital!

2 Jack, this guy I know, invited me out for coffee the other night. When I got to the café, he was there with a group of people – including my ex-boyfriend. It was *not* a comfortable evening!

3 I asked one of my accountants, Gisela, to work late yesterday. She wasn't very happy about it but I insisted. Then this morning when she came in, I heard someone asking her if she'd had a good birthday yesterday.

4 I remember doing an exam where I finished way before everyone else. A classmate told me later there were three more questions on the back of the paper – but I hadn't checked the back.

5 I went on a skiing holiday to Switzerland with some friends last winter. They were better than me and I tried as hard as I could to keep up with them. Eventually, though, I had a fall and guess what? I broke my leg.

6 I bought several advance tickets to a popular theme park for my grandchildren and their friends. But before we could go, the theme park suddenly closed down. Those tickets were so expensive!

Unit 9

3.1

BRIAN Right, can you all see? Now, the book we're printing here has 320 pages. The number of pages is important because when you're making a book, you print it in sections. So with a book like this, we'd print it in ten sections. So each section is ... anyone?

PERSON 1 32 pages.

B That's right. Ten sections, 32 pages, gives you a 320-page book. So, here we're using a B1 printing press. Er, first of all the operator pours ink and water into the machine so it covers the plates and rollers and then the paper – very large sheets of paper, as you can see – goes into the printing press, which, er, prints the pages onto the paper.

PERSON 2 So it does all 32 pages at once, right?

B That's right. The machine prints 16 pages on one side, turns the paper over, and prints 16 pages on the other side – so, yeah, 32 pages.

PERSON 3 How fast does it go?

B Well, in an hour, this machine'll do about 10,000 sheets.

B So, when the paper emerges from the press, it's ready for the next stage, which is folding.

PERSON 4 Folding the large sheets, you mean?

B That's it. So we put the sheets into this machine, which folds them in half and then folds them again, and then again, and again.

P1 So that's ... four folds.

B Yes, and if you fold a sheet of paper four times, you'll end up with a 32-page section.

P2 So how do you get the pages in the right order?

B Good question. Er, yes, obviously page 1 needs to come before page 2, then page 3 and so on. Now, when you see a large *unfolded* sheet, it looks like random pages all over the place. But in fact, we arrange the pages so that, when they're folded four times, they end up in the right order.

P3 That's clever.

B Well, it's just er, a formula that you follow. Another thing is, as the paper passes through the folding machine, it cuts a little notch into the spine – the back – of the section. That's actually quite important but, er, I'll come back to that later.

B So, we print and fold the ten sections of the book one after the other, and each of your ten sections is given a letter, so the first section is A, the second section is B, third is C and so on. So, the next step is, all the folded sections go to the gathering machine.

P4 And that puts all the sections together?

B That's right. You have the ten sections, A to J, in front of the gathering machine. Then the machine picks up an A section, then a B section and so on, and puts together a complete set. Now, does anyone know what we call ... ?

P1 A book block?

B Right. The set's called a book block, and it's basically just a very crude book, erm, it isn't glued, there's no cover, it's not trimmed round the edges.

P1 Right.

B Now, you remember I told you, er, during the folding stage, about the notches cut into the spine of each section?

P1 Yes.

P2 Yep.

B Well, what happens next is, the machine grabs the book block and runs it over very hot glue. Er, the glue goes into the notches, and then the machine attaches the cover to the book block.

P2 Right, so the glue holds everything together.

B Exactly. All the sections – ten in this case – and the cover.

P3 How hot is the glue?

B Er, it's about 250 degrees.

P4 Celsius?

B Celsius, yes, though it cools down pretty quickly. Erm, the book moves along a conveyor belt slowly while the glue cools down and hardens, then it drops into what's called the three-knife trimmer – and the trimmer cuts off the edges of the book block.

P1 So, the top and the bottom?

B And the right-hand side, yes. So the trimmer gives the book its final size and then it's ready to be packed up and shipped to, er, whoever wants it. And that's the whole process. Any questions?

3.3

JOSETTE Well, I'd say I've got three or four important roles in my life. Professionally speaking, I work as a writer, these days mostly working on screenplays for films, but the most important thing in my life is that I'm a parent of two young boys. Fortunately my husband and I both work from home so we're able to spend a lot of time with them, and in fact I've recently taken on the role of their teacher as well, as we decided we'd like our kids to be educated at home, erm, at least for a few years. Erm, I'm a member of the Screenwriters' Guild. In fact, I play quite an active part in the Guild ... from time to time, for example, I act as a representative for our members at different events. Er ... what else? I belong to a local charity which works with homeless people so I occasionally do voluntary work for them. And that's it, really. Oh, I'm a lifelong supporter of Crystal Palace football club. But I don't know if that counts, does it?

3.4

ADAM Thanks for your introduction, Mary, and thanks, everyone, for coming. Erm, I think for the first ten or fifteen minutes I'd like to talk about four main things: first, what it's like to be a travel writer, er, the lifestyle; then money, very important; how to get into travel writing, of course; and finally, how I think the profession's changing at the moment. After that, we can throw it open and talk about anything you want to. Is that all right, Mary?

MARY Sounds perfect.

3.5

ADAM So, let's begin with the lifestyle. Er, of course people always say, 'Wow! Travel writer! Must be the best job in the world!' Well, er, I think it *is* the best job in the world but it's important to understand that it's not as glamorous as most people seem to think. As a travel writer your job is basically to collect as much accurate information as you can in the fastest way possible: bus timetables, prices, opening times, and so on. On a typical day, I'll be on my feet maybe twelve hours and I might visit ten hotels, half a dozen cafés and the local tourist office. Then, in the evening, while the real tourists are relaxing and having a good time, I'll be in my hotel, typing up my notes. So, it can be a great job but it's not like being on holiday! Any questions so far? Yes?

MARY Do travel writers take holidays?

A Good question. Erm, yes, yes, they do. If I want to be a tourist, I take a holiday, just like anyone else. In fact, I've just had a holiday and I had to fight the urge to pick up leaflets everywhere I went. OK, er, that's the lifestyle. The next thing is money. Again, er, hm, unless you're very successful, you'll never be rich and in fact most people do find it hard just to make a living. You really need to have regular work from one of the top travel magazines or write guidebooks. Yes?

STUDENT 1 When you're working on a guidebook, do the publishers generally pay their writers' expenses?

A Not exactly. As a rule, they just give you a sum of money to cover the cost of your trip and your fee, and you get on with it. So obviously, if you want to keep any money for yourself, you don't stay in five-star hotels. And by the way, most travel writers don't get free hotel rooms or meals in restaurants. They have to pay for them. Yes?

STUDENT 2 Roughly how much would a travel writer make in a year?

A Er, there's so much variety, that's really impossible to answer. But to give you some idea, mm, there's a very successful travel writer some of you may have heard of, Tom Brosnahan, and he calculated that after all their expenses, an established travel writer might make about six dollars an hour, so, not very much. That's all I wanted to say about money for now. Erm, I'm really not trying to put you off but

travel writing really does have to be something you want to do passionately. So, assuming you're still interested, let's move on to how you can get into the business. Most people start off by writing for travel magazines, so it's useful to know what kind of thing they're looking for, and what kind of thing they really don't want.

3.6

Write down:
the name of someone who has made money in an unusual way.
the name of someone who's good at thinking in original ways.
something you prefer to do in the quickest way possible.
the name of someone who sings or writes in an interesting way.
something you got in an unexpected way.
the name of someone who dresses in a very distinctive way.

3.8

bookcase   bullet   bully   childhood
cookie   cushion   misunderstood
overtook   rosebush   wooden

Unit 10

3.11

OK, so, er, this is some basic information about Leif Eriksson from the Internet. Erm, depending on who you ask, he was born around 970 or 975, and, erm, he was probably the first European to explore North America. He lived in Greenland but in around the year 1000 he sailed to Norway. Then there are two different stories about what happened next. According to one version, while Eriksson was trying to get back to Greenland, he was blown off course by bad weather and ended up in North America. But other sources claim that he was following the route of an earlier explorer and deliberately sailed to North America, so, not by mistake. He wasn't alone of course, erm, yeah, in one article, it mentions that he sailed with thirty-five men, though interestingly, several sites make no mention of any companions. So, they first came to a land covered with flat rocks, which might have been Baffin Island. Then they arrived at a place with trees and, er, white sandy beaches, which was probably Labrador. And finally they reached a third place, which Eriksson called Vinland. They built a small settlement there and then explored the area a bit. It seems to have been a very pleasant place with a mild climate, green grass, wild grapes, rivers, salmon. They stayed there for the winter, then returned to Greenland. Erm, most sources are in agreement that Leif Eriksson died in about 1020. One of the most interesting questions is, where exactly was Vinland? Er, in the 1950s and

60s, some archaeologists discovered a Viking settlement at the northern tip of Newfoundland in Canada – so that's one possibility. Sources vary on this question, though. Some just say that Vinland *was* in Newfoundland, others say it's only a possibility. So that could be an interesting angle, I think. Er, and that's it, really.

3.12

GAVIN Erm, here in England we have the so-called 'right to roam', which means that hikers have the right to walk on public or privately owned land in the open countryside. We can't walk on all privately owned land, like, er, people's gardens or special hunting and fishing areas – but landowners are obliged to let us walk on their land in the mountains, hills and forests or along the coast – even on some kinds of farmland. Walkers usually follow paths through these areas, which is good because that way, they have a minimum impact on the land. Er, they're also expected to obey the countryside code. So, for example, if they close all gates carefully, don't drop litter, don't disturb the animals, don't damage plants and so on, then they're free to pass through people's land.

HIKARI My husband's a civil servant and we live in an apartment building for civil servants. But because there's no building manager, the families who live there have to take care of the grounds and pavements around the building themselves ... oh, and also the children's play area in the back. It's our duty to organise this in turn, so once a month the person in charge – usually it's a woman – she decides what day and time we should meet to clean up the area. Then we all go out and pick up rubbish, pull out weeds, er, sweep up leaves in the autumn and so on. She also collects a small amount of money from each household for various common expenses, like stair lights. I suppose we have the option of hiring someone to do the cleaning but it's not that much trouble ... and anyway, it gives us a chance to chat together.

RYAN Friends from other countries are often surprised when I tell them it's compulsory to vote here in Australia. It's been like that since the mid-1920s, and the reason was because of poor voter turnout in the 1922 election – around 60% – so the government decided to take action. Nowadays, about 95% of registered voters go out and vote. If you don't, you have to explain why and if your explanation's not good enough, you probably have to pay a small fine. My brother thinks we should have the freedom to vote or not, as we choose. But personally I like our system because it means that election results reflect the wishes of almost all the people, not just a few. Anyway, Australia's not the only country that has compulsory voting. Belgium has, and Argentina, Singapore and others.

Unit 11

3.13

ANTONIA   Did you always imagine you would end up working in this field?

ANDIE   I always wanted to. I left school in 1966, not quite knowing what to do next and I applied to go and work on one of the North Sea pirate ships and in fact got offered something from one of them but that caused such a kerfuffle at home that I didn't go. I think these days people like me would have just said, 'Well, tough, I'm going,' but it was different in those days and I always wanted to work on radio. But I had twenty-eight years when I was a primary school teacher but all the time I was doing it, I wanted to work on radio and so I used to apply for jobs, having had no experience but telling them how good I was going to be. And so, when I eventually entered radio, it was towards the end of my teaching career but I managed to combine them both for a number of years.

ANTONIA   You say 'people like you'. Is it very much the person that you are that you bring to air?

ANDIE   Yes, I think so. Erm, having had years of teaching, then I had a certain style anyway and I used to know how to handle people and obviously get the best out of people, even though they were children. And then it was quite easy for me in many ways to transpose that to becoming a broadcaster. But ultimately I'm interested in people and I want to know what people have got to say for themselves.

ANTONIA   Do you interview all sorts of people?

ANDIE   I started here as the sports producer. And for five or six years, I absolutely loved it but it did become repetitive. The current show is completely varied and I can talk to politicians, to listeners, to health experts. We talk about consumer problems. I might well interview somebody who's appearing on television. So it's an across-the-board thing.

ANTONIA   So you love this aspect far more. Your eyes are lighting up!

ANDIE   Absolutely. To think that I can come to work and talk to almost anybody is terrific. I love politics, I love current affairs and I could think of nothing better, really.

ANTONIA   Do you rely on basic questions that you've prepared in your mind or does it just happen?

ANDIE   I never have any basic questions in my mind. I never have any basic questions written down. Whoever I interview – and very often I'm given a person to interview with perhaps thirty seconds or a minute's notice – I quickly decide on an opening question and take it from there. The opening question, I often feel, has to be something which maybe puts the interviewee at ease sli ... maybe slightly, erm, jocular if you like, but get them talking and then I just see where the interview takes me.

ANTONIA   What about those tough times, when the guest just clams up?

ANDIE   Happens rarely, but it has happened to me. I remember interviewing Alan Sugar many years ago now and he was really difficult. But that didn't put me off. I just kept going, getting to where I wanted to go.

ANTONIA   What do you mean? How did you do that?

ANDIE   Because I was persistent and even though his – I say his body language – his voice language maybe wasn't very warm, I still kept going.

ANTONIA   You have a producer. Is that right?

ANDIE   I do. He tells me who the person is, I get into the interview and occasionally we have a system here whereby ... we call it Talkback but basically he can put a question up on the screen. Sometimes he will put up something that he specifically wants me to ask but that happens very occasionally.

ANTONIA   Do you think you ever stop learning?

ANDIE   No. Never. I learn things every day. And I don't know how many times I actually say on air, 'It's amazing, but I've learnt things today.' And you don't just learn those things from experts. You learn them from ordinary people and that's one of the pure joys of this show. I really seriously don't know how many times I say, 'Good lord, I've learnt something today.'

ANTONIA   Andie, thank you.

3.15

VICKI   OK, well, as you know, I put together some questions to ask the people who live round here as well as the people who come in to work for local businesses. In the end I spoke to just over a hundred and fifty people.

TREVOR   Wow.

V   Most of them I spoke to on the street just outside the shop – so, local people – and I also visited all the shops and offices on the main street. All of them were pretty happy to talk to me, actually.

GINA   Great work.

V   So, the first question was about where people buy their ordinary day-to-day bread. No surprises here, really. Eight out of ten people said they usually got their bread at the supermarket.

G   Hm. Did they say why?

V   Cost, convenience. The supermarkets are cheaper and most people prefer to do their shopping all at once.

T   Alright. Have you got any good news?

V   Actually, yes! Erm, when I spoke to people who work round here, I wanted to know how many of them bought their lunches here and what we could do to encourage more of them to buy from us.

G   Right.

V   So I spoke to forty people from local businesses. Just under half of them buy their lunches here. From the rest, a couple of people said they just preferred to bring their own lunch from home, but ten people said we were a bit too far away from where they worked and they couldn't be bothered to walk. The other ten – this is the interesting bit – said they think we could offer slightly healthier food.

T   Healthier?

V   Yes. Fruit, fruit juices, things like that, maybe salads ...

T   Salads? This is a bakery, not a café.

V   Well, that's what they said. For example, quite a few of those people were vegetarians, whereas nearly all the sandwiches we make have meat in them. So we're not offering those people much choice, really.

G   That is true, Trevor.

V   So, related to that, another question was whether people would be interested if we were to take orders and deliver their lunches to them where they work. And nearly everyone said yes!

T   OK, interesting. Anything else?

V   Yes, about cakes for special occasions – birthdays, weddings and so on. Again, it looks like we're missing some opportunities here. Three quarters of local people said they need cakes for special occasions two or more times a year ...

G   Right.

V   ... and nearly all of them said they'd be interested in buying from us ...

G   Great!

V   ... but they also nearly all said they didn't know we did 'big, fancy' cakes!

T   Hm. That surprises me, I must say.

G   Yes, me too.

v Well, that was it, basically. I've made a little summary of all the results for you to have a look at.

g Ah, that's great, thanks.

t Yes, thank you. We've got a lot to think about.

g Why don't we think about things over the weekend and have another talk next week?

v Good idea.

t Sounds good to me. Now, Vicki, can I give you a lift?

3.17

1 The TV you can use but the DVD player's not working.

2 The milk you'll find in the fridge and the sugar's on the shelf.

3 This door you open with the big key and that door you open with the small key.

4 Yesterday's newspaper, what did you do with it?

5 This coffee machine, can you tell me how it works?

6 These chairs, where do you want me to put them?

3.18

building   fiftieth   fingernail   income innocent   opinion   physical symphony   typical   women

Unit 12

3.20

FAY Hello ... hello and welcome to you all and thank you very much for coming to see our school. It's good to see some children here as well as parents. My name's Fay Greenlie and I'm not the head teacher – we don't have a head teacher! – but I am the longest-serving member of staff. Now, as you know, here at Southglen we have an approach to education which is rather unusual, we think rather special, so I'd just like to say a few words about that now by way of an introduction. After that, I'll be taking you on a tour of the school, then lunch, and then we'll be coming back here to talk about the application process and discuss any questions you might have.

3.21

FAY Well, Southglen was founded nearly thirty years ago by people who believed that students of any age, whether children or teenagers or adults, learn best when they're allowed to take responsibility for their own learning. In practice, what that means is that we're a democratic school. We address each other using our first names. There's no head teacher, but the school is managed at weekly meetings called 'parliaments'. Anyone connected

with the school – teachers, students, parents, kitchen staff, cleaners – can attend the parliament and anyone can make a proposal, but only teachers and students may vote. Now, we have 15 members of staff and about 150 students, so you can see that decisions about the running of the school are very much up to the students. To some people this is a strange – even frightening – idea, but my experience is that rights and responsibilities go hand in hand. When our students are given the right to decide important issues – how to spend the school budget, whether to hire a new teacher, how to deal with cases of bullying – they take their responsibilities very seriously and are capable of making decisions for the good of the school as a whole. People are sometimes surprised at the kinds of ideas our students have. For example, any student who has a cooked lunch here in school is expected to help with the washing up afterwards. This is a policy that was proposed and approved by our students. And during tomorrow's parliament, we'll be discussing a proposal from a student – not a teacher or a parent – to introduce a school uniform. In many other ways, we're just like other schools. We have a timetable and classes in a range of different subjects. Of course, there's a lot of evidence that people learn in different ways, so we use a variety of different techniques in lessons, from traditional lectures to hands-on projects and research. However, it's for the students to decide which subjects they'd like to study. We offer guidance, of course. We encourage everyone to try out a wide range of subjects at the beginning of their time here so they can work out where their talents and interests lie. Once they've made their choices, our students are expected to attend all lessons, and they're given regular homework assignments on which they're expected to work independently outside the classroom. Our system means some students study fewer subjects than others but, when they're not in class, they're expected to work on further projects connected with their studies or make a practical contribution to the school, for example taking care of the school gardens. Again, this is not something that we've imposed from above – it's a system the students have worked out for themselves and are happy with. Well, that's all I wanted to say for now. I can see some of you are

bursting with curiosity, so let's begin our tour and show you the school at work. Now, we'd like to divide you into two groups. I'll be taking one group and, er, Jenny here will be taking the other.

3.22

JI-SUN ... so having looked at various activities, I think the four listed on this document are the best. The first is the Acting Workshop, where everyone works together to put on a play of their own choice.

BRYN Sounds quite entertaining.

J Yes, creative too. The only thing is that not everyone feels comfortable on stage and I'm afraid it could be dominated by a few strong personalities. So I'd rule it out since it might not involve everyone equally.

B Hm.

J The next possibility is the Weekend Camp. Now this one's interesting because its success depends on each person's ability to use and share their skills. They decide together how to spend their budget – on food, cooking equipment and so on – so it requires lots of group planning and cooperation. They share skills like cooking, putting up tents, building fires ... and they have to supply their own entertainment – music, games, whatever they want. I was quite keen on this option but ...

B But? Is there a downside?

J Yes, the temperature at this time of year. It can be quite chilly outside, and at night, well, some people might not appreciate sleeping in a cold tent.

B All right. What about the third option, ballroom dancing?

J Well, ballroom dancing's very popular these days and several people would be keen to do it. It would be fun and, and very good for fitness but it's basically a pair activity, not a team activity. So, unfortunately, I'd advise against it because it's not really what we're looking for.

B Right. And there was one other option.

J Yes, the last option, the Treasure Hunt, sounds childish but it's a tried and tested team-building activity for adults. The aim is to find the key to a treasure chest by working in small teams and using maps to search for clues in a forest.

B Right.

J Then the teams find out the only way to get the treasure is by working together, so eventually they combine their clues to find the key.

B And who gets the treasure?

J Everyone shares it. Anyway, it takes full day and we could have a feedba meeting and lunch at the Forest Centre the next day.

B   So that's the one you're recommending?

J   I'd strongly recommend it, yes. Basically, I think the choice is between the Weekend Camp and the Treasure Hunt. I'd reject the first on the grounds that it could be too cold so if I were you, I'd go for the second, the Treasure Hunt, as it offers value for money and is ideal for our purpose.

B   Well, that makes sense. Let me think about it for a while and we'll talk again tomorrow.

3.23

BRYN   Right, well, first of all, thanks very much for all your work finding out about the activities.

JI-SUN   That's OK. It was interesting.

B   Now, I've had a look at the promotional material and considered the four options, especially the Camp and Treasure Hunt ...

J   Right.

B   ... and I've decided to go for the Weekend Camp.

J   OK.

B   Sorry to go against your recommendation but I'd like us to spend a full weekend working together, not just a day. I also think, erm, the camping weekend will involve a greater variety of team-building activities.

J   Yeah, that makes sense. I think we'll have a good time.

B   However, I think we should keep the Treasure Hunt in mind for another occasion as it has many good points.

3.24

ESBETH   Erm, I think people are more health-conscious in Holland, erm, now than they were twenty years go, erm, but I'm not quite sure hether they're actually healthier. I ink they, erm, they sort of seem to ow a lot more about diseases and v to stay healthy but I think the tyles are actually less healthy they used to be because people less and walk less, erm, and robably drink, smoke more and till smoke a lot even though ned in public places now. So, suppose people are more conscious but whether they're r, I'm not so sure.

that it's definitely true that d to worry far too much health and, in part, this ibuted to the role of the are constantly hammering ds that we're all going to every single thing known s cancer, particularly if

you're reading certain newspapers, and in that sense I think it's really crucial that, er, even though we are more aware of our health, we tend to stress more, and this stress has a negative effect on our health – and in that sense I'm not so sure that our health is improving.

SAHANA   In India, there's a big distinction between the rural and urban worlds, and a lot of people in rural India may actually prefer to use traditional or alternative medicines that they've been using, erm, in their families for centuries, erm, and they tend to, I think, put a lot of more faith in traditional healers than in, erm, medical doctors simply because a lot of people probably have never seen medical doctors before because the reach of healthcare in India, especially in rural India, is a fairly recent phenomenon and even now it isn't complete so, erm, while a lot of rural India will tend to regard medical doctors with a lot of respect and awe, but they will still tend to put their faith in traditional methods of healing because it also is often associated with religious, erm, connotations so, yes, definitely I think in rural India particularly, erm, traditional medicines would hold sway over, er, medicine.

REGINALD   In Nigeria, when people have minor illnesses, they go to the general hospitals, not to the same doctors. That's because people do not have, family doctors as opposed to developed countries. Yeah, in Nigeria, people cannot get all their healthcare from the state paid for by taxes. Erm, the government really don't have provisions for that. People care for themselves when they are ill.

Unit 13

3.25

LIESBETH   A few years ago, erm, there was a problem on our, on our road. I live on a, on a cul-de-sac and at the end of the cul-de-sac is a green. And all the children, er, of all different ages spent, used to spend a lot of time playing on this green. Erm, some of the people at the end of the road who lived in little bungalows, er, wanted to, erm, they sort of went to the council and wanted this whole green to be paved over into a car park but unfortunately they didn't talk to anybody else on the road about this, so next thing ... the first thing we heard about it – those of us who didn't live at the end of the road – was the plans to pave over this whole green. So those of us with children didn't obviously,

erm, weren't too impressed by this idea. So, I tried to think how we could kind of solve this problem, not having it all turned into a car park but also keep the peace on the road and keep everybody happy. So I, erm, printed a load of leaflets explaining the different plans and the different ideas people had and I got everyone's opinion and I called a meeting of everybody on the road [hm mm] who wanted to come to it, including the ones that wanted a car park, and we sat round the table, we sort of thrashed it out and came up with a compromise plan which we proposed to the council – a little bit of car park and still a lot of green for the children to play. And that's what they implemented. Well, at the end of the day, I didn't want any car park but I was, I also thought it was important to keep everybody in the road happy with the result and make sure everybody had something of what they wanted, so, er, yeah, I was, I was happy and I was quite pleased to sort of have done that. Yeah, everybody felt they had got something out of the, er ... and it actually brought people in the road closer together, talking to each other more, so I thought it was a good deal all round.

3.26

YOUSEF   Er, Leo, do you have a minute?

LEO   Ah, Yousef, how are you?

Y   Fine, thanks. Erm, I've got Mr McKenzie coming in for a meeting in a while ...

L   Right.

Y   ... and we really need somewhere where we can sit down and talk.

L   OK. When's the meeting?

Y   About three.

L   Right, well, I'm going out in five minutes, so you can use this office. I'll tell Janet.

Y   Ah, that's great, thanks. Actually, I've been thinking, erm, would it be possible for me to have my own office at some point?

L   We just don't have the room, Yousef. And besides, it's not just you. Agustin and Rachel should really have their own offices too.

Y   Yes, I've thought about that. Apparently, the company upstairs wants to rent out some of its rooms. Couldn't we take those?

L   Well, of course we could, but we won't get them for nothing.

Y   Couldn't we at least ask about the price?

L   Come on, Yousef, you know how things are with money at the moment. Even if I thought it was a good idea, I'm afraid there's no way Karin would agree.

Y   Hm. Well, in that case, I've got another idea.

L OK …

Y I could move into the little photocopying room.

L But what about the photocopier? We'd have to move it *somewhere*.

Y That's no problem. It could go in the corridor, next to the drinks machine.

L Are you sure it would fit? In any case, that room's too small. There'd only be enough space for you. What about Agustin and Rachel?

Y Well, if I moved out of the main office, we'd all have more space –

L I'm not sure they'd see it that way.

Y No, maybe not.

L Look, how would it be if *I* take over the photocopying room?

Y Oh. OK. Hm.

L This office is far bigger than I need. Then the three of you could move in here.

Y Ah, that could work, yeah.

L Now, obviously, you wouldn't each have your own office, but you *would* have a lot more space and it'd be a lot quieter. And if the photocopier won't fit in the corridor, it can go where your desks are at the moment.

Y Mm, that sounds great, if it's OK with you.

L OK, well, er, I'll discuss it with the others later.

Y Right. Thanks, Leo.

🔊 3.27

// I've been <u>thinking</u> // would it be <u>possible</u> // for me to have my own <u>office</u>? // // We just don't have the <u>room</u> // And <u>besides</u> // it's not just <u>you</u> //

🔊 3.28

ETHAN So you see, Caitlin, we've looked into it and I can't express how sorry we are about the confusion. Er, apparently one of our staff made a mistake when he took your booking and recorded the number of dinner guests as seventy-five …

CAITLIN … rather than a hundred and seventy-five.

E Yes. So when you all arrived, I'm afraid we weren't prepared for such a large group. We did set up a buffet in another room, but of course …

C Yes, the buffet was set up quite quickly and we appreciated that, but unfortunately almost forty of our guests did choose not to wait and went home … and because of that, we certainly lost some important donations.

E I'm so sorry. I know how important your work is and how much you depend on donations. Erm, I gather you'd like to work out some compensation.

C Yes. We believe we should be compensated for our losses and the inconvenience to our guests.

E Could you, erm … what exactly did you have in mind?

C Well, we'd like you to cancel the cost of food, drink and room rental for the emergency buffet meal. It was $2,843 in total.

E I see.

C In addition, we feel we're entitled to a 50% refund of the cost of the sit-down dinner for seventy-five people in the dining room. It was $5,856 – here's a copy of the bill. A 50% refund would be $2,928.

E Well, to begin with, I'm afraid we can't agree to cancel the entire cost of the buffet meal. We have our own expenses to cover. However, we can offer a refund on the buffet room rental, which was $750, and we're prepared to add an extra $250 to round it up to $1000. As for the meal in the dining room, those seventy-five guests had their meal as planned and I don't honestly see why we should give you a 50% refund for that. However, we can offer another $1500 as compensation for the inconvenience.

C I don't think we can accept that, Ethan. You see, we estimate our charity has lost five to six thousand dollars as a result of your employee's error. Now, as you know, this is the third time we've held our fundraising dinner at your hotel and until last weekend, we had nothing to complain of …

E Obviously, we hope we can host your dinner again.

C Well, that depends on what we agree. Of course, we'd be willing to come here again provided we can sort out this problem.

E I see. Well, let's compromise. If you agree to accept the $2500 I mentioned, then we propose a 20% discount on your next booking with us.

C Do you mean 20% off the cost of the food, drink *and* room rental?

E Yes, 20% off the entire cost of your event. What do you say?

C Well … yes. I think we can agree to that.

E Excellent. As I said, I am really sorry. Now, let's sort out the payment …

🔊 3.29

1 Oh, it was terrible. We had to put half the guests in a little side room which we don't usually use. We did manage to organise a pretty decent buffet at very short notice – but we were still putting things on the tables when most of the guests arrived. A lot of the guests took one look at it and went home. They'd been promised a proper dinner, so I can't say I blame them.

2 I'm quite angry about the way they're trying to put the blame on us. I know the guy who took the booking, and

he's absolutely certain they said 75 guests, not 175. So I think it was their mistake. Of course, now they're putting pressure on the management for compensation. I don't think they should get anything but they're old clients so, well, I guess they will.

3 I didn't go to the dinner but I share an office with Caitlin and I can tell you, it put her in a terrible mood for the rest of the week, and I'm not surprised. The hotel put her in a really difficult situation with some very big donors of ours. It was so embarrassing, but what could she do? We'll be asking for compensation, of course. I made the booking for the dinner myself and I'm sure I said 175 guests.

4 Obviously, I'm very concerned. We've put a lot of time, money and effort into our catering services recently, building good relationships with local businesses, local charities and so on and obviously something like this involving so many people, well, it puts our reputation at risk. They'll ask for massive compensation, of course, which we can't give them, but I've instructed the hotel manager to be as generous as possible – and, in future, to ask our clients to confirm their bookings in writing.

🔊 3.31

1 Look, I'm trying to work. Will you go away?

2 Please join us. You can bring a friend along, of course.

3 I've never liked Rick. I don't know why she puts up with him.

4 Look, it's silly to argue. Let's sit down and talk about this.

5 Well, nobody told me! Apparently, it's been going on for ages!

6 I think we need another meeting. Can you set one up, Julia?

7 No, I haven't got fifty pounds! It's time for you to face up to your responsibilities!

🔊 3.32

shadow tobacco float motivate throat toast hollow portfolio owner although overcome

Unit 14

🔊 3.33

EAMONN I tend to be quite spontaneous in terms of the decisions I make because I'm of a really emotional nature and so I usually react to circumstances, react to the way things are going. And I don't find it's very useful to plan everything because when the plans don't work out, you get really upset. However, I do have a few ideas about how my future might go. For one thing, I'm a writer, so hopefully I'll have published another novel by the end of next year – ideally a bestseller. And, erm, yeah, let me see ... erm, I think in about ten years' time, my wife and I will probably be living in Portugal, maybe in the Algarve. And by that time, I'll have saved up enough money to buy a place with a sea view. It's something I've always wanted. And, erm, I guess that's all. I'm fairly sure about those three things but as I said, I usually act on the spur of the moment.

LILIYA   I like to plan ahead because then I have a long time to look forward to things and also I can make sure everything's in place so things will go smoothly. They don't always turn out as I plan ... but that doesn't stop me planning! For instance, I'm a member of a home exchange club, where you, er, in order to go on holiday, you exchange houses with a family in another country. It normally takes about eight months of planning from when you first contact the people and I really enjoy that whole process. But sometimes I like to respond to things spontaneously on a day-to-day basis. Anyway, looking into the future ... by the end of the year, I should have earned my helicopter pilot's licence. I am really excited about that. And in a year or so, I'll be running my whole department at work, the accounting department. As for my life in general, I hope to bring up my children well, so they're happy and healthy and, you know, treat other people well. But I guess most parents would say that.

🔊 3.35

IAIN   So on your CV do you have a, a special section that sells yourself or promotes yourself?

BARBARA   Usually we write a main objective, what we are looking for, and after that we talk about our experience and also our academic references.

I   How, er, long is your CV? How, how com- ... How many pages?

B   Well, it's recommended to have, er, one or two pages. Yeah.

I   That's, er, certainly the same with, er, with my experience. It's two pages maximum. Erm, do you have a covering letter with it as well?

B   Yeah, it is recommended.

I   How about when you get to, er, interviews then? Do you still have to be very, er, persuasive and very forward?

B   Yes, yes. It's very important to be, and you have to be very dynamic.

I   I would find that quite tiring. I know when I've been in interviews, it's quite tough to be dynamic for an hour or so.

B   Sure, sure. It is. And also the other thing is that there is no real, real conversation, it is quite strange. I have found, I, I found out that here in England it's more like a conversation, like, in order to really, er, demonstrate that you can really deal with the clients and talk with people, you know.

I   Do you ever ask about salary or money or that kind of thing?

B   Well, usually people don't ask about salary and, er, it's not really in, in the advert. So ... but it's discussed later when they offer you something.

I   Oh, right, so it's not in the advertisement.

B   No, no, usually we don't have it in the advertisement.

LIXING   Well, in China, you can imagine the, er, competition for the job is fierce, so actually the interviews are quite different for those who directly graduate from the universities or for those who have experience of working and he or she just wants to, to change job. And for the graduate students, the interview is more or less focused on their psychology or their personality instead of their knowledge because they, erm, most of them have more or less the same grades.

CIAN   So for, erm, the graduate students, is a CV not as important? Because I find, erm, in Ireland the, er, the CV is crucial and the cover letter, if you don't put a lot of work into it and really sell yourself through that, you, you won't get to the interview stage but it's different in China, is it? It's more of a case of ...

L   ... the students are now probably required to have some, er, internship experience prior to this interview but, er, mostly the employers just look at the ... the personality of the student. Actually, according to Chinese culture, we do not like people who appear to be so bossy, like, who appear so aggressive, so the people are really careful about that too.

C   Yeah, we'd be the same. We have group discussions and usually the loudest person or the, the person who answers the most isn't the most desirable for the employer. They want a mix. They want somebody who can interact and step back and know when to talk and when to make a good point, so I think we're both very similar there.

🔊 3.36

atmosphere   earpiece   gear   hero
interfere   interior   overhear   steer
volunteer   experience

Vowels

Short vowels

/ə/	/æ/	/ʊ/	/ɒ/	/ɪ/	/i/	/e/	/ʌ/
teacher ago	married am	book could	on got	in swim	happy easy	wet any	cup under

Long vowels

/ɜː/	/ɑː/	/uː/	/ɔː/	/iː/
her shirt	arm car	blue too	or walk	eat meet

Diphthongs

/eə/	/ɪə/	/ʊə/	/ɔɪ/	/aɪ/	/eɪ/	/əʊ/	/aʊ/
chair where	near we're	tour sure	boy noisy	nine eye	eight day	go over	out brown

Consonants voiced unvoiced

/b/	/ð/	/v/	/dʒ/	/d/	/z/	/g/	/ʒ/
be bit	mother the	very live	job page	down red	magazine	girl bag	television

/p/	/θ/	/f/	/tʃ/	/t/	/s/	/k/	/ʃ/
park shop	think both	face laugh	chips teach	time white	see rice	cold look	shoe fish

/m/	/n/	/ŋ/	/l/	/r/	/w/	/j/	/h/
me name	now rain	thing drink	late hello	carry write	we white	you yes	hot hand

Irregular verbs

Infinitive	Past simple	Past participle
All forms are the same		

	bet
	burst
	cost
	cut
	hit
	hurt
	let
	put
	set
	shut
	split
	spread

Past simple and past participle are the same

bend	bent
bring	brought
build	built
burn	burned/burnt
buy	bought
catch	caught
deal	dealt
dig	dug
dream	dreamed/dreamt
feed	fed
feel	felt
fight	fought
find	found
get	got
hang	hung
have	had
hear	heard
hold	held
keep	kept
kneel	kneeled/knelt
lay	laid
lead	led
learn	learned/learnt
leave	left
lend	lent
light	lit
lose	lost
make	made
mean	meant
meet	met
pay	paid
read /riːd/	read /red/
say	said
sell	sold
send	sent
shine	shone
shoot	shot
sit	sat
sleep	slept
slide	slid
smell	smelled/smelt
spell	spelled/spelt
spend	spent
spill	spilled/spilt
spoil	spoiled/spoilt
stand	stood
stick	stuck
strike	struck
teach	taught
tell	told
think	thought
understand	understood
win	won

All forms are different

Infinitive	Past simple	Past participle
be	was/were	been
begin	began	begun
blow	blew	blown
break	broke	broken
can	could	been able to
choose	chose	chosen
do	did	done
draw	drew	drawn
drink	drank	drunk
drive	drove	driven
eat	ate	eaten
fall	fell	fallen
fly	flew	flown
forget	forgot	forgotten
forgive	forgave	forgiven
freeze	froze	frozen
give	gave	given
go	went	been/gone
grow	grew	grown
hide	hid	hidden
know	knew	known
lie	lay	lain
ride	rode	ridden
ring	rang	rung
rise	rose	risen
see	saw	seen
shake	shook	shaken
show	showed	shown
shrink	shrank	shrunk
sing	sang	sung
sink	sank	sunk
speak	spoke	spoken
steal	stole	stolen
swear	swore	sworn
swell	swelled	swelled/swollen
swim	swam	swum
take	took	taken
tear	tore	torn
throw	threw	thrown
wake	woke	woken
wear	wore	worn
write	wrote	written

Infinitive and past participle are the same

Infinitive	Past simple	Past participle
become	became	become
come	came	come
run	ran	run

Infinitive and past simple are the same

Infinitive	Past simple	Past participle
beat		beaten